Garden Suburbs of Tomorrow?

Faced with acute housing shortages, the idea of new garden cities and suburbs is on the UK planning agenda once again, but what of the garden suburbs that already exist?

Over the first six decades of the twentieth century, councils across Britain created a new and optimistic form of housing – the cottage estates of 'corporation suburbia'. By the early 1960s these estates provided homes with gardens for some 3 million mainly working-class households. It was a mammoth achievement. But, because of what then happened to council housing over the later years of the century, this is not very often appreciated.

In *Garden Suburbs of Tomorrow?* Martin Crookston suggests that making the most of the assets which this housing offers is a positive story – it can be positive for housing policy; for councils and their 'place-making' endeavours; and for the residents of the estates. This is especially important when all housing market and development options are so constrained, and likely to remain so for the next decade or more.

Following an examination of what the estates of 'corporation suburbia' are and what they are like, there follow chapters on specific examples from different parts of the country, on how they are affected by the workings of the housing market, and then – not unconnectedly – on how attitudes to this socially-built stock have evolved. Then the final chapters try to draw out the potentials, and to suggest what future we might look for in corporation suburbia in the twenty-first century.

Martin Crookston is an independent strategic planning consultant. Recent assignments have focused on housing market renewal in the North and Midlands, on London's Olympic 'Legacy' plans, and on urban strategy in the UAE. He was a member of the Urban Task Force, and is a Trustee of the CPRE and a Board Member of Architecture and Design Scotland.

Planning, History and Environment Series

Editor:
Ann Rudkin, Alexandrine Press, Marcham, UK

Editorial Board:
Professor Arturo Almandoz, Universidad Simón Bolivar, Caracas, Venezuela and
  Pontificia Universidad Católica de Chile, Santiago, Chile
Professor Nezar AlSayyad, University of California, Berkeley, USA
Professor Scott A. Bollens, University of California, Irvine, USA
Professor Robert Bruegmann, University of Illinois at Chicago, USA
Professor Meredith Clausen, University of Washington, Seattle, USA
Professor Yasser Elsheshtawy, UAE University, Al Ain, UAE
Professor Robert Freestone, University of New South Wales, Sydney, Australia
Professor John R. Gold, Oxford Brookes University, Oxford, UK
Professor Sir Peter Hall, University College London, UK
Professor Michael Hebbert, University College London, UK

Selection of Published Titles

Garden Suburbs of Tomorrow?
A New Future for the Cottage Estates

Martin Crookston

Routledge
Taylor & Francis Group

LONDON AND NEW YORK

First published in paperback 2016
First published 2014
by Routledge
2 Park Square, Milton Park, Abingdon, Oxfordshire OX14 4RN

and by Routledge
711 Third Avenue, New York, NY 10017

Routledge is an imprint of the Taylor & Francis Group, an informa business

This book was commissioned and edited by Alexandrine Press, Marcham, Oxfordshire

British Library Cataloguing in Publication Data
A catalogue record of this book is available from the British Library

Library of Congress Cataloging in Publication Data
Crookston, Martin.
    Garden suburbs of tomorrow? : a new future for the cottage estates / Martin Crookston.
      pages cm. — (Planning, history and environment)
    Includes bibliographical references and index.
    ISBN 978–0–415–85893–9 (hb : alk. paper) 1. Housing policy — Great Britain.
      2. Suburban homes — Great Britain. 3. City planning — Great Britain. 4. Cities and
      towns Growth — History — 21st century. I. Title.
HD7333.A3C76 2014
307.740942 — dc23

                                                                              2013028988

ISBN: 978–0–415–85893–9 (hbk)
ISBN: 978–1–138–68891–9 (pbk)
ISBN: 978–1–315–81997–6 (ebk)

Typeset in Aldine and Swiss by PNR Design, Didcot

MIX
Paper from
responsible sources
FSC   FSC® C013056
www.fsc.org

Printed and bound in Great Britain by
TJ International Ltd, Padstow, Cornwall

D
307.

Contents

Foreword

Martin Crookston has written an astonishing book. Astonishing, because he has discovered a forgotten piece of England, a piece that is large and important and right in front of our eyes, but which we have somehow succeeded in airbrushing out of the mental picture we have created of our own country. It is home to some 3 million people, one in six of us, almost none of them rich, not too many poor, most of middling circumstances: the true Middle England, you might say. And they live very much like the rest of us, in homely houses with gardens on the suburban edges of our towns and cities. Many of these homes and these estates were outstandingly well designed – especially those, around a quarter of them, built between the two World Wars – and, even eighty years later, stand the test of time.

Yet not only are they forgotten: when the rest of us recall them, our image is almost universally negative. These are 'council houses' on 'council estates' – the places where none of us would ever dream of living, or wish for our children or our grandchildren. The strange fact is that they are not that, any more: half the homes in them are now owner-occupied. Most of them are unproblematic, untroubled places: good places to spend lives and to bring up children. As Martin Crookston says, they represent an 'impressive inheritance'.

And so – this is the important message – they represent what he calls a huge 'lazy asset'. They are a national resource, yet we are not getting the most out of them, either socially or economically. Especially in the northern half of England, many of them are still council housing – and they should remain that, areas of choice for those in the social-rented market. They could also serve as stepping-stones, to help meet the growing demand for houses in the 'intermediate' housing market – for sale, but not at full market pricing. And finally, as houses are sold – particularly by those who originally acquired them, under Thatcher's 'Right to Buy', they could and should progressively become part of the 'regular' housing market around them. As one study, quoted by Crookston, puts it: they should 'become a place where households wish to stay given the means, as opposed to leaving as soon as they get a chance'.

This book is being published at a propitious time, just as the country gears up to a pre-election year: a year which will surely see a fundamental debate on every aspect of our economic and social life. Housing will surely form a prominent part of that debate, and Martin Crookston has made a vital – even indispensible – contribution to it. No one seriously concerned with the way we live, and should live, can afford to miss it.

Professor Sir Peter Hall
London
July 2013

Acknowledgements

This book has relied on support, help and advice from very many people. Thank you to all of them.

In particular, I must thank Peter O'Brien of Place Futures for analytical and intellectual support right from the earliest idea of a study, Tom Carter who once again drew maps that illuminate the work, and Ann Rudkin of Alexandrine Press who steered a novice through the mysterious world of publishing with constant advice and reassurance.

Special thanks also to three readers for their reviews and their suggestions on early drafts, which helped shape and guide the argument: Bill Brisbane, Adam Hilton, and the *egregio maestro* Professor Sir Peter Hall.

Other colleagues whose ideas in discussion influenced the direction and balance include Professors Michael Hebbert and Alan Murie; Keith Thorpe and Shane Brownie, the 'men from the ministry' (CLG); Jim Coulter, and Nicholas Falk.

I am also enormously grateful to my 'witnesses': several of the chapters would have been more or less impossible without the contributions of a group of people who shared their experience of life – then and now – on the estates of corporation suburbia: Matthew Bradby, Secretary of the Tower Gardens Residents' Group; Alan Cooke of the Craven Vale Community Association; Jane Ely, Michelle Griffiths, Peter Griffiths, Neil Sinden, Dr Chris Smith, Sandra Walmsley, Brian Wilden, Tim Williams, and Paul Wright at The Hub in Bromford; et les trois dames de l'avenue Paty à Stains.

For information, local knowledge and help on particular areas, thanks go to Reverend Al Barrett of Hodge Hill Church; Ruth Crowley; Councillor Tim Evans, Bev Carroll, Sharon Freedman and Beverley Walker of Birmingham City Council; Jennie Coombs at Barking & Dagenham Council; Michael Donachie, Kevin Dawson and Sasha Rayner at Gentoo Sunderland; and Councillors Denny Wilson and Paul Watson, Sunderland Council; Richard Finlow of Gateshead Housing Company; Kathryn Forte and Lisa Beck at Home Group; Andrew Marshall, Peter Mennell and Councillor Brian Coates, Gateshead Council; Brendan Nevin; Richard at Burchell Edwards in Erdington; Councillor Anne Stennett, Sule Nişancıoğlu and Nairita Chakraborty, Haringey Council; and Garry Taylor, Hull Council.

And for all sorts of other assistance: Steve Atherton; Lucy Ayre (LSE Library); Di Barnes; Charlie Baker and David Rudlin (Urbed); Adam Carey; Tony Clifford (Barking & Dagenham Libraries); Hugh Daglish (Gateshead Council); Richard Flouriot; Alison Gelder (Housing Justice); Ros Grimes; Lorraine Hart; Paul Jeffrey; Sheila Johnston; Mary Lester; Nick Matthews (TCPA); Clive Rand; Alison Ravetz; Richard Shield; Russell Taylor (Leicester City Council); Sophie Shillito (CPRE);

Richard Turkington; Roger Hull (Liverpool Record Office); John McGill (NLSA); and Tom's CAD-monkeys. To others who I may have forgotten to mention, and to all those residents and passers-by who I pestered up and down the country – thank you as well.

Martin Crookston
London
July 2013

Chapter 1

Introduction

A Mammoth Achievement

Over the first six decades of the twentieth century, councils all across Britain spent enormous amounts of time, effort and money building a new and optimistic form of housing – the cottage estates of 'corporation suburbia'. Drawing on the models of garden cities and garden suburbs, by the early 1960s they had provided family homes with gardens for some 3 million mainly working-class households. It was a mammoth achievement. Some of the places it produced are of great character and quality.

Because of what then happened to council housing over the later years of the century, this is not very often appreciated. This book looks at that achievement to try and understand how these places work today. It also seeks to work out how the people who live there now, and the communities they are part of, can get the most out of this impressive inheritance.

The last few years have seen a lot of talk about planning new garden cities and suburbs. It seems like a good time to explore the potential of the garden suburbs we have already got.

This Book, and Our Questions

The genesis of this book lay in questions and ideas that came up during research about the links between housing and the economy in the three regions of Northern England.[1] Dozens of localities were studied, across the North from Hull to Blackpool and from Tyneside to Merseyside. Eight of them, studied in some detail, were what were airily called 'type 2' areas: 'near-market municipally-built' suburbs – the familiar suburban council estates which are in or near every town and city in the country (Urban Studio, 2009*a*).

And the question that kept nagging was: these are (usually) well-built houses, on (generally) biggish plots, often with pleasant views out to the Pennines or the North Sea – why does it seem as though people do not choose to live here, what is it that does not work, and is it fixable? Lynsey Hanley, in *Estates*, nails it as usual: 'There has to be some reason why people who waited years for a coveted home from 'the Corpy' wouldn't wish the same for their own grandchildren' (Hanley, 2007).

Coupled with that was the sense that these places might be something of a 'lazy asset' for their areas and communities. We do not seem to be getting the most out of them, socially or economically. In some of them, maybe many, there are of course deep-seated problems, and attitudes, to tackle. But the idea was about missed potential, not simply glum failure, and the wish now is to explore that potential and not just once again revisit the estates wearing problem-shaped lenses.

When I were a Lad…

This is not just academic. It is also about the shared experience of the post-war years. Growing up in Lancashire in the 1950s, your schoolmates were as likely to be from the – fairly recently built – estate as from the private housing in the surrounding roads and lanes. What stigma there was probably attached itself to the visibly poorer and scruffier little terraced streets and – especially – back courts as yet untouched by 'slum clearance'. And mums on the estate were just as insistent on hankies and proper shoes (not tatty plimsolls) as any in the private semis. The separations that undoubtedly came later were associated with 16+ choices (work vs university, going away vs staying), by aspirations and class, as much as or more than by where you lived. Maybe, already, the distinction between Alma Hill (built to house 'slum dwellers') and Hall Green (the bigger town expansion to house the more respectable working-class) lurked somewhere there. However, the label of council tenant was not the key to that, or to our attitudes and experience in general. The estate was different, but it wasn't that different, and it wasn't stigmatized.

And indeed the literature from those years has almost as a trope the provincial working-class boy from the estate who looks back on those years, perhaps with a nostalgic glow. Yet his angst and regret are not noticeably tinged with a feeling that his home, or his estate, was the distinguishing feature of growing up – or of the life later exchanged for metropolitan excitements. Growing up on a cottage estate might end up with you up and out. But it was up and out from Wigan, not especially from *those* streets, *that* estate.

So there are questions here about the past of corporation suburbia, about what happened and why, which might help to inform what could happen in future.

A Starting-Point

The study in the North suggested that the opportunity for these localities could be of three kinds. First, they are still, a lot of them, council housing: they can – and should – remain areas of choice for people in the social-rented market. Second, alongside that, a stepping-stone role: they might be able to help meet growing demand for houses in the 'intermediate' housing market (for sale, but not full market pricing). And third, as houses are bought and sold: they ought to be able to integrate more fully into the 'regular' housing market around them. The aim would be for them 'to become a place where households wish to stay given the means, as opposed to leaving as soon as they get a chance' (Urban Studio, 2009a).

This in turn could change how they 'work' in another way: areas of choice, well-placed for access to jobs in the cities, they could play new roles in the labour market, for a wider range of working families.

People, Houses and Places

So the interest is partly about the issues of 'mix' and tenure change in these estates, where guidance has pre-eminently come from the work of Alan Murie and Colin Jones on the processes and effects of the 'Right to Buy' (Jones and Murie, 2005). It is partly about the areas' roles in the labour and housing markets, and how these might change. And it is, inevitably, partly about some deep-seated problems which, it must be recognized, are not all confined to the inner-city tower blocks, as is clear from, for example, Lynsey Hanley's analysis of her native outer-suburban Chelmsley Wood. But, and to stress: it is also about the potentials that one might be trying to release, and the positive side of the story.

'Corporation Suburbia'

So the focus is on the 'corporation suburbs', as Richard Turkington labelled this form of housing in his work in the 1990s: the council-built estates, almost always in a 'cottage' format even if some flats are included in amongst the houses (Turkington, 1999). They are generally the ones that are not so stereotypically 'problem estates'. The interest is in the ones that 'work', or could do so: their potential, and the threats they face. The thinking seeks to go beyond labels like 'sink estate', or 'edge city'. These are not just pejorative – they are too simplistic to describe all our municipally-built environments.

Places that Work?

The case here is that making the most of the assets which this housing offers is a positive story. It can be positive for housing policy; for councils and their 'place-making' endeavours; and for the residents of the estates. This is especially important when *all* housing market and development options are so constrained, and likely to remain so for the next decade or more.

The next chapter looks at what the estates of 'corporation suburbia' are and what they are like. Then follow chapters which home in on specific examples from different parts of the country, on how they are affected by the workings of the housing market, and then – not unconnectedly – on how *attitudes* to this socially-built stock have evolved. The final chapters try to draw out the potentials, and to suggest what future we might look for in corporation suburbia in the twenty-first century.

Note

1. Commissioned by The Northern Way initiative in 2007–2009 Llewelyn Davies carried out a series of studies which were published by Llewelyn Davies Yeang and Urban Studio; these are cited individually in the bibliography.

Chapter 2

The Cottage Estates
and Their Successors

Corporation Suburbia's 'Cottage Estates'

Corporation suburbia is made up largely – but not exclusively – of 'cottage estates': large swathes of family houses on their own plots, generally with only a few flats mixed in, though with a marked change in style and feel during the post-war years and into the 1960s and 1970s.

The aim is to show what's special and valuable about these places. Starting with an attempt to define what England's corporation suburbia *is*, and whether it is like social housing anywhere else, the chapter then pokes around at the magic, and loaded, 'estate' word, to try and understand what that load is all about.

The rest of the chapter looks at what makes up these estates, and where they came from, leading into three chapters which explore a number of them in more detail.

What, How Much, Where?

The council estates which might be broadly defined as 'corporation suburbia' are a sizeable chunk of our total housing stock. We are dealing with about a sixth of all of England's homes. (Unless otherwise stated, the figures in this chapter relate to England, not the whole UK.)

John Hills's key report gives the 2003 figures. There were then 21.5 million dwellings of all kinds in England, of which 4.8 million were in 'predominantly council-built areas'. Of these, 3.25 million were in areas which were 'mainly houses' (as opposed to his other two categories of 'mainly flats' and 'houses & flats'). So just over 15 per cent of all homes were in what might be regarded as corporation suburbia. These areas are also a big majority of the country's social housing: the same figures show that they made up 68 per cent of all the council and housing association stock (Hills, 2007).

Though predominantly council-built, they are not, obviously, all now mainly council-owned. Hills's 2003 figures record that 50 per cent of the homes in his 'mainly houses' council-built category were still in the social sector, but the other half were by

Figure 2.1. Familiar all over the country: council-built homes (Upney, in London's Becontree).

then in the private sector. In contrast, the 'mainly flats' areas still showed a big majority in social rather than private ownership, in a 73:27 ratio.

This has of course largely been a Right-To-Buy induced switch. But even after that very strong movement, these 'mainly houses' areas still accounted for 40 per cent of all the country's socially-owned homes. And their location, as expected, is predominantly (69 per cent) described in the Hills report as 'suburban residential': that is, not 'city/other urban centre' or 'rural'.

Figure 2.2. Classic inter-war: Norris Green reached out into Liverpool's green hinterland – with the familiar geometric plan and groupings of these estates. (*Source:* Liverpool Record Office)

Built When?

As to when corporation suburbia dates from: pre-1945 building accounts for 27 per cent of these estates; 1945–1964 for another 49 per cent; and post-1964 for 22 per cent (Hills, 2007). The classic inter-war cottage estates are thus less than a third of the total in the council-built suburbs.

Their post-war (that is, post-1945) successors are generally recognizable by their more stripped-down exteriors. Later on, the layouts changed too, with the 1950s/1960s shift to designs such as 'Radburn' planning which sought to separate cars and pedestrians. Altogether, the post-war building actually accounts for much more in total than the pre-1939 construction.

Figure 2.3. The 1960s Radburn ideal: carefree play in car-free walkway streets. (*Source*: Town & Country Planning Association)

Part of Suburban Life

In their various forms, then, these suburbs are a big and characteristic part of the English housing scene. Along with their privately-built neighbours, they dramatically changed the shape of urban Britain in the 20 years after the end of the First World War: 'The residential growth of towns and cities in interwar England was practically synonymous with the creation of garden suburbs' (Whitehand and Carr, 1999). The municipal building effort also forms a very significant proportion of all our suburbs. Definitions are difficult: but as one careful study of twentieth-century suburbs points out, the timing and scale of suburbia varies a lot between places, notably in the case of London whose suburbs grew faster and earlier than anywhere else between the wars (Whitehand and Carr, 2001). But a look at a medium-sized middle-England sort of a place like Leicester can perhaps give a feel for the sort of scale of presence that these estates have in suburbia as a whole.

Leicester is one of a group of Midlands cities in the 250–350,000 population range, and it is the biggest, at almost 330,000 (ONS, 2012). As a long-established city – not one whose serious history starts with the Industrial Revolution – it dominates a rural hinterland of about a million people, and has quite a varied local economy (ranked eleventh out of fifty-plus 'Primary Urban Areas' in terms of job numbers), including a shopping core which is in the top dozen in the country (L&LP, 2010). As in many urban areas, there is a large ethnic-minority population: the distinguishing feature of Leicester is that has the largest population of Indian heritage of any local authority area in England and Wales (about 25 per cent); and as in many urban areas deprivation is a serious problem across some of the city. So it is not necessarily an average or typical city in every way – nowhere is; but it can help to illustrate how the council-built estates fit in to their urban setting.

Council Estates as Part of Suburbia: Leicester

Leicester's compact central area extends east–west from London Road main line station to the River Soar, and north–south from Abbey Park to the Royal Infirmary: about 1 km by 1.5 km. Around that is a ring, a kilometre or two wide, which makes up the inner city that was built up by about 1920: largely tight little streets of terraces and industry, but also with some comfortable Victorian and Edwardian neighbourhoods to the south. Together, these central and inner parts account for something over 1,500 hectares (21 per cent) of the city's total of 7,300 hectares and 41,000 (35 per cent) of the 116,000 dwellings.

Beyond again, the outer areas cover about 5,800 hectares – of which about 1,300 ha are industrial estates, major hospitals, shopping centres, city-scale parks and golf courses. That leaves the 'suburban Leicester' that people live in as about 4,500 ha, with something like 75,000 dwellings. This is the context within which sit the twenty-three suburban council-built housing estates (out of a city total of twenty-nine).

It is apparent that in this 'post-1920' Leicester the cottage estates were an early and very significant component. The Victoria County History (VCH) comments that: 'The provision of housing was perhaps the most important task undertaken by the municipality in the years between the wars'. Starting in 1919–1924 in North Evington (Coleman Road) and West Humberstone (Tailby Estate), both of them east of the centre, the council increasingly looked at areas outside as well as inside its boundary, with Saffron Lane to the south and from 1925, the triple cluster around Braunstone in the southwest. By 1935 the inevitable expansion of the city limits matched the residential expansion. The city had built over 9,000 homes by 1939, and subsidized private construction had added another 3,000 or so. 'The construction of extensive housing estates with a distinctive character to the south and south-east of the city was a new development in Leicester's urban growth and one that was to become increasingly important after 1945' (VCH, 1958).

Of course the ownership pattern is not now the same as formerly. Before the Right-To-Buy the city council was the landlord for nearly 40,000 homes; it now has just over 22,000. What was sold, between 1979 and 2011, was predominantly houses rather than flats: 12,873 out of the 13,354 sales, inevitably mostly from the outer estates. There are now just over 11,000 houses in council ownership, to which can be added some of the 9,000 housing association properties in the city.

'Corporation suburbia' (irrespective of its tenure now) is about a third of the total area of suburban Leicester. These twenty-three estates occupy 1,577 hectares of land, out of the total area (4,500 ha) of the residential suburbs. The proportion of the housing itself is actually markedly higher, at about 43 per cent: 32,700 of the suburbs' 75,000 or so homes were originally council stock.[1]

The proportions will naturally vary from town to town. But if Leicester can be taken as some sort of broad indication, then the cottage estates of corporation suburbia

Figure 2.4. Council estates in Leicester. (*Source*: Leicester City Council)

will often form at least a third of the housing areas in our suburban world. This makes them an important element of our settlements' structures, and a very characteristic part of the places that we see as we travel around from day to day.

All Our Own Work? – European Comparisons

They are also a very English (or rather, British Isles) form. In France, for example, 86 per cent of the social housing is in the form of flats: 97 per cent in Paris (Murie, 2008). In Germany, the estates are almost always flats and tend to be large by European comparison (Droste and Knorr-Siedow, 2007). Only in Holland, where the whole housing stock is dominated by single-family houses, does the proportion of the social-rented stock which is houses rather than flats (47 per cent) appear in any way comparable to Britain's; and it is not generally built in 'estates', but interspersed in mixed neighbourhoods (Elsinga and Wassenberg, 2007).

This is not to say that the 'cottage estate' form has no parallels in neighbouring countries. It does, and often very consciously modelled on the British pioneers. But it is never a major component of the stock in the way it is in this country.

Two examples from Paris's near suburbs (known as the 'Petite Couronne', as opposed to the Grande Couronne which is more or less equivalent to London's Outer Metropolitan Area) show this. In 1916 Henri Sellier, who was both public health minister and mayor of Suresnes – and who had learned his trade at the Unwin/Parker studio in Hampstead Garden Suburb – founded the Office Publique d'Habitations à Bon Marché de la Seine, and organized fifteen *cités-jardins* in the suburbs. He surrounded himself with a dozen like-minded architects: *'Directement inspirée par les réalisations britanniques et le mythe du "cottage"'*. They planned picturesque villages with winding roads and individual houses in a vernacular style: steep roofs and high chimneys.[2]

At Stains, on the north side between the city and the airport about 10 km from the centre, the scheme that went up between 1921 and 1927 contains 1,676 units in 456 houses and nineteen blocks of four or five floors. Practically unchanged since its creation (though with a very recent renovation), its heritage value was recognized in 1976 when it was listed.

The *mythe du 'cottage'* is certainly realized as if we were in outer London. There are similarities to the contemporaneous Becontree estate in Dagenham – indeed, at one point (rue Rolland) there is even a short cul-de-sac of the sort known in Becontree as a 'banjo'.

Similarities also to the cosiness of Tower Gardens in Tottenham: both London estates are studied further in the next chapter. One elderly lady in avenue Paty said that before she moved in (from a nearby tower block) she used to say to her children *'allez, on va se promener en Angleterre'* and take them round the *cité-jardin*.

The conscious use of little greens and planting is also very reminiscent of the English estates: the layout at Place Rolland, and its feel, are wholly comparable with some of those illustrated in the following chapter, in East London.

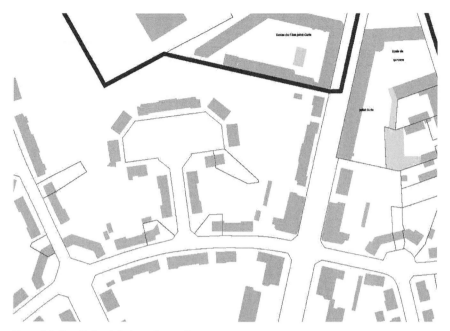

Figure 2.5. Rue Rolland, Stains: echoes of Becontree.

Figure 2.6. Stains, avenue Paty: 'let's go for a walk in England'.

On the other hand, it is unusual in Becontree to see a guy puffing calmly at a *shisha* on the pavement, as one might in the rue Duchêne. Stains is very mixed: indeed probably more so now than are many of the *grands-ensembles*, which seem to be predominantly black or predominantly *maghrébin*; here there is still a broad split between (generally older) white working-class and a wide range of more recent arrivals.

Arcueil, another location in the early suburban *cité-jardins* programme, is about 7 km south of central Paris, alongside the Autoroute du Soleil and with fast RER access to the city. It dates from 1921–1923, and has undergone rather more modification since it was built (Inventaire général du patrimoine culturel, 2012). If Stains is England, Arcueil is Scotland. The houses are plainer than in Stains, and often rendered like Scots estates.

Figure 2.7. A little piece of Scotland? Cité-jardin de l'Aqueduc, Arcueil.

It is actually less coherent than Stains, both in layout and in individual groupings, and so less legible as you walk around. But it has one borrowing from the garden suburb – little back lanes – which must be great if you are 7 or 8 (as very large numbers of its denizens seem to be). Socially and racially it too is very mixed. If there is a difference it might be that whilst the more recent arrivals in Stains are from all over, Arcueil's non-white residents seem to be predominantly black (probably from the *départements* in the Caribbean, judging from the Creole being spoken on-street) within a generally suburban upper working class/lower middle class range – which is partly the difference between the north and south of the Petite Couronne.

A privately-constructed example, on the Seine downstream, is the cité de la Petite Campagne built for the well-paid and exceptionally well-housed workers at Standard Oil's Port Jérôme refinery in Notre-Dame-de-Gravenchon near Le Havre. Again, although this township was not started until 1930, the houses and the layout are a lasting tribute to cross-Channel influences (Base Mérimée, 2012).

So the resonance with the British cottage estates is considerable, and was deliberate. But the essential difference is the context. Both physically and in terms of the overall stock, the *cités-jardins* are now swamped by *tours* and *barres* (towers and slabs), as well as by complex 1980s high-density medium-rise architecture. They are a minor and quirky variant (albeit a pretty successful one, especially compared with the lineal descendants of Le Corbusier) in France's housing story: they are now starting to be appreciated as a valued part of the *patrimoine* – the heritage;[3] and since 1994 the number of individual houses built annually in France has consistently been higher than for flats (Fribourg, 2008). But houses in the garden estate form are not a major contributor to the supply as in Britain and Ireland.

Other examples can be found dotted across France (such as the railway township at Tergnier in the northern Aisne *département*), Belgium (e.g. Watermael-Boitsfort, in Brussels), Holland and Germany. In Holland, the Westelijke Tuinsteden (Western Garden Suburbs) was a very large-scale development originally inspired by the British garden city movement, but as the great 1928 Amsterdam Plan was implemented over the 1930s, the balance of apartments and individual houses shifted heavily towards flat-building and this, together with the open-block planning rather than perimeter-blocks, suggests that the scheme was rather hi-jacked by the modernists, as time went on and the product became markedly more 'European' and less 'English' (Oudenampsen, 2010). Others, such as Slotermeer, Amstelveen and Bijlmermeer, are even less like garden suburbs or cottage estates.

In Germany, Hellerau in northern Dresden is probably the most complete attempt outside England to realize a garden suburb. Started in 1908, it was consciously based on Howard's ideas; it involved an Arts and Crafts-type linkage to a woodworking factory; and its cottagey houses facing onto curving streets are about half of the total of some 800 units completed by 1913. A similar 'garden village' for Krupp workers was built at Margarethenhöhe in Essen, which Hall says 'faithfully followed the Unwin-Parker tradition to create a magic little town…'. But again, these are outliers in the range of German social housing forms, where the 'estates' (*siedlungen*) are almost entirely apartments in open blocks (Galonska and Elstner, 2007; GHDI, 2012; Hall, 2002). This story, of an initial interest in the English garden city movement being overtaken by higher-density more urban modernism in the 1930s and onward, is paralleled all over continental Europe (Panerai *et al.*, 1997).

Thus we come back to the overall point: despite the interesting comparisons elsewhere, corporation suburbia is pretty much all our own work, and its role is pretty much specific to this country.

The 'Estate' and Social Polarization

Our particular 'estate' form has particular social consequences. In Britain, there is a tendency to see council tenancy, estates, working-class-ness and low income as inevitably and irrevocably intertwined. But if true now, it wasn't always thus – and ain't always thus elsewhere.

Ruth Lupton's research for the Joseph Rowntree Foundation and the Tenant Services Agency, drawing on four British birth cohort studies to examine the role of social housing for four generations of families since the Second World War, tracks what happened.

Four generations ago, families in social housing included almost the full social range. Council and housing association homes offered high quality. However, from the 1960s, home ownership took over from social housing as the main type of housing for families. Over time, the more advantaged families moved out. Increasingly, encouraged by policy, social housing has acted as a 'safety net'. It has also lost out in term of relative desirability... Society is also now more unequal than it was. The result is that the gap between the socioeconomic circumstances of children in social housing and other tenures is wider than for any previous generation.

She argues that her research offers no support for reducing the attractiveness of social renting or the number of homes available – rather the reverse: 'we need to help social housing catch up with the desirability of home-ownership housing, and increase its social mix' (Lupton *et al.*, 2009).

John Hills (2007) makes comparisons over time (1979–1999), and between countries, drawing on work by Stephens *et al.* (2002). He shows how much the social, economic and policy changes of the late twentieth century have affected who lives where. In 1979, the population living in Britain's social housing was spread across the income distribution to quite a surprising extent. So the people who lived on estates were from quite a wide band of incomes and social groups: 'polarization' was not that marked. But 'by the late 1990s, the income differences between tenures were greater in the UK than in [five other European countries studied], and social tenants had the lowest incomes in relation to the average. In the other countries the differential with owner-occupiers was smaller, and there was little if any difference between the incomes of those in private and social renting' (Hills, 2007).

It is apparent that the social polarization has become much more marked in the last two or three decades. Not only that, but the British form of social housing helped to accentuate this effect. In a country where so much of the stock is in the estate format, this has made a huge difference – on both the 'mainly houses' and 'mainly flats' estates.

If social housing had not been predominantly built as estates, but instead had been 'pepperpotted' (as some housing association street property acquired in the 1960s and 1970s was), this polarization by income would not necessarily have meant polarization on the ground. But the combination with location of properties has meant that it is. (Hills, 2007)

There we have it. We have seen that two-thirds of all social housing is located within areas built as estates. And therefore even though such areas are no longer solely owned by social landlords, and even though the cottage estates in particular have seen high penetration of Right-To-Buy, the effect of having 'estates' as the basic format for social housing provision has been to tend to reinforce polarization. This despite many years of worthy intentions about 'social mix' – the idea, and aim, that places would be healthier and more balanced if they housed a variety of people in terms of their income, age, social class and employment status. A good thing, most agree; but not an outcome of the real processes that have been at work.

What They Are

'Estate' can of course mean many different forms and locations, and the Hills report offers some important distinctions and data to help scale the differences. The focus here – within his 'mainly houses/predominantly council-built' grouping – is on the cottage estates of corporation suburbia, and especially those built in the 'classic' format of the inter-war and immediate post-war years.

It is important to note their location. The persistent image is of peripheral estates lost 'out there' somewhere. But they are by no means all now 'outer' suburbs: they generally *were* when built, because they tended to be on cheap farmland at the urban edge. Some still are – like Lynsey Hanley's native Chelmsley Wood on the Birmingham-Solihull fringes: which she uses brilliantly in her 'Estates' book to convey the texture of life there (Hanley, 2007). But many of these places are now embedded in a wider metropolitan context, with the city extending well beyond them – as with Tottenham's Tower Gardens estate (see Chapter 3 below), built on farmland before the first World War, but now 5 miles (8 km) in from London's green-belt-defined outer edge. This is a familiar pattern throughout history, whether in what were once the *faubourgs* outside the walls of Paris and even Québec, or in what was a century ago Mr Pooter's genteel Holloway – the epitome of peripheral suburbia when the Grossmiths were writing their affable satire, now very much part of inner-city London.

But they are definitely suburbs, and they are often still outer ones. They can be described in terms of several types – partly based on their form and location, partly on their history. The 'typology' used here, with examples, is:

- *Corporation suburb I: set in prosperous regions*
  Tower Gardens, North London
  Becontree, East London

- *Corporation suburb II: set in less prosperous areas*
  Deckham/Carr Hill, Gateshead
  Hylton Castle, Sunderland

- *Radburnland: the later post-war suburbs*
  Bromford, Birmingham
  Orchard Park, Hull

These estates are the places described in more detail in the next three chapters.

What They Are Like; Where They Came From

What you see when you visit more than a couple of these estates is impressive. They are the result of huge effort, investment and achievement, and of real municipal care and attention, which made up one of the big twentieth-century welfare state components.

They are often seen as having started with the 'Homes fit for Heroes' initiative after the First World War – but their story actually begins earlier, at the start of the twentieth century. Then, they reflected two main things: the drive to slum clearance – the Housing of the Working Classes Act had passed in 1890 (Jackson, 1991) – and the councils' response to the garden suburb movement – where 'two men … firmly put council housing in the mould of the garden city … Ebenezer Howard (1850–1928) and Raymond Unwin (1863–1940)' (Ravetz, 2001): Howard as town-planner and theorist, Unwin as architect and master planner. The design response, starting in Bedford Park in 1877–1880, with what Pevsner called 'an estate of friendly, semi-detached brick houses embedded in trees', soon included workers' housing at Port Sunlight and Bournville, which showed how urban living and quasi-rural greenery might be combined, even for the less well-off (Richards, 1965; Pevsner, 1991).

This was not just a London region effort. Birmingham, too, was in the forefront:

The city has two important garden suburbs at Bournville and Harborne, which are just as important in their own way as Letchworth and Hampstead respectively. (Bournville predates Letchworth by almost a decade and was a key inspiration; the Harborne Garden Suburb was built at roughly the same time as Hampstead Garden Suburb although it is much smaller.) Moreover, the city's vast 1930s suburban belt – almost as extensive, proportional to its population, as London's – is remarkably spacious and well-planned, and it too is a legacy, in part, of the efforts of the late Victorian and Edwardian reformers. (Neale, 2012)

And in Manchester as well, the pre-First World War period had seen social housing experiments at Burnage Garden Village and Chorltonville in south Manchester, and at Blackley to the north, a wave of building in 1910–1911 which adopted this cottage-and-garden style inspired by the new thinking (Hebbert and Hopkins, 2012). However it was primarily in the capital that the *municipal* adoption of these strands took early hold. Sheffield Corporation had in fact started the little Wincobank cottage estate in the east of the city following a design competition organized for 'a miniature garden city' as early as 1905. But by 1914 the London County Council (LCC) had started substantial cottage estates in Tooting, Tottenham, and Old Oak in Acton, and during the war the government built a similar estate at Eltham Well Hall for munitions workers (SYAS, 2009; Jackson, 1991; Oliver *et al.*, 1981).

As to what they looked like, and feel like now: the LCC's Totterdown Fields in Tooting, the pioneer, is made up of small cottages in terraces, with little attempt at adornment or elaborate street layouts. Their second, Tower Gardens in Tottenham, though still laid-out on a plain grid, shows much more thought about the external appearance and a distinctly 'Arts & Crafts' look with hanging slates and deep gables very like Hampstead Garden Suburb.

By the time the third was started, at Old Oak, the garden suburb ideals were more explicitly adopted with the street plan moving away from a grid to more curves and closes; this is also the one where, as later stages were designed, the picturesque Arts & Crafts look gave way to the more restrained 'neo-Georgian' one which became more or less standard in the inter-war years. The LCC had built about 3,400 homes under these arrangements by 1915 (Jackson, 1991).

Figure 2.8. Pre First World War: the LCC's Tower Gardens in Tottenham.

After the First World War came the 'Homes fit for Heroes' rhetoric of Lloyd George, a perception that the threat of revolution required measures to keep the populace happy, and even a speech from King George V about 'an adequate solution to the housing question' (Oliver *et al.*, 1981).

The inter-war years produced very large numbers of council houses, including over 153,000 in the London area alone: averaging more than 7,500 a year there. Manchester embarked on the huge (25,000 homes) and ambitious Wythenshawe Garden City, designed by Barry Parker who, with Unwin, had already been responsible for New Earswick in York, Letchworth Garden City and Hampstead Garden Suburb. Started in 1932, it was half-built at around 12–13,000 homes by the outbreak of war, by which time the city had also built over 20,000 council homes in other locations (Hebbert and Hopkins, 2012).

On a smaller scale, this was repeated all over the country, so that by 1939 there were over a million households in socially-rented homes. This was over a quarter of the nearly four million dwellings built in the two decades. The great majority of this inter-war municipal effort was on cottage estates (Jackson, 1991; Ravetz, 2001). At the same time, private house-building was roaring ahead too, and 'garden suburbs in a broad sense were an almost ubiquitous form of development in England after the First World War. Their open spaces and frequently curvilinear roads were in marked contrast to the predominantly rectilinear, compact streetscapes of the Edwardian period' (Whitehand and Carr, 2001).

They produced, too, the classic package for these estates: a combination of the plainish neo-Georgian appearance of the houses, plus the garden suburb's rather geometric layouts, as at Becontree in East London and Norris Green in Liverpool. That package was institutionalized in the 1918 Tudor Walters Report and is now the immediately-recognizable template for the council estates of the first half of the twentieth century. And these years produced the design rationale 'where characteristics such as a clear formal order, unity and consistency were defined as "good design"' (Oliver *et al.*, 1981). This is beautifully shown in CPRE Lancashire's pre-war contrasting of 'rational' and 'irrational' housing layouts (CPRE, 1937).

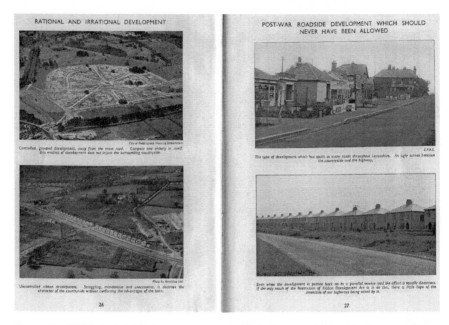

Figure 2.9. CPRE's 'orderly' design was contrasted with the horrors of ribbon development. (*Source*: CPRE Lancashire)

And what this inter-war period produced, too, was the basic 'deal' and mind-set for tenants and their landlords. As Lynsey Hanley says: 'The council homes of the interwar period were part of a contract: we will give you a good home if you look after it' (Hanley, 2007).

The stylistic to-ing and fro-ing of the early years might be thought rather specialized architectural history: the tension between the formality and simplicity of the 'Liverpool manner' and the loaded historicism of 'Queen Anne' references; the picturesque Arts & Crafts of some estates versus the 'simplified classicism' of neo-Georgian which replaced it in local authority building after the Great War. But they are not *just* architectural history: they are also very important social markers, too. Because what they looked like meant 'council estate'. And if there was one thing private housing developers and owners did not want, it was to look like *that*.

So, as Ian Bentley pointed out in that wonderful book *Dunroamin*, 'most local authority estates were designed in a rather stripped-down version of Neo-Georgian; so Neo-Georgian was perhaps the *least* frequent stylistic influence in the Dunroamin estate'. Bentley quotes an eminent lawyer of the period: '… the kind of house … that is bought just because its exterior is so different from the decent exterior of the council house that the casual observer must see at a glance that its owner is *not* living in a council house' (Oliver *et al.*, 1981). Chapter 8 returns to this cluster of attitudes.

The Years after the Second World War: A Lot of Building

After the Second World War, building styles and layouts initially continued as more of the same, though somewhat more simplified and even plainer. But quickly in the 1950s new forms emerged on the suburban estates – coupled of course with the huge push on tower-block flats and the political emphasis on the numbers of new-build. From the million-plus social homes in 1939, and starting only in 1949, the numbers rose to 2.24 million in 1953, 4.64 million in 1971 and 5.46 million in 1981. The building-rate was astonishingly fast: from a standing start in 1949 councils (and to a much lesser extent housing associations) built 176,800 in that year and similar or higher for the next 30 years or so, peaking at nearly 262,000 in 1953 and 1954 (DCLG, 2011 – UK figures, not just England).

These output figures are inevitably relevant today. The very high annual home-building rate of these years was primarily a product of the political determination to make it happen. The chart from Kate Barker's Interim Report, showing the long-run

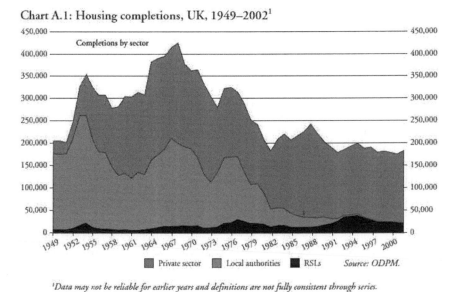

Chart A.1: Housing completions, UK, 1949–2002[1]

¹Data may not be reliable for earlier years and definitions are not fully consistent through series.

Figure 2.10. Public and private house-building since the Second World War. (*Source*: Barker, 2004)

building figures, gives a graphic overview of the way in which Council (and housing association) building contributed to the post-war housing drive (Barker, 2004).

Figure 2.10 illustrates how private house-building took about a decade to reach 150,000 per annum (by 1959) and then stayed in the range 175–225,000 units per annum for year after year, until the late-1980s slump. The socially-built production was what made the difference. It peaked at nearly 262,000 in 1953 and 1954, and sustained an average of over 170,000 (and so a total volume of 5.1 million) over the three decades 1949–1978. So the annual house-building output from all sources was never below 250,000 per annum from 1952 onwards, for the next 25 years. Then, since 1980, the social output slumped – even with increased funding for RSLs (Registered Social Landlords, primarily housing associations) – and the *overall* annual total has never exceeded the 250,000 mark since 1979 (DCLG, 2011).

Post-War Designs and Layouts: *What* Was Built

Increasingly, as the 1950s went on, the model for council architects, and even more so for those planning the new towns (Hall and Ward, 1998), was 'Radburn'. This was 'a planned urban layout … first applied in Radburn, New Jersey, USA 1928. It separates pedestrians from cars and trucks by arranging "super blocks" of housing … around a central green. Each super block has its outer roads, off which come service culs-de-sac. The central green has pedestrian access only… The experience of Radburn NJ itself has been a success…' (Llewelyn Davies, 2005) – there, there is a strong community focus, predominance of owner-occupiers, and an annual residents' fee towards year-round recreation and management programmes. The Llewelyn Davies team went on: 'The Radburn layout concept was later widely adopted in the planning of post-war housing areas in Britain… It was thus imported as an approach to urban design and layout – separated from its context, the house designs, and the ownership/community structures with which it was associated in its native land'.

Alison Ravetz is even more critical:

This layout, in a misunderstood and corrupted form, was re-imported to Britain… The British version of Radburn made two changes that were crucial to its operation: houses were built in short rows or terraces rather than in pairs or detached, and garages were grouped in courts at some distance from and often out of sight of the houses … one of the problem points of estates in the years to come. (Ravetz 2001)

Nonetheless, and rather as with Tudor Walters and the approach after the First World War, the concept had holy water sprinkled on it by a government document: in this case the 1961 *Homes for Today and Tomorrow*, notably in Section V (Parker Morris, 1961). This, combined with the very *very* plain (generally still brick, but not always) treatment of the buildings, established the characteristic look of the final phase of social building on the grand scale.

To a user, most of these post-war estates feel very like Lynsey Hanley's description of Chelmsley Wood: 'a long boomerang-shaped crescent from which car-free stalks of

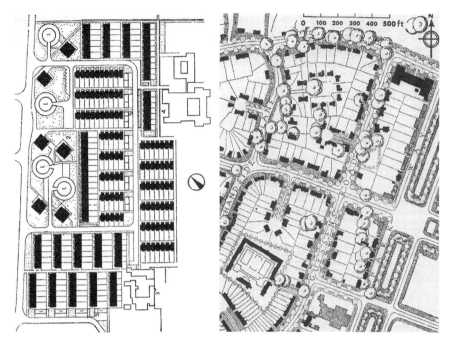

Figure 2.11. 'Radburn' in Cumbernauld, compared with early 'garden city' in Welwyn. (*Source*: Osborn and Whittick, 1963)

terrace housing spring out … criss-crossing macadamed walks with boxy brown rows set on either side' (Hanley, 2007).

The homes' appearance had indeed changed a lot, as well as the layout: these post-war houses are generally very plain indeed: a mix of two and three storeys with occasional four-storey town houses and maisonettes; low-pitch roofs with brown concrete interlocking tiling; 'fronts' that face onto the greens and the walks, but are used less than the 'backs' reached from the parking courts.

Some are well-realized, within the overall Radburn design concept, and by now have matured into neighbourhoods which offer pleasant places to live. Peter Hall makes the interesting point that New Earswick in York – 'beautifully preserved, sympathetically restored … a small gem, dazzling to the eye at the age of more than eighty' – has a layout of communal greens, pedestrian ways and some culs-de-sac 'anticipating the Radburn layout by more than a quarter of a century' (Hall, 2002).

But even where the houses and green spaces work well, other aspects have turned out to be pretty unsatisfactory. The Llewelyn Davies report for CABE listed a series of problems, noting especially the crime and insecurity associated with separating off pedestrians, alleys with no natural surveillance, and anonymous open space backing straight onto people's gardens and yards (Llewelyn Davies, 2005). And as early as the 1970s, there were criticisms: David Thompson quotes an 'ex-resident of a new town' as remarking that 'Our Radburn layout looked lovely, but it meant that no-one ever passed our house by chance. My wife felt wholly cut off' (Thompson, 1976).

We are a long way from 'cottages' by this time; though admittedly still trying to provide something like the same product, in a post-war form.

The End Product, 1900–1970

Looked at from the planning and urban design end of the telescope, the cottage estates and their post-war successors were the product of a very great deal of attention, thought and design effort. Unlike the tower blocks and the deck-access slabs, they were not just a weird result of architectural modernism mating with a political push on housing numbers. They 'should have worked'.

Looked at from the consumer end, they probably did at first, but as society changed they later mainly did not. Hanley sketches the changing attitudes and expectations:

They had been given homes, but not the caretakers to look after them. They had been given front doors, but only on the condition that every one was the same colour… There was a sense that what they really wanted – to be individuals, with individual property and individual wealth … – could only be achieved by retreating from the state that had given them the space, the health and the freedom to make such decisions. (Hanley, 2007)

The Places Themselves: Six Estates

Now to look at particular examples from corporation suburbia. Six estates are described and discussed in the chapters that follow. Two are 'Corporation Suburb I – set in a prosperous region' in the typology above: they are Tower Gardens and Becontree in London, dealt with in Chapter 3. Two are 'Corporation Suburb II – set in less prosperous areas': with Deckham/Carr Hill and Hylton Castle in Tyne and Wear – Chapter 4. And two are in Chapter 5's category 'Radburnland – the later post-war suburbs': Bromford in the West Midlands, and Orchard Park on the edge of Hull.

Notes

1. Figures supplied by Leicester City Council, in *From Start of Sale of Council Houses* table and map *Council Estates – Leicester*.
2. See http://www.tourisme93.com/stains/printemps-cites-jardins-2012.html.
3. See http://www.ville-stains.fr/site/index.php?option=com_content&view=article&id=250&Item id=376.

Chapter 3

Two London Estates

The first two estates explored – Tower Gardens in North London, and Becontree in East London – have in common their setting in the generally-prosperous London region; but they are surprisingly different in scale and feel.

Tower Gardens

The Tower Gardens estate is in Tottenham, part of the London Borough of Haringey. It contains a little under 1,000 homes. It is the earliest and most 'cottagey' part of a very extensive area of council-built housing (the LCC's – 'White Hart Lane Estate') which extends north from Lordship Lane along Roundway and Great Cambridge Road: this later and bigger extension has the classic feel of 'council semis on the bypass' not shared by Tower Gardens.

It sits in the typology as 'corporation suburb in a prosperous area' – the prosperous area being London and the South East, with the most jobs and highest wages of any

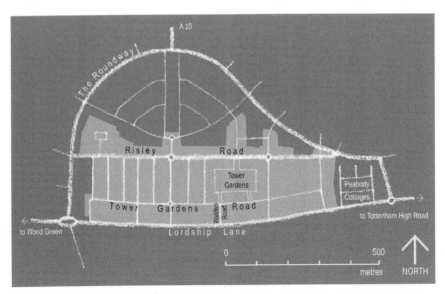

Figure 3.1. Tower Gardens, Tottenham.

British region. Tottenham itself, of course, has an unenviably high profile as the *non-prosperous* part of Haringey and as a generally deprived and troubled part of the capital.

Tower Gardens itself is not in this highly problematic category. Figures for the two 'best fit' census tracts (an area slightly larger than the estate) paint a more nuanced picture. Unemployment, at 14 per cent in 2011, was and is troublingly high, and double the London average. But there is actually quite a range of people here: 23 per cent 'managerial & professional', 32 per cent in other administration and skilled jobs, 46 per cent in service and unskilled occupations. Just over a third work within 5 km – essentially, within Haringey borough – but most (58 per cent) travel further afield, to the rest of the city. This being London, public transport dominates the journey to work (51 per cent), with a third using car or motorbike, etc, and a surprisingly low 7 per cent on foot or bike: presumably a reflection of most jobs being well outside the estate (these are 2001 figures, as the Census 2011 office is still hard at it on the abacus 2 years later. But the patterns will not have changed much).

The area is very mixed ethnically: 46 per cent 'white', 27 per cent 'black/black British', 9 per cent 'mixed', 11 per cent 'Asian/Asian British'. It is, in particular, and like the wider Tottenham area, the long established home to a lot of households of black-Caribbean heritage or origin. The newer changes in London's population are reflected too, and on a big scale: 31 per cent of the residents were born outside Europe, over 1,000 people, up from 654 a decade ago. The mix includes, for example, groups of young Bulgarian workers, and Roma families, sub-letting ex-Right-to-Buy properties, and a 'Romanian Shop' catering to national tastes on Lordship Lane.

The Census data for tenure also show a mixture, with just over half the households in social homes (52 per cent, down from 59 per cent in 2001), approaching a third owner-occupiers (28 per cent, slightly down over the decade), and the balance in private lets or 'other'. The private-rented proportion was the one that rose, from 141 to 233 properties (19 per cent) – a reflection of how dynamic this sector has now become in the London market in particular.

The Census tables give other hints about the changes and pressures in this part of London. Car ownership, already below 50 per cent in 2001, fell again to 47 per cent of households. The social and occupational mix 'stretched', with more residents in the upper (managerial & professional) strata and in the lower less-skilled ones, but 7 per cent fewer in the mid-range technical and admin categories. Household size increased (as in England and Wales as a whole) but much faster than average, and is now almost 2.8 persons per household. Tower Gardens seems to be showing in some ways the polarization, and overall tightening of conditions, that twenty-first century Londoners are experiencing.

One of the First Garden Suburbs

This first part of the White Hart Lane estate is over a century old. Over the period from 1904 to 1915, the 40 acres (16 ha) fronting Lordship Lane were developed as Tower Gardens: '963 cottages and five shops with flats above… Rents for two to five rooms varied from 6s to 13s' (Jackson, 1991). Today's equivalent would be about £30–£60/ week – so at its upper end, not far off council rents today. At about the same time, the Peabody Donation Fund added 154 more little terraced cottages off Lordship Lane, immediately to the east, completed in 1907. The Peabody homes are still there – a tranquil enclave which continues to be managed by the Trust. The big expansion came between the wars, when the White Hart Lane Estate more than doubled in size, with a further 1,266 houses and flats added and sixteen more shops, so that by 1938 the estate housed just over 10,000 people (Jackson, 1991).

The original (pre-First World War) estate is now a Conservation Area. Haringey Council's Supplementary Planning Guidance (SPG) note on it says 'it has a very special place in the history of Council Housing building. It was one of the first "garden suburbs" in the world and its architecture is of extremely high quality'. The SPG relates it to the Arts & Crafts and Garden City movements, and to the LCC's wish to 'improve housing conditions for the working classes by providing well-constructed,

Figure 3.2. A mini Hampstead Garden Suburb in N17. (*Source*: London Borough of Haringey)

healthful homes in pleasant surroundings to rent'. It was the first LCC estate built outside the county (Tooting was just inside). A special aspect of its history, and of what was developed, was that 'the Jewish entrepreneur Samuel Montagu … donated £10,000 to purchase land and build at a lower density to provide accommodation in a "garden suburb" setting. This donation was tied to the rehousing of Jewish workers resident in the Tower Hamlets parishes and required an area of land to be set aside for public gardens: hence the name Tower Gardens' (Haringey Council, 1997).

What *was* developed was a simple but very coherent little estate. It is quite densely-built, compared with later 'mainstream' corporation cottage estates: the net density of each block is about 75 dwellings per hectare (about 30 to the acre), much higher than the post-First World War (Tudor Walters) indication of 12 per acre (30 dph or dwellings per hectare). Some of that tight form (and small garden size) is offset by having the 3 acres (1.3 ha) of public gardens right within the estate.

Tower Gardens Today

The layout is a simple grid of straight streets, so it predates the geometric circles and swirls of later layouts. The houses are mostly in short runs of terraces, with what variety there is coming mainly from the carefully-chosen (Arts & Crafts again) materials – walls of red or yellow stock bricks, or roughcast, or washed render; roofs in tile or grey slate; and from the varying use of bays, cross-gables, porches and roof depths in the succession of little terraces. It adds up to a very satisfying mix of variety within unity.

The feel is of quite tight little streets, when compared with later council housing 'road' or 'avenue' layouts: although not if compared with, say, the inner-city streets

Figure 3.3. The twentieth century lives on – Tower Gardens Road at Walden Road, Spring 2012.

its earliest residents would have left behind in Whitechapel. Lots of planting (street trees, garden bushes) and the Arts & Crafts house forms give a 'cosy' feel which is very attractive; a working-class Hampstead Garden Suburb. The Tower Gardens park is pleasant and well-used, and the area is quite lively, with people on the streets and some traffic (though little rat-running by London standards).

The 'Peabody Cottages' streets to the immediate east are a delightful extra, with the feel of a time capsule where the milkman's horse-and-cart could come round the corner at any time.

Northwards, as noted, the Roundway housing is more a typical inter-war council estate in style and feel – the density is approximately 17 to the acre (42 dph), according to the SPG, though still generally looking cared-for and popular.

Now, a century of London's growth later, Tower Gardens is of course far from the peripheral edge-of-London location it once was: 'A nearby farm, together with open views to the south and north, contributed to an almost rural setting, disturbed only by the electric tramcars on the main road' (Jackson, 1991). But it is suburban, not inner-urban, in its connections (a 15-minute walk to rail; or bus, or bus-then-tube, for Central London and its million-plus jobs; and similarly a bus trip for anything more than local shopping at Wood Green). However, it has far more local shops and services nearby than do most council estates, because of what is now a sort of 'semi-inner-city' location, embedded in the London context.

What Do Residents Think?

A retired nurse, who has lived in the locality most of the time since she arrived from the West Indies, said 'yes it's a nice little area – you know, on this street [Tower Gardens Road] there were professional people, a piano teacher, a teacher – there was a little stream, but they diverted it…'.

The 'kind of people' comes up again in the recollections of Charlie Roberts, who moved to the area in 1946 from bomb-damaged Hoxton: 'Most of the people living in Tower Gardens were East End characters that had moved because of bomb damage in the East End, and professional people such as teachers, bank clerks and Police Chief Constables and Councillors' – with memories of 'a very close community. Front garden competitions were a regular feature. Tower Gardens Park (the Little Rec) was the setting for school sports days – people were not normally permitted to walk on the grass' (Haringey Council, 2012).

One of the ward councillors ('a Haringey girl' herself, as she said) confirmed that people *do* stay, and that a strong residents' group reflects commitment: 'it's an area people are very passionate about – it's seen as a bit special compared to the Roundway houses to the north'. She felt that 'with some of the newer families there's a bit of – not exactly tension – but a bit less pride, maybe?' and recent problems and arguments over dumping of rubbish on street had got caught up in that.

The residents' group secretary has lived in the area for some 9 years, in a sold-on RTB purchase, the previous owner having moved to Enfield – reflecting the pattern with the long-established (generally white skilled working-class) families, of whom there are now very few left; they have mainly moved further north or out to Hertfordshire. His immediate neighbours in the terrace of four are two council tenant families and one original RTB-purchaser: the son of a tenant who moved in during the 1930s.

There has clearly been some limited 'colonization' by young professionals like him, but fairly recently. Before, there would not have been enough private houses on the market for much change to occur. For him, Tower Gardens is 'a nice affordable place to live, with reasonably good transport links… I guess I thought at the time – I can either live in a one bedroom flat in Muswell Hill, or I can live in this nice cottage in Tottenham! Of course Tower Gardens seemed very green and almost suburban, quite different from the central part of Tottenham further to the east'. No, it is not scary: 'there *is* a rough element, and if you just read the local paper you'd never go out. But visitors say "is it always this quiet?" and I say "yes it is, really!". Tottenham itself, yes, has 'a dreadful dreadful reputation, and it's worse than ever, with burnt-out buildings and so on'. But he has never felt vulnerable around here yet.

Other members of the residents' group had perhaps more critical comments. One woman, a tenant in social housing, said that she intends to stay in the area, but thinks it has got worse rather than better over time, highlighting *'noise, squatters, difficult landlords and cars'* as all being concerns: but *'good neighbours'* as the best feature of the locality. When asked what her reaction would be if the area became more popular with buyers from outside, that would be fine: but if the area were to carry on housing a lot of people who – like her – are tenants, and cannot afford to buy, she would be worried.

Another resident, an architect who had bought his 'ex-Right-to-Buy' house on the open market, echoed some of these concerns. On the 'better, or worse?' question, his comment was that 'sometimes there's a glimmer of improvement – improved shops on Lordship Lane, more young working families moving in – but it's often quashed by something negative occurring: increase in squatting, burglary and car damage, increase in anti-social behaviour'.

His thinking laid a lot of stress on the need for an area like Tower Gardens to be *managed*, not just left to bumble along. Issues like a relatively large transient population – whether asylum-seekers, or European journeyman workers – putting uncomfortable demand on services; and like the burden on local schools of transient non-English-speaking children, which he saw as 'causing families who might otherwise settle to be forced to up and move to less transient areas when their children reach school age. I worry that this could have an unfortunate impact on the sense of community in the long term'. Indeed, he saw himself as moving on in future.

Like his neighbour, he raised the nuisances caused by 'a small number of residents, typically council tenants, [who] have a blatant disregard for the property and space of others, yet the council seems powerless to manage this'. So again, if the area carries on housing a lot of people who are tenants and cannot afford to buy, while for him there is 'no concern about this per se … it requires a very well-structured management system by the local authority in terms of property maintenance, anti-social behaviour control, community building, and improvement in services'. These are serious concerns and well-argued logics; and in later chapters it will be evident that they relate to some recurrent, and widespread, problems that need to be tackled before these estates' potentials can be released.

On the other hand, his list of what is good about Tower Gardens is a long one too. 'The sense of calm experienced when entering the estate...'; the fact that 'the small scale of housing tends to prevent the splitting of properties' so that 'there tends to be a longer lifespan of occupancy which helps to build community'. Perhaps not surprisingly given his design background, the list included many attractive features of the physical form: the requirement for hedges, presence of trees, prevention of parking in gardens, properties with clearly defensible space, and 'the subtle changes of detailing, massing and materials that give special character to each street, without compromising the unity of the whole'.

And even though 'the Conservation Area status is regularly disregarded by occupiers and tenants, and the planning authority seem relatively powerless to enforce remedial action', it does seem that 'to an extent, the Conservation Area status holds back the potential for neglect, decay and mismanagement of properties'.

So...

In summary: Tower Gardens is extremely attractive to the outside eye; it looks mature, homely and friendly; and it seems as though it ought to be convenient and appealing to quite a range of households. But it cannot just be taken for granted – it needs care, attention and hands-on management.

Becontree

The Becontree estate is at the opposite end of the spectrum to cosy little Tower Gardens. It is huge. It makes up about half the area of the London Borough of Barking and Dagenham, and is 'by far the largest of all the estates developed by the London County Council' (Jackson, 1991). By the end of the 1930s nearly 26,000 houses had been built, in less than two decades from autumn 1920. They stretch from the A13 Ripple Road northwards to Chadwell Heath, and west–east from the boundary with Ilford to the strip of green belt at Eastbrookend.

It accounted for 40 per cent of the LCC's inter-war cottage-estate building; other large ones were St Helier, Downham, Bellingham, and Mottingham in south and southeast London, and Watling in the northwest. Borough councils in outer London contributed another 48,000 out of the 122,000 total. This was the period when London doubled in size on the ground – though the spatial expansion was not matched by comparable population growth, as the cottage estates and their private-sector equivalents lowered the conurbation's density throughout the inter-war years (White, 2008).

Becontree, like Tower Gardens, sits in the typology as a 'corporation suburb in a prosperous area' – the prosperous area again being London and the South East. But the East London which surrounds it has a long history of being the more industrial, poorer, less attractive side of London. And Becontree's development is as much as anything part of the story of attempts to deal with that 'old East End' legacy.

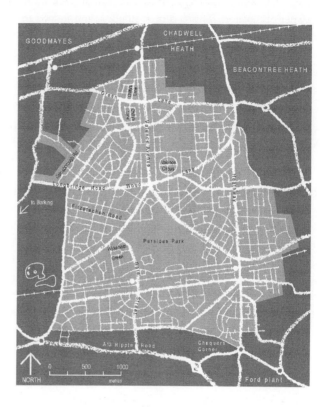

Figure 3.4. Becontree, East London.

The total population of the Becontree estate is now rising again, after drifting downwards in the post-war years. It is once more above 100,000, having risen by over 10,000 (+11 per cent) since the 2001 Census. As elsewhere in London, this growth in the numbers of people has been much faster than the increase in households or housing stock: the number of households rose by less than a thousand over the decade, so the average household size went up from 2.46 (already above the national average of 2.36 in 2001) to 2.67 (nationally now 2.40).

This population has also changed dramatically too, in ways that were not expected and are still not always very obvious on the ground. What was still in 2001 a 90 per cent 'white' estate recorded a 64 per cent figure for this ethnicity in the 2011 Census. 'Black/ black British' respondents rose from 5 per cent to 18 per cent; and 'Asian/ British Asian' from 2 per cent to 13 per cent. Residents born in the UK and Ireland, who formed 93 per cent of the population in 2001, are now 74 per cent: about 10,000 fewer in number. The really big additions are of those born outside Europe – now nearly 20,000 people or over 19 per cent, and arrivals from the EU Accession countries who are now 5 per cent of the area's population: over 4,800 people compared to 475 a decade ago.

There is change, too, in the housing market; and again, not in expected ways. Becontree people were among the 'early adopters' of the Right-to-Buy (RTB), with the 1980s and 1990s seeing a massive switch from monolithic municipal tenure to owner-occupation. That has now stopped, and indeed in a sense gone into reverse: owner-occupation actually fell in the first decade of the 2000s, and is now back below 50 per cent, having been at 56 per cent in 2001. Social renting continued to lose ground, though slowly (38 per cent down to 35 per cent). But it is private renting which has grown enormously – up from 2,080 households (6 per cent) to 6,095 (16 per cent) – an even bigger jump than in Tower Gardens. The RTB stock is now clearly an important component of this market.

Socially and economically, Becontree's data are an intriguing mix of the predictable and the surprising. The socio-economic classification in the 'NS-SeC' tables of the 2011 Census confirms that the estate's social structure is, as it has been for a long time, light on people in the higher-end 'managerial and administrative' classifications; around the national average for the mid-range ones ('intermediate', 'self-employed', 'lower supervisory', etc); and heavy on the lower-end of the range ('routine', 'semi-routine', and so on). Unemployment, at 11 per cent on the 2011 Census basis of 'unemployed as percentage of economically active', remains higher than the London (7 per cent) or England & Wales (6 per cent) levels. But as in Tower Gardens, the striking 2001–2011 changes described above have been accompanied by a sort of 'stretch' or polarization in the occupational structure of working residents. Here, the three lowest (paid) groups have increased (42 per cent to 46 per cent), as have the uppermost two (15 per cent to 19 per cent), whilst the middle three have slipped from 43 per cent to 35 per cent. Once again, we see the estate becoming more varied, less homogenous – moving ever further from its original municipal conception.

Enormous – In Conception and Realization

The estate's history began with LCC decisions in 1919 to undertake a massive programme of working-class housing and to concentrate it east of Barking. From the outset it was a mammoth and ambitious scheme. The LCC's architect referred to '*a township with a population of 120,000*' in his report in early 1920, and the council described it as '*a township more or less complete in itself*' quite early on (Home, 1997).

In 1919–1920 the necessary CPOs went through; in 1921 the first houses were finished, at Chitty's Lane in the northwest (Ilford/Barking) corner; the initial target of 18,000 houses was reached in 1934. Edwin Hardy Amies, whose father was Resident Agent from very early on, recalls that they lived initially in 'a very nice farmhouse in Gale Street. The land about us was flat and uninteresting but it was genuine Essex countryside…' where his father found the farmers mainly ready to sell the land and very happy with the money they got. As with the Alton Estate after the Second World War, the scheme had an international profile: '…he often had to entertain visitors from overseas that came to see what was considered at that time a remarkable project. It was a big estate and my father was quite proud of it and the foreigners thought it was marvellous' (quoted in Rubinstein, 1991).

More and more houses were then added over the next 30 years, first by the LCC (1,400 more) and then by the pre-1965 Dagenham Council (another 4,000, mainly post-war). By the end of the 1930s the population had reached 116,000 (Jackson, 1991).

Figure 3.5. The first houses, and their LCC plaque (Chitty's Lane, 1921).

So the development was enormous, in conception and realization. Alan Jackson (1991) says 'the 1931 census found it already larger than Darlington or Bath'; Robert Home (1997) remarks that 'it has tended to attract impressive, if rather tedious, size comparisons'. It was not, as has often been assumed, conceived as the housing for workers at Ford's giant Dagenham car plant (which was really only under way after 1931), and even in 1937 61 per cent of tenants worked in Central London, not locally or in the rest of the East End (Jackson, 1991). The 'working-class' the estate was aimed at were its upper strata – working in manufacturing or transport, many of them busmen.

This aspect of class differentiation is dealt with more fully in Chapter 8 on 'Attitudes'.

And the achievement, even with all its weaknesses, was enormous too. Andrzej Olechnowitz quotes Terence Young's 1934 judgement: 'If it [Becontree] had happened in Vienna, the Labour and left Liberal press would have boosted it as an example of what municipal socialism could accomplish', but he adds 'In interwar Britain there was not the slightest chance of "public opinion" endorsing that judgement'. He quotes a raft of contemporary criticisms about monotony: its not being a community, the one-class (= working-class) nature, badly planned, no local government structures, and so on (Olechnowitz, 1997).

Over the post-war years, Becontree's role and status inevitably shifted. By the late 1980s, one of the long-standing residents interviewed for *Just Like The Country* said: 'When the estate houses were first built everyone was very proud and they looked after them. Maybe it was because we had a brand new house, and we did our utmost to keep it spick and span. As for today some of the houses are run down a bit. People aren't taking so much care of them with many of the front gardens left unattended' (quoted in Rubinstein, 1991). But it is still a popular choice for tenants moving; according to borough staff, it is generally top of the list in the 'More Choice in Letting' system except for the few who might choose Thames View because of their links to Barking centre, or a flat in the centre because of community links, mosque attendance, etc. In the open market, it is attracting new groups: for example African families, because of the combination of having more space than in Inner London, quite good schools, and relatively low house prices.

A Sense of Place?

One of the effects of the great size was, and is, a fairly weak sense of place. Jackson's formulation is 'because it was so extensive & diffuse … a sense of community grew with difficulty'. But at this scale, it was never likely that it would be seen as one place, with a common sense of 'community', particularly because it has never really had its own single dominant town centre.

What is perhaps more interesting is that few of its sub-divisions seem to have much distinguishing character either – whether designed-in, or evolving over time. Few if any of the sub-areas have a particular name: if you want to find out where someone lives, you will probably ask them 'what's it off of?' – and they will say 'Green Lane', or 'behind Five Elms shops'. It is noticeable that the areas that do have tenants' and residents' associations are in the flatted developments, not the main swathes of housing. No doubt it is in the flats that there are management issues best dealt with en bloc; but it does also suggest that in general the cottage estate has not really generated much sense of local community at the small-group-of-streets level.

Olechnowitz says of the early years:

As the estate became divided between three boroughs, tenants thought of themselves as living in East Barking, New Ilford, or Dagenham. London was also a barrier. Many tenants were proud to be 'East Londoners... There were definite 'rough' and 'respectable' parts of the estate. One respondent wrote 'obviously the "suntrap" houses immediately north of Becontree station were more attractive... Also by 1940 some streets were known to house criminals and got bad reputations'... The Becontree area was where the 'elite of the estate' lived. The Gale Street area was 'for people earning higher wages, more of a middle class'. The Heathway area was 'rough'. (Olechnowicz, 1997)

Fifteen years later, this is still the pattern. One resident in the centre of the estate said '*it is Dagenham, but I never say I live there, I say Becontree*' – because Dagenham (the 'Nam') is still associated with the Heathway, which is still seen as 'really rough'; and the Chequers Corner area near the Ford Dagenham plant as dismal.

This question of identity links in a way to the to-ing and fro-ing over the name. The LCC decided on 'Becontree'. But even now locals tend to alternate between reserving that name for the smallish area round Becontree underground station (referring to the whole area as 'Dagenham'), and making the stigma-driven distinction described above. In his recent walk-across-London saga, Mark Mason claims that the older name of Beacontree was the intention, but was too long for bus destination boards... (Mason, 2011).

The estate's design reflects the main elements of post-First World War thinking, with a plainer 'neo-Georgian' look to the houses, with the Tudor Walters report's 12-to-the-acre, and with a garden-city-influenced move away from plain grid layouts towards the 'curvilinear' expressed in sweeping bends, 'circuses' and crescents. The classic form of this – which is always shown in plans and aerial photos – is Valence Circus in the middle of the estate. Of course, not much of this is actually visible at ground level. As long ago as 1944, Patrick Abercrombie remarked on the inter-war estates having 'elaborate geometry which can only be seen from the air' (LCC, 1944).

It is clear that the LCC designers worked very hard at the layout. They carefully linked their broad sometimes-dualled new avenues to the older country-lane alignments, often with 'Y' junctions that seem to have been trying to give a sense of place. They used short culs-de-sac to create local groupings and perhaps a feeling of community. Their shape led to their always being known as 'banjos', which seems to be a term unique to Becontree. The banjo format is not an unalloyed success these days: kids playing noisily on the quite narrow common green adjoining some of the houses, and car parking pressure on the tight little neck of entry road, mean that in some of them the main road will be looking after itself whilst the banjo has neighbour problems. A banjo homeowner suggested that rather than engendering community spirit, the form (especially in some of its less well-realized variants) actually needed rather more local management and attention, not less: preferably in consultation with residents.

The designers also interspersed a lot of small green spaces between the houses and on corners – although children were reportedly discouraged from playing on them so they were rather more feature than functional (Home, 1997). As with the curves and circles, though, all this form is pretty hard to pick up at ground level, as the roads and houses go on and on and on over the Essex lowland. Peter Hall's cruel but fair conclusion is 'The housing was worthy enough, and it conformed to Unwin's pattern books; it, and the layouts within which it was embodied, were just plain dull' (Hall, 2002).

Area differentiation, as discussed already, is not a strong feature. In most parts of the country, the 'status' of localities varies with factors like location and convenience for transport; or like reputation and (in a sort of feedback loop) the extent of Right-to-Buy; and/or to a limited extent like stock type (certain sorts of semi seem quite sought-after). In Becontree, things are perhaps not so clear. There is no doubt that attempts at variation began early: at Gale Street, near Becontree station, '800 houses of larger type intended for remunerative letting to the highest-paid workers' were developed in the late 1930s (Jackson, 1991). Now this Wykeham Green locality is the one really distinct neighbourhood that everyone can identify, the one which is the most desirable, and the one with the highest penetration of Right-to-Buy. Other roads facing onto parks, such as Ivy House Road, which like Wykeham Green adjoins Parsloes Park, are also seen as better locations; as are, broadly, roads which combine closeness to parks, schools and convenient access to the Underground. However these do not seem to add up to whole neighbourhoods seen as 'better' or 'worse'. Some variations between sub-areas can be seen, though not dramatically, in sale values; even less so in rentals (see Chapter 7).

Within the overall size and apparent uniformity, though, and despite the shortage of focal points and strong places, there *is* variety and range. But the variation seems

Figure 3.6. Gale Street/Wykeham Green 'suntrap' homes: top of the range in Becontree.

to be hyper-local, street by street, not between neighbourhoods as big (say) as Tower Gardens but smaller than the whole of Becontree. Some side-roads are stark and unappealing, and yet they are quite near good little collections. A 'frinstance', as they say in the East End, of this fine grain of difference lies close to the estate's western edge. Here the dull and unloved-looking Gainsborough Road runs behind Becontree Avenue, an epitome of the common image of the monotonous council scheme. But across it runs Sylvan Way, where one of the small corner greens really does create a pleasant little 'place' which looks as though people appreciate it. Similarly, 600 metres to the south, Fitzstephen Road is drab, shabby, tree-less and poorly maintained, even though it is just north of the popular Gale Street: in neither case is any 'area effect' detectable.

The Right-to-Buy and Social Change

Sometimes, obviously, the differences come not – or not just – from the design, but from the tenure. The council managed 47,000 homes before the major Right-to-Buy wave; it now has 19,000. In common with the provinces (as in Leicester, see Chapter 2), but unlike Inner London, almost all of the flats have stayed in the social stock, with the vast majority of sales having been of houses. Post-RTB, Becontree sports the familiar personalization of many of the homes: colour, planting, little extensions, cladding; homeowners clearly happy to own here and wanting to show it.

In places, a grouping of houses that now looks to be all or mostly owned rather than rented gives an impression of an area where social change is well under way and where individual household decisions are adding up to more than just cosmetic change. So whole localities could potentially be differentiating. One has to be careful though: even after 30 years of RTB, the social composition has not changed as much as the tenure. Over the last 15 years or so, the first generation of RTB purchasers have been selling up and moving on, and borough staff believe that at least half have gone into the private-rented sector, not to another owner-occupier. One of the residents pointed out that the smaller (two-bedroom) houses were less likely to be privately rented, in the centre of the estate away from stations and shops anyway.

So it is still hard, as we have seen, to identify actual neighbourhoods (except Gale Street) that are now seen as more or less desirable. And the market evidence reported in Chapter 7 suggests that there remains a marked price differential between this property and nearby non-council-built houses of a similar sort.

Overall, the feel is still of the big rather uniform working-class estate, though not a particularly poor one. Mark Mason, as he trudges along the route of the District Line out from the city, captures it rather well:

After Barking the ethnic mix returns to monochrome. This is the land that twentieth-century municipal socialism built. On the huge Becontree Estate … the interwar council houses now bear Cyfrowy Polsat dishes, but there are almost no black or Asian faces to be seen. It feels very Essex, very working-class, very 1960s. There's obviously not much money about, but neither

Figure 3.7. Differentials? About 20 per cent on prices between the Valence Avenue 'RTB' row (*above*) and non-council-built Ventnor Gardens, towards Barking town centre (*below*).

is there much graffiti or rubbish. Florists offer wreaths saying 'Mum', 'Dad', 'Nan'… A garden gnome wears a West Ham kit. You half expect a front door to open and a young lad to run out shouting that the Russian linesman has allowed England's third goal. (Mason, 2011)

Robert Home offers a slightly more academic judgement: he notes that in 1945, despite the shortage of social facilities, Mass Observation reported that 85 per cent liked their homes, 63 per cent liked their neighbourhood, and 14 per cent wanted to be owners; and goes on to say 'Sixty or seventy years later, the inter-war cottage estates are generally still intact and popular, and increasingly being bought by their sitting tenants' (Home, 1997).

What Do Residents Think?

A woman who moved from Inner London, and bought her house 11 years ago as an affordable sound 'doer-upper', was very clear that the estate is still stigmatized by its history as a council product – and some areas within it even more so, by their 'rough' reputation. Yet if you were to come in and drive around, much of it looks OK: and *'it's quiet, there's no aggro, not even kids hanging around, which would worry a lot of people'*. But the estate does not offer much, and there has been little or no development of facilities; in the centre of the estate, *'there's a café on Green Lanes which is well attended and an OAP's club, and it's miles to a pub, the Bridge House – and that's it. There's a lot of nice open space, but there's too much of it: they should break Parsloes Park up and develop some of it, and make nice little spaces like in Bethnal Green, with cafés and so on – there's nothing, no toilet, no tea bar, no playground'*. Barking's East Street market, a quarter-hour's bus-ride away, is the only place with some character and something to do, *'just to have a little wander, especially if you've not got much money'* – though even that is hardly cappuccino culture, as she said.

Figure 3.8. Parsloes Park: 'there's nothing…'.

As for a sense of community: this obviously very outgoing person said *'I mean, I'm not saying I want to bake cakes and go to community do's, but there's no community round here'*; while acknowledging that, without young children, she probably misses out on the only local focus, the primary-school gate. Her perception is that young migrant households are now buying in to the area, which to them is good value with good schools: especially Polish and Lithuanian families, who are now staying long enough that you see the kids growing up (and the bloke's mum, who's come over to mind them). Nearby Goodmayes, an Edwardian suburb just outside the estate, has much more life and community, but that is because it has attracted Muslim families and the associated shops, mosque and so on.

On the other hand, young English-born people who grew up on the estate do not stay, their aspiration is still Hornchurch, 'down the line' to the east. The houses may or may not be good value, but for them *'the area's still the area'*.

A somewhat more rosy view came from residents interviewed by a journalist: contrasting the early feeling of what palaces the homes seemed in the old days, the man in the cab office acknowledged the size issue mentioned above: *'These days they're small and poky: a very small kitchen, a very small front room, three bedrooms, one large, two small'*; but added that *'having lived in mine 25 years it makes not a jot of difference… If I won the lottery, I'd tour the world and come back here and put a granny flat on my house'*. And a couple living in one of the Gale Street 'suntrap' houses were very positive about the community aspect: *'We've had a lot of people move in from other countries … an Indian family lives on one side and Brazilians on the other; across the street is a Nigerian family. We enjoy it'* – with mention of joint parties and neighbourhood barbecues. *'It is a lovely feeling to have neighbours on all sides who are friends'* (Barton, 2009).

This is cheering, and it is no doubt the sort of thing *The Guardian*'s readers like to see – but the predominant impression from most of Becontree is rather more like the preceding narrative.

In Summary

It is hard to summarize Becontree. It is not all one thing – but it is not a lot of very distinct separate things either. The proportion of Right-to-Buy is high, with less than 40 per cent of all the homes now socially-rented, the majority of them flats (though owner-occupation has actually dropped since 2001), and many of the neighbourhoods have indeed stood the test of time reasonably well. The proportion of people in jobs is comparable with surrounding parts of (non-municipal) East London, and it continues to have strong labour market links with Central London (and new Docklands) employment. On the other hand, the penetration of the private-rented sector (tripled since 2001; and see also rentals information in Chapter 7 below) suggests that a simple assumption of continued *embourgeoisement* is not a safe bet for the future, and that some of the localities within Becontree could be headed for less stability not more. What is more, the borough's management of the estate environment is noticeably less impressive than that provided by some of its equivalents further north. If only because of its size, Becontree raises many of the issues about potentials and threats that corporation suburbia as a whole may be confronting.

Chapter 4

In the North East

The next two localities considered are 'Corporation Suburbs' set in a much less prosperous region: the North East of England. They are Tyneside's Deckham/Carr Hill, an inner suburb not far from Gateshead town centre, and Wearside's Hylton Castle on the outskirts of Sunderland.

Deckham and Carr Hill

Gateshead is Newcastle's southern twin, but the unfancied one across the Tyne. Its grimy industrial past meant that everyone had a poke at it, from Samuel Johnson to J.B. Priestley (he said 'Every future historian of modern England should be compelled to take a good long slow walk round Gateshead...' and – the quote that is always dragged out, and here we go again – that it 'appeared to have been carefully planned by an enemy of the human race') (Priestley, 1934). In the T. Dan Smith era, the council compounded this image by building a dreadful shuttered-concrete shopping centre and the notorious 'Get Carter' multi-storey car park: both happily now demolished.

But Gateshead also built a suite of interesting and often attractive housing estates. Among them are the Deckham and Carr Hill group: perched on top of and behind the Gateshead ridge, east of the Old Durham Road (the original Great North Road, precursor to the A1) as it runs south out of the town. Deckham and Carr Hill are made up primarily of a garden-suburb layout of semis and short terraces in a group of contiguous cottage estates. The neighbourhood also includes some late Victorian terraced blocks of Tyneside flats – at Deckham Terrace and between the two Durham Roads at Northbourne and the post-war 'Radburn'-layout Medway area.

The whole area is within 2 km of central Gateshead, with good radial bus services to the centre and the Metro interchange. In work for the Housing Market Renewal Pathfinder, it was characterized as part of the Inner Ring of Newcastle-Gateshead – 'a short ride to town' (BNG, 2010).

The 2011 Census describes a 'middle-layer super output area', Gateshead 011, which covers the Deckham and Carr Hill areas well, with small additions to north and west. The overall picture is of much more stability than in the London estates. The population has risen slightly over the last 10 years, by about 3 per cent, so less than the averages for Gateshead or the whole country, and is now just over 6,400. Household

Figure 4.1. Perched on the ridge, overlooking the Tyne and Newcastle.

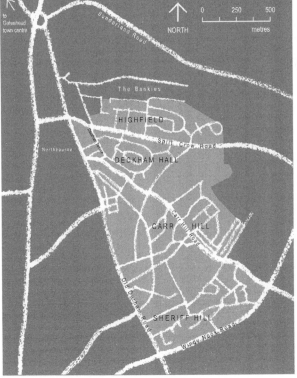

Figure 4.2. The Gateshead estates: Deckham and Carr Hill.

size has actually gone down slightly, in contrast to the recent national trend, to 2.32 persons per household (nationally, 2.4). The figures show strikingly how this remains a white district (96 per cent) in a white town (Gateshead 96 per cent) in a white region (95 per cent) – these figures have only edged down marginally since 2001. Similarly, 95 per cent of the residents are British or Irish born (it was 98 per cent in 2001); there are however now measurable small proportions born in the Accession countries (1 per cent) and outside Europe (3 per cent), reflecting slightly the presence in Gateshead of some 8,000 people from these two groups of countries.

The occupational mix confirms that this remains a primarily but not exclusively working-class group of neighbourhoods. The jobs that people do spread over three main groupings in a way which is similar to the pattern for the whole North East region but somewhat skewed to the lower (paid) end: 53 per cent in the census headings of elementary, machine operations, sales, caring and other service activities (41 per cent in the North East); 25 per cent in the skilled and admin groups (24 per cent in the North East), and 22 per cent in the three best-paid groups (35 per cent in the North East). The unemployment rate of 12 per cent (using the 2011 Census figures for 'unemployed as percentage of economically active') is higher than the national (6 per cent) and Gateshead (7 per cent) averages, but is not the extreme case found in some parts of the region – though in some sub-areas, such as Deckham Hall, it is as high as 15 per cent.

Housing tenure, too, has seen little change, compared with national patterns. The proportion of houses that are owner-occupied is still below 40 per cent (37 per cent in 2011, hardly changed from 2001). Social renting is now at 52 per cent (from 57 per cent) with a concomitant rise in the private-rented sector, which has always had a small presence on the western fringes of the area (6 per cent up to 10 per cent over the decade). Car-owning households have now reached 50 per cent (44 per cent in 2001), but still lag the Gateshead (63 per cent) and regional (69 per cent) averages.

History and Character of the Estates

Although the estates were, as usual, built on farmland adjoining the town, the first area developed, known as Carr Hill, was actually further south, with Deckham Hall being 'backfilled' between it and the older town later on, in the 1930s.

This southern estate, the first council housing built in the town, now tends to be called Sheriff Hill, to distinguish it from the main - and slightly later – Carr Hill estate which is either side of Carr Hill Road itself, just to the east. ('Sheriff's Highway' is the name of the section of the Old Durham Road that runs steeply up past the Carr Hill area.) Wide curving tree-lined avenues intersect between varied cottage pairings and terraces in a relaxed example of garden suburb design.

Deckham Hall estate, run by the Home Group housing association, is further back into town and reflects more the austerity of the late 1930s, with dwelling types sturdy but heavily standardized, little architectural detail and minimal landscape treatment. Highfield, also mainly owned by Home Group, dates from the immediate post-war

Figure 4.3. Millway, one of the early Carr Hill estate avenues.

era and, compared with Deckham Hall, has more varied house types and street layouts, some with larger gardens.

Indeed, these different estates east of the Old Durham Road are something of a local history-book of the sort of design changes, at national level, discussed in Chapter 2. The story starts, as usual, in 1919: Richard Wylie RIBA was appointed to lay out the new estate and build the houses, and the first 232 had been completed at Carr Hill ('Sheriff Hill') by the end of 1923. The effect is like a looser more open Tower Gardens. Houses are in semi-detached pairs or terraces of four or eight. Terrace-ends, as in many of the early cottage estates, are treated as 'pavilions' and often projected forward. They are usually distinguished by steep gables or hips to the street, as are some of the centre-terrace houses (Taylor and Lovie, 2004).

Then, between 1923 and 1927 a second phase was built at Carr Hill ('Carr Hill estate') – 342 houses and seven shops. These were somewhat different in character and appearance. Almost all were semi-detached pairs (only two terraces of four were built), and a harder type of red brick was used, with many houses rendered on the first floor. There were still attempts to avoid monotony, such as different styles of house being built in alternating pairs; and again the streets were well planted with trees.

The third wave was at Deckham Hall, between 1936 and 1939. It followed the move, already remarked on in for example Becontree, towards geometric forms, being laid out as a series of irregular concentric rings. According to a local resident, this is why it is known as the 'Frying Pan' or the 'African Village' (with the huts in a circle).

It is slightly more densely-built than Carr Hill: over 30 dwellings per hectare, whereas the earlier layouts were a little below.

The houses were of very uniform appearance compared with those built at Carr Hill. Orange brick was used throughout and less attention was given to landscaping, with only a few green spaces and evidently no tree planting, producing an austere effect overall. Houses were either semi-detached , built in terraces of four or as flats in pairs of two. Pairs of semi-detached houses of L-shaped plan were built to flank the few semicircular green spaces that were provided. (Taylor and Lovie, 2004)

Figure 4.4. Deckham Hall: 'an austere effect overall'.

The last of Deckham's building came after the Second World War, with the rapid restart of social house-building. The first new estates (1948) were Highfield – across Split Crow Road from Deckham Hall – and Blue Quarries Road, in a gentle style like its pre-war Sheriff Hill neighbours, down at the far southern edge of the area. In the 1950s, the calmly neutral – but very popular – Hodkin Gardens was added to the east of the earliest 1920s scheme and its little Hodkin Park; with the final additions being at the northern Mount Pleasant edge, adjoining the sharp drop of the 'Bankies' woodland down towards the Tyne Gorge.

The area largely escaped the post-war trend to non-traditional house-building techniques, though there are a few concrete 'Dorran' houses (1952–1954) in Carr Hill Road: plain, rather cheap-looking, some of them still not yet re-clad as part of the area's facelift.

English Heritage's Simon Taylor and David Lovie, in their history of Gateshead's architecture and development, comment that:

The well-planned estates at Carr Hill and Bensham are attractive good examples of 1920s garden suburbs, and must have made a dramatic impact when first built. Providing a consistent and airy setting, the housing contrasted starkly with the town-centre slums as well as the regimented pre-war terraces of Bensham and Shipcote. The later change of emphasis and decline in architectural quality, represented by the high-density and less attractive Deckham Hall Estate of the 1930s, reflects the more utilitarian attitudes to housing that dominated the decade before the Second World War.

Now the area is generally quite poor, with council reports noting it as featuring in the upper end of the national deprivation ratings. In Deckham Hall in particular, Home Group's tenants are often not in work, either benefits claimants or pensioners, and they expect both welfare reform and government housing changes to have a sharp impact over the next few years.

The council's urban designers draw an unfavourable contrast between the Deckham Hall part, with its 'long curved streets and repetitive blocks of houses of similar materials [which] give little sense of place, and are disorientating', and the more characterful Victorian and Edwardian part along Old Durham Road, with its shops, cafés and so on. This seems rather charitable to the older area, which is no great shakes as a local centre for shopping and services; but perhaps not that *un*charitable on

Figure 4.5. Deckham Hall's higher density, accentuated by concentric layout.

the inter-war housing, which is admittedly somewhat stark, if scarcely 'disorienting' (Gateshead Council, 2011).

Several reviews of the area comment on the limited number of shops, and imply a criticism of the initial planning. At the start of the twenty-first century, this looks much less like a mistake than twentieth-century planners might have thought. Britain's estates are studded with failing (purpose-built) shopping parades, buried inside poorish estates with no passing trade. The Gateshead reliance on the existing main road shops (Old Durham Road, Carr Hill Road), low-key though they are, looks in retrospect like a sound scheme – with at least the basis for businesses to upgrade and invest in response to changing demand.

An earlier consultancy report for the BNG Pathfinder was also quite critical of 'The poor environment of the two socially rented estates ... caused by low grade boundaries and public realm materials, under-investment in upkeep and a lack of attractive landscaping in both public areas and private gardens'; but it does emphasize that the critique is of these detailed failings 'rather than fundamental structural weaknesses in the layout and design of spaces'. And the impression is that Home Group and others have responded to this over the last few years, so that some improvement has clearly occurred.

Similarly parking pressure has led to the replacement of grass verges by low-grade parking surfacing 'which has eroded the garden suburb character and quality of the public realm'. They add that fences, hedges and walls are in poor condition, as are (or were at the time) some of the houses. Coupled with paving and street furniture 'of the lowest quality ... this creates a harsh environment lacking quality and distinction. This impacts on its market appeal and confidence in the neighbourhood in general' (GVA Grimley, 2006a).

Another report by the same consultancy gave data for the 1930s Deckham Hall part of the area, which was then (2001 Census) 82 per cent social rented. A sharp distinction was drawn with the 1920s Carr Hill locality to the south, with more privately-owned houses and '...higher prices, exhibiting the characteristics of a high demand and popular market area' (GVA Grimley, 2006b).

It is apparent that there is a lot of differentiation within the overall Deckham/ Carr Hill locality. The southern (earliest-built) part, now more generally termed Sheriff Hill, seems always to have been very stable and popular, classic territory for the Right-To-Buy purchaser who stays in situ. At its northern edges, the northern end of Millway and the streets immediately off Carr Hill Road are less leafy and less apparently successful, though the change is not dramatic. Then across Carr Hill Road, Deckham Hall to the north is recognizably poorer, plainer and less sure of its future. And Highfield, according to the local councillor, is less popular because – built on the steep slope down towards the Tyne – its houses have as many as twenty steps down to the front door, with problems for pushchairs, bins and posties: 'when I'm leafleting at election time, it hits home!'.

But even within Home Group's Deckham Hall/Highfield management area, staff say that tenants may well differentiate: for example, a feeling that Split Crow Road and Carr Hill Road, as main roads and bus routes, get more attention than 'inside' the estates; and a recognition of the better-cared-for feel of, say, Hendon Road which got consistent garden fencing to replace scrappy boundary treatments, as part of Pathfinder investment.

Managing the Estates: Deckham Hall and Highfield

Home Group's role is important. The housing association – which is a major national RSL – do seem to regard Gateshead, and especially this estate, as their roots. They grew out of the pioneering pre-war North East Housing Association, which actually built Deckham Hall (not the council, unusually for this period). They have 582 homes in Deckham Hall and Highfield; in addition eighty-two houses have been sold (RTB), and a small number of homes are privately-rented (on Hendon Road, Edgeware Road, and Split Crow Road). So this is still a predominantly social housing area.

Their local staff – thoughtful, knowledgeable, committed – operate a Neighbourhood Management Initiative, based in a Split Crow Road house, to complement conventional housing management in Deckham Hall and adjoining Highfield. Such a switch to better and more welcoming management, stressing local contact and capacity-building, seems to run alongside a greater readiness to accept that the estates cannot just be left to potter along. The previous hands-off approach had tended to lead to *ad hoc* responses: examples being paving-over the D-shaped greens to increase parking supply, and then deciding that the area needed 'greening'; or demolishing problematic walk-up flat-blocks without any plan for what do with the sites, so leaving a gappy effect.

Figure 4.6. Highfield: paving over for parking, then deciding area needs 'greening'…

The neighbourhood management approach has been coupled with an attempt to look more strategically at the area and its needs, with a consultancy report under way. There is undoubtedly a balance to be struck on Deckham Hall, between closing up some of the gaps with development, and using at least some of these spaces as green space (with a function) in what is one of the tighter cottage estates.

There are very few empty houses, and indeed Home Group have never had many 'voids' here compared with other big estates. Deckham Hall and Highfield properties let very quickly. There is a high proportion of mutual exchanges, and not very quick turnover anyway. A lot of residents were born on the estate; they may have moved within the area, as the household changed; 20–30 year-olds born in Deckham Hall will move off the estate but may well come back when they have kids. Council staff confirmed an impression that it is now quite stable, though *still not a place of choice, even if not frightening* (!). To them, the 'package' offered by Deckham Hall/Highfield is below par: hardly a GP in the area, the Old Durham Road shops weak, and the local open spaces sometimes problematic.

As for the issue of stigma: Home Group people recognize that Deckham historically had a bad reputation, and that this sticks, so that it may still be seen as a rough area by outsiders. But they think that it is not really reflective of the reality. Crime and anti-social behaviour (ASB), which triggered an elaborate CCTV response 10 years ago, are sufficiently far down the agenda now for the system to be switched off, with tenants having responded inconclusively to a consultation on it. Even where there are still problems, they are highly localized and generally a product of one dysfunctional household – but this can affect a street's reputation for years. This happened at, for example, Edgeware Road, the north–south cross street across the end of the Deckham Hall 'geometry'. Here, a history of large and noisy families in (now-demolished) flats, and a private tenant whose son was involved in petty crime, mean that Edgeware Road is still rather problematic; seen as such by many; and so possibly stuck in a bit of a cycle of lower popularity.

The local co-ordinator observed, of what is actually a fairly stable estate, in reasonable condition: *'When it started, I didn't get it – why a Neighbourhood Management Initiative? But you need to scratch away at the surface'*: she meant the high level of benefit dependency, the low educational level and aspirations, and so on. These form much of the rationale for the initiative, not the burnt-out cars or boarded-up properties that mark neighbourhood failure in say, the West End of Newcastle. This looks very like classic 'community development', but focusing on life chances, working with young people, and partnership with other agencies to benefit residents across a broad spectrum, not just as housing provider.

So although development options are being studied, this is not the core agenda. The future is seen as being about two main things: the people and helping them get more into the labour market; together with focusing on the existing stock and making it more attractive (wall and fence treatments, access improvements, loft insulation, 'paint-a-gate' schemes with kids, and so on).

Managing the Estates: Carr Hill/Sheriff Hill

Gateshead Housing Company are the 'arm's-length management organization' (ALMO) which runs the former council stock on behalf of Gateshead Council. They have around 630 properties: about 150 in Carr Hill, and some 480 in Sheriff Hill. They see the Old Durham Road (Sheriff's Highway) frontage – the western boundary of the estate – as one of the 'gateways' to the town, and make a point of keeping it well groomed and the wide verge carefully mown (cuts permitting…). Demand is high and steady, with no real pockets of lesser popularity, and even one-bed properties now in demand, after earlier decades when they were hard to fill. Turnover is low (half the borough average in Carr Hill, just below it in Sheriff Hill); voids are more or less non-existent; and the estates' stability, at 78–79 per cent of tenants resident for 3 years or more, is again slightly above the Gateshead-wide figure. The age pyramid for the 'main tenant' is dominated by the middle-age-bands (25–54 year-olds, 61 per cent; over-65s, 21 per cent); they judge about a hundred of the houses to be under-occupied.

The management district now has Hodkin Park as its southern boundary, but they and residents would regard the actual change from Carr Hill/Sheriff Hill as being a bit further on, marked by the massive Queen Elizabeth Hospital site: it, and the estates beyond it, are no longer inner Gateshead, but form the more outer-suburban Windy Nook, Wrekenton and Beacon Lough. Within Carr Hill, there do not seem to be particular sub-areas with a better or worse image: '*maybe the bottom end of Pottersway and Fosse Terrace are a bit less well-thought-of, but demand's pretty solid throughout. And even places in Sheriff Hill which had a bit of a bad reputation fifteen years ago are now much better*'. Nor are there particular locations with an anti-social behaviour problem: as at December 2012, there were only four ASB cases spread across the 600+ properties, two of them noise/unruly kids, two property damage or condition.

Right-To-Buy take-up is often an indicator of more popular streets, and '*a fair number have gone by now in Millway and round there*' (mainly in the tree-lined curving streets of the earliest construction phase, and the late-period Hodkin Gardens: the least 'council-estate' in feel of all of them).

Figure 4.7. 1950s Hodkin Gardens: 'calmly neutral, but very popular'.

The actual proportion sold over the whole of Gateshead Housing's local holding is 34 per cent. It ranges from 24 per cent in the Blue Quarries Road sub-area – probably a reflection of the number of small OAP homes here – and 30 per cent in the northern part of Deckham, through 33 per cent in Carr Hill and Sheriff Hill, to (the only significant variation) 58 per cent, i.e. forty-three out of the seventy-four houses, in Hodkin Gardens. After a long lull, sales are now slowly restarting because of reintroduced discounts.

The area is managed as part of the 'Central' district, with a team of Estate Officers (EO) who handle about 700 properties each. There are also two Neighbourhood Relations staff who handle ASB cases once they have passed the stage where EOs are handling them without enforcement action – which is the preferred model wherever possible. The estate is generally in good condition, with the structural issues affecting some of the Sheriff Hill part having been largely rectified by government-funded Decent Homes spending to meet national standards. The councillor observed that this is reflected in the higher esteem of what are now more comfortable properties. It receives a weekly street-by-street visit from the EO, and occasional members' estate tours and clean-up drives.

The much better performance and position is attributed to a mixture of things (in addition to the higher basic demand because of the tightness of the wider housing market): the Decent Homes work, more regular attention from EOs, and the approach to Anti-Social Behaviour (ASB). The company has a 'robust' attitude on ASB – the Autumn 2012 edition of their news magazine contains four separate one-page articles under the 'Respect – ASB charter for housing' rubric, describing evictions or injunctions, naming the tenants, showing a picture of their street, and underlining the message to everyone else with captions like '*Residents of Grasmere Court in Winlaton are hoping for a bit of peace and quiet after a troublesome family was evicted by the housing company*'.[1] However, staff were keen to stress that these are last-resort responses, and that the majority of cases can be resolved without enforcement action of any kind, thanks to a multi-agency approach, very good information and record systems, and the fact that staff get real satisfaction from closing a case with a settlement that restores neighbour relations by working with both victim and perpetrator. As noted earlier, the Carr Hill estates are not anyway hugely plagued by this issue, and the recent average incidence (1.7–2.0 cases per 100 households) is well below the borough average of 2.5.

It is noticeable that the ALMO is still engaged in managing much of the non-housing environment, even though a substantial proportion of the individual houses are now privately owned. They work with other council departments, of course, on the street scene, cleansing, trees and planting, and so on. Beyond that, they are quite prepared to write to or call on private owners or tenants about, for example, the condition of front gardens or rear alleys: they regard this as a legitimate way of protecting their own investment, and in fact they do have a legal 'hook' for it in that formerly council-owned stock is always sold with a covenant dealing with external treatment.

Gateshead Housing Company are clearly positive and enthusiastic about Carr Hill and Sheriff Hill. They see the area as attracting not just people with family connections, though this is still very important. It is well located and stable feeling. Around Millway, for example, it is perfectly possible that people will drive around and see quite a few of the streets as attractive to them as 'incomers' too – though of course there are *'pockets where that's still not so likely'*.

What Do Residents Think?

Home Group staff remarked that Deckham Hall has no residents' association (the RSL having tried and failed to get one going) but that people are perfectly ready to respond on an issue-by-issue basis, for example on the CCTV. There are outspoken tenants who will always let them know what they think, and individuals who contribute, for example, old photos of the estate or recollections for oral histories. A 'Deckham born and bred' resident of Split Crow Road, whose parents had moved into their home when it was new in 1937, had lived in several houses on the estate over time and would not dream of living anywhere else. One of his neighbours, a 90-year-old lady, had never lived anywhere but Deckham Hall either. He saw the whole issue of family connections as being an essential part of the estate's appeal, and described it as *'friendly, if you can get away from the "nakkers"'* – the few badly-behaved families (especially 10–14 year-olds) who to him meant that *'Edgeware Road's a bastard'*.

On the estates further south, the councillor's summary was *'yes there are issues, but generally, happy we're here, in substantial houses from the 20s 30s and 40s, with a Carr Hill community centre that's in full use, with good community spirit'*; and even in the Fosse Terrace cul-de-sac, which has had its problems, five of the twelve families have lived there for years.

Property Prices and Agents' Views

Prices are generally lowest at the Deckham Hall end, where there are smaller properties (more two-bedroom houses) and a higher proportion of social tenancies. The average on a small sample of actual prices achieved over the last 2 years – information mainly from Rightmove, plus local agents' websites – is approximately £60,000: though the range is quite wide (£40,000 to £77,500). The earlier, greener estate at the Sheriff Hill end further south gets consistently higher prices, in the range £59,000–£89,950, averaging £71,000: still strikingly low for what are decent houses often in very appealing street settings. Hodkin Gardens, one of the last areas built, the one that looks least like a classic council estate and which is somewhat separate from the rest, is mainly in private ownership and averages over £103,000. In comparison, two-, three- and four-bedroom non-council-built homes in the adjacent suburbs off Old Durham Road/Sheriff's Highway or towards Felling fall into a wide range between £90,000 and £160,000, averaging about £117,000. Less than a kilometre to the southwest, prices in the middle-class suburb of Low Fell are at least double this.

The view of one thoughtful property professional was that there are actually few areas in the whole region where an 'incomer' young couple would be likely to include an ex-council property on an estate in their house search patterns. He did, though, add: *'Mind you, £212,000 for one in Corbridge…'* (referring to a small estate in the very 'hot' Tyne Valley market west of Newcastle). Essentially, though, the general point was that *'unless you know somewhere'* (brought up in the locality, got family there), the wide range of alternative property available would make it unusual for people to explore such an area.

Overall

So, in summary: this 1.2 km² chunk of inner Gateshead displays a continuum of publicly-built cottage estate environments from the very well-realized, and pretty successful, Sheriff Hill/Carr Hill avenues in the south to the harder, denser and still quite stigmatized (though stable) Deckham Hall. In between are groups of houses from the late 1920s through to the 1950s, all of which 'work' in slightly different ways. Apart from the southern avenues, though, and despite the rolling topography and views out to north, west and east, the overall impression is still one of too much homogeneity, not enough distinctiveness; it does seem to go on and on. And very many streets are too stark: *'a garden suburb without greenery!'* as a council staffer observed.

Tenure remains predominantly social, and much of the area – though reasonably well let – is not really an area of choice, except for some streets in the oldest part of Carr Hill/Sheriff Hill, the most 'garden suburb' in its feel – and Hodkin Gardens: the least like a council estate.

And yet most of the rest, too, is potentially a pleasant convenient inner suburb, where a range of families could choose to lead much of their lives (whether house-buyers or renters). Interestingly, one of the councillors commented, in an echo of the Becontree resident's view (Chapter 3), that Polish families with no prejudgments of stigma did appreciate the area and used its facilities. It could provide choice of tenure and of house/flat size which can allow local moves over quite a long period of the lifecycle, from say young couple to family with older children. It has two good primaries (one 'outstanding') in South Street and Carr Hill. Given more attractive local shopping and services than Old Durham Road currently provides, some new housing to widen choice a bit more, more greenery, continuing careful management, and local treatments to increase area differentiation, Deckham/Carr Hill would seem to have a lot going for it.

Hylton Castle

Ten kilometres south-eastwards from Deckham, a journey through a landscape of urban sprawl and scrappy 'green belt', Hylton Castle is a post-Second World War estate in outer Sunderland. It is some 5 km from the city centre, beside the main A19 trunk road/western bypass which bounds it to the west. To the south are the playing-fields and parkland along the Hylton Dene Burn – they separate it from neighbouring Castletown. Another kilometre further on is the incised valley of the River Wear.

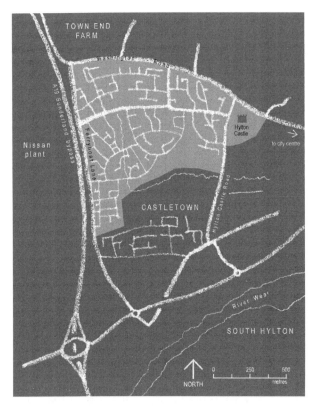

Figure 4.8. Hylton Castle, Sunderland.

It formed part of Sunderland's huge and rapid expansion over the open ground inland behind the Victorian port and town, made up primarily of council estates to deal with clearance of the slums in the centre and around the shipyards. A 'vast programme of public building, perhaps 7,000 new houses by 1939, and almost 20,000 during the 20 years from 1945', meant that Sunderland was 'the third highest house-builder among 157 towns' (VCH, 2012). A table in Norman Dennis's magisterial review of the city's housing issues has it at the top of a list of twenty-eight large towns in terms of new homes built per 1,000 population by 1961: Sunderland with 382 per 1,000, Coventry 339, Newcastle halfway down the list at 231, and on down to Salford with 105 per 1,000 (Dennis, 1970).

By 1966 this development had spread as far out as the city's expanded boundary and the bypass (A19), taking in what are now the Pennywell, Grindon, Springwell Farm, Thorney Close, Farringdon, Carley Hill, Witherwack, Hylton Castle itself, Hylton Red House and Town End Farm estates. Dennis's study makes an interesting observation about the role the new estates played in working-class Sunderland life. It is one which is perhaps different from the usual expectation of dislocation and regret (and although the hapless Town End Farm Estate came up time and again as provoking exactly that reaction, it was unusual in that regard amongst Sunderland estates, it seems). 'Losing contact with relatives was mentioned even less… [NB only two cases]… as the main disadvantage of living on a council estate… It is possible to speculate that because of

Sunderland's history and the distances involved … rehousing does not seriously affect the more important kin contacts'. And one of his interviewers' notes, from an inner area, is 'Grants me an interview while her granddaughter from Hylton Castle (who works in the town) is getting her dinner' (Dennis, 1970).

Hylton Castle's first tenants arrived in 1953, and its expansion continued for more than a decade. One or two of the original residents are still around, including a 92-year-old lady who had spent the war working in the shipyards – Sunderland's own 'Rosie the Riveter'. Like all the city's stock, it was transferred from direct council management first to the Sunderland Housing Group (2002) and then to Gentoo Sunderland, the housing association within the Gentoo Group (2008).

Figure 4.9. Unusually, there actually *is* a Hylton Castle.

Unusually, since twentieth-century developments seem to make a habit of obliterating the feature they are named for, there actually *is* a Hylton Castle. The castle itself is a fourteenth-century gatehouse tower, rather tinkered with in the nineteenth century but still an impressive marker, and minor visitor attraction, at the eastern corner of the neighbourhood. A Scheduled Ancient Monument and Grade I listed building (Pevsner, 1985), it is now in the hands of English Heritage. The estate's 'Cauld Lad' pub (the Caad Lad, in Dennis's book – no doubt an interview transcript) along Caithness Road commemorates some unfortunate local who was hacked to death by a knightly Hylton in the early 1600s. A locally-led Lottery bid is trying to get funding for a major renovation which would not just be about heritage; it would aim to use the restored castle as a focus where kids are wanted and want to go, with facilities like public toilets and a café, which would work alongside the Dene's wild open spaces to make the whole area more attractive.

'Residential Futures'

The two estates – Castletown and Hylton Castle (CHC) – were selected in the Northern Way's 'Residential Futures' studies as an example of, and case-study for, what the studies called 'type 2' localities. These were defined as representing:

the better of our municipally built housing stock ... predominantly suburban environments, where the basic build quality and fabric are positive, but where the areas suffer from the stigma of being 'council stock'. (Urban Studio, 2009*b*)

The thesis was that such localities have begun to become, or have the potential to become, part of the lower end of the private sector market, partly via the Right-To-Buy, and sometimes as a result of infill developments by volume homebuilders. They were of interest, too, because their relative stability means that they tend not to appear on a 'needs-based' analysis – the concern being that, thus overlooked, they might not make the progress they could because of a lack of clarity about their potential role despite their inherent qualities.

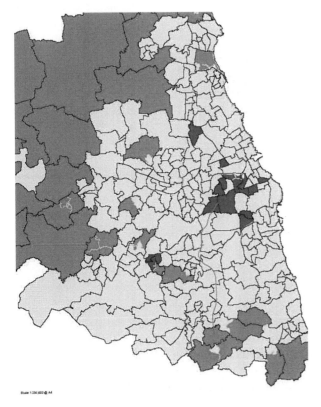

Figure 4.10. 'Type 2' estates along the A19 corridor.

The studies looked across the North at this locality 'type'. They identified, across the Tyne & Wear city region, quite a substantial concentration of places of this sort along the A19 corridor. The policy conclusion was that where 'Type 2' characteristics are so prevalent, and the neighbourhoods clustered in this way, there might well be a case for a cross-boundary initiative to provide a strategic spatial and regeneration framework for the whole 'cluster'. And that the Homes & Communities Agency (HCA) should engage with its RSL/housing association and local authority partners to think creatively about the future role of such estates in their market context.

Focusing on Hylton Castle Itself

Although the 'Residential Futures' work took Hylton Castle and Castletown for joint study (as 'CHC'), there have historically been quite substantial differences between Hylton Castle to the north and Castletown to the south. The former was rather closer to the sort of opportunity that the studies were trying to explore, while Castletown had more problems: more substantial and entrenched issues of social exclusion and deprivation – though now substantially reduced, as discussed below. Hylton Castle is quite a distinct entity: Castletown is clearly separated from it by the green space along the Hylton Dene Burn, and Town End Farm is across Washington Road and 50 feet (15 m) higher up the sharp incline of Hylton Lane.

The impression from Dennis's tables and reporting is that Hylton Castle probably always was one of the better performers as a council estate. In the rankings by residents (of all areas, not just the outer council estates), it was tenth out of eighteen for access to work, thirteenth out of twenty for privacy, and sixth out of sixteen for access to everyday shops – though next to bottom for access to central Sunderland. And it seems to have had a fan-base from early on: a 1967 letter to the Sunderland Echo about waiting-lists and allocations asked 'why should people be sent to live at Gilley Law if their hearts are in Hylton Castle, Fulwell or Grangetown?' (Dennis, 1970). This was over 40 years ago, of course; but coupled with the attitudes noted earlier about kinship links, they do give the sense that in this city the gradations may not be as acute between different sorts of locality as in some places.

Gentoo Sunderland staff confirmed this. They do not see the sharp distinctions between estates that can be seen in some cities, and they regard Hylton Castle as a sought-after estate: behind their new-build estates in residents' choices, but on a par with Castletown and ahead of nearby Town End Farm – which, yes, *was* massively stigmatized, but is now much less problematic, having had a lot of money spent on it, Decent Homes upgrades, and demolition of unpopular flats and small bungalows to be replaced by houses.

Although Hylton Castle is generally of good quality, and seems to be very stable, it does suffer from a lack of structure and character. The street pattern produces a layout which, though not as wilfully annoying as some Radburn layouts, does have quite low permeability and, in places, a rather unwelcoming pedestrian environment. Despite the apparent attempt by the original designers to create little clusters and groups, the enclosure effect is not particularly marked, with wide roads running between low storey-height houses and no attempt to express corner features or key junctions.

The 2011 Census gives a broad picture of a fairly stable, and homogenous, working-class suburb. The population, at around 4,400, has barely changed since 2001, and the household size has gone down slightly as it has in Deckham. The people are 98 per cent 'white' and 98 per cent British or Irish born – both figures were 99 per cent in 2001 – with those in all the other ethnic categories rising from 34 to 76: almost all of this very small increase was people born outside Europe. So Hylton Castle, unlike most of the rest of Britain, seems to manage to survive without Poles or Lithuanians.

The jobs that people do are mainly but not exclusively in lower-paid occupations, with the census headings of elementary, machine operations, sales, caring and other service activities predominant. Sixty per cent work in these fields (compared to the national average of 35 per cent), with average proportions in the skilled and admin groups, and 16 per cent in the three best-paid groups (compared to 41 per cent nationally).

Housing tenure has changed, as everywhere, over the intercensal decade, but not dramatically: half the houses are now owner-occupied (44 per cent in 2001) with the social-rent category falling from 52 to 42 per cent. The most marked shift is in the private-rented sector, which now accounts for 9 per cent of the stock (3 per cent in 2001) – pointing, as elsewhere, to how this tenure is steadily taking up a bigger and bigger proportion of the council-built housing. The number of car-owning households has risen steadily but again not strikingly: 56 per cent in 2011 (up from 45 per cent in 2001), so still well below city (65 per cent) and regional (69 per cent) averages.

As would be expected from its location and residential character, the area is a net exporter of employees. Working residents are largely concentrated in routine or semi-routine categories (47 per cent in 2011, almost double the average proportion for England & Wales). They travel to a wide variety of destinations, with the biggest flows being to the city centre, Hendon, Nissan, Washington and Doxford Business Park. There are secondary links with Newcastle-Gateshead, as the economic core of the city-region, and travel to Metro Centre and the Team Valley also reflects the location on the strategic road network.

The range of the 'residential offer' of housing types is quite restricted, as is generally the case on such estates, where there is limited variety in the stock and a historic dominance of socially rented homes. The standard is good, a product of three factors: a reasonable quantity of private-sector new-build; the investment by Gentoo in meeting Decent Homes standards; and the locality's history of development: the relative newness of the stock has meant that one does not see extreme quality concerns as in some of the inner parts of the conurbation. As in much of the rest of Sunderland, properties available for purchase within the private sector are largely affordable.

Buying, Owning, Trading

The Right-To-Buy has made sizeable inroads: 54 per cent of the original stock total has been sold. This is higher than the citywide average (44 per cent), but then that also includes flatted estates, where sales are much lower.[2] As in other places reviewed, this has not really happened on a sub-area basis within Hylton Castle; the differentiation is more street by street, with some streets now two-thirds privately owned. Gentoo staff in fact could not think of any city locality where a whole 'sub-area' had been bought, except possibly (and pleasingly!) the last remaining post-war prefabs, in Springwell; and Washington's Upper (sold) and Lower (not sold) Oxclose. And they remarked that in one place – Grindon, further south along the A19 – a collection of houses which had been 'RTB-ed' had all now dropped into the private-rented sector.

Housing market information gives a very clearly differentiated pattern. Rightmove's listings at the end of 2012 showed not a single ex-council three-bed semi in Hylton Castle offered in six figures: the range of asking prices was £75,000 to £99,950, and the average £88,100. Highest prices seemed to be being asked for the most modified – maybe the ones looking the least like the conventional image of the council house. Immediately to the south, in a ten-street chunk of privately-built housing (and some self-build) that the estate agents are pleased to call 'Hylton Manor' and 'Fulford Grange', the prices sought ranged from £130,000 to £199,950, averaging £161,000. Then there are two other categories, in between in price terms: first, within Hylton Castle itself, non-council-built homes in infill culs-de-sac (average, £133,000); and second, ex-council houses in neighbouring Castletown: average £117,000 (Rightmove, 2012). The differential *within* Hylton Castle, between council-built and non-council-built, is thus very wide: of the order of 34 per cent. The local councillor attributed this to '*not*

Figure 4.11. Hylton Castle, Cheam Road: could easily be market housing of the same period.

much more than snobbery: they'll move out of the ex-council house to a smaller one, that's built of cardboard, that they can't afford, it gets called Cornbeef City cos it's all they can pay for after the mortgage': another example of how local even these moves and perceptions can often be.

Also relevant, perhaps, is the comparison between those privately-built homes in Hylton Castle, in smallish groups on culs-de-sac, and the ex-council ones in Castletown, which are also in smaller groupings. Here the differential is less, of the order of 12 per cent. This suggests that there are two effects in play: the 'estate' impact on prices of just being on a big all-of-a-piece estate like Hylton Castle, as opposed to Castletown with its more mixed feel; and the simple 'council-built' difference made by being or not being municipally-built in the first place.

On first impressions, the differentials are quite surprising. It is true that the private construction will tend to be more recent than the bulk of the council's effort: 1970s to 1990s rather than 1950s and 1960s. So some of the price difference will reflect that. But Hylton Castle is post-war, the houses are quite 'modern' looking without being stark, and in general they (like Hodkin Gardens in Gateshead) look much more like market housing of the same period than, say, the pre-war 'cottages' do. It does look as though the 'estate effect' is quite strong in this area; more important, indeed, than the fact that the corporation built the house.

Liveability and the Environment

The 'Residential Futures' studies scored Hylton Castle's 'liveability' position as mid-ranking, but suggested that concerns about crime were at that time (2009) likely to affect this locality's future desirability for the family market.

On the positive side, the area contains or adjoins meadows, woodland and playing fields, all easily accessible for the local community. There is also a lot of open space within the locality itself: mostly shapeless slices of mown grass, though one or two of better quality: for example where, in a thoughtful piece of design, a linear green space follows a little tributary of the Burn and provides a useful cut-through on foot.

Public transport is reasonable, with regular and frequent bus services linking the area to Sunderland city centre (four routes, notably the 56 every 10–15 minutes, connecting to both the centre (15 minutes) and outward to Nissan (under 10 minutes) and Newcastle (50 minutes)). Shops and services in Hylton Castle are of a decent standard, though not attractive enough in themselves to add to the appeal of the area as a place to live. The Chiswick Square local shopping is just about big enough to have avoided the fate of some 'in-estate' parades, though it is rather drab and could do with a facelift.

On the more negative side, the quality of place and the perception of the locality lack any real or valuable character or identity to draw on: other than the castle, which the Lottery bid has hit on. The quite low density, combined with not very 'legible' routes, especially north–south, and the width and traffic-speeds on the more important roads, makes for an environment which is quite hard work on foot – nowhere is near anywhere else. The quality and maintenance of the public and private realm in Hylton

Figure 4.12. Chiswick Square shops: drab, but not in crisis.

Castle is reasonable, but crime rates have been relatively high and seem to have had a negative impact on the overall liveability, and image, of the locality. The police state that 'Anti-social behaviour in Castletown and Hylton Castle has reduced significantly during the year [2011]'. 'Extra police have been on patrol in the areas where the disorder has been worse and young people have been encouraged to get involved in the many youth activities available'.[3]

The poor quality of parts of nearby Castletown was until recently felt to have an impact on the wider area. Now, Gentoo staff think that the Castletown issue is in the past, and indeed that Castletown is at least as high up the 'hierarchy' of localities as Hylton Castle. That change has come about mainly because the problematic and poorly-built 'Aviary' housing (Thrush Grove, Chaffinch Road – why do the worst estates always have the daftest names?) has been demolished and replaced by the St Catherine's scheme where two- and three-bed houses are being sold at £110,000 upwards. It did take a long time to clear, so got worse and was inviting trouble; but coupled with a general sharp fall in youth disorder (reflecting city and national patterns) they see the whole issue as being history. Hylton Castle was not affected as far as they are concerned – the only (occasional) ASB issues tend to be neighbour-to-neighbour 'clash of lifestyle' incidents, of which there is one live case at present.

There is also a concern that although there has been some new development (Barratt, and Cheviot HA), which is a positive signal, the tendency has been for the recent schemes not to integrate, so that rather than adding to the wider sense of place within the suburb, they tend to exist as mono-tenure 'bubbles' within the area – a missed opportunity, but a frequent occurrence in recent urban development, and not just in Sunderland.

Gentoo Sunderland manage 820 properties in Hylton Castle (out of an estate total of about 1,770), so less than half the original stock now (46 per cent). They see it as a place needing 'normal' good practice, not intensive multi-agency management. It is a very stable estate, with few serious issues that worry either the managers or the tenants. Like Gateshead Housing, Gentoo see themselves as custodians of the whole estate's environment, not just their own housing asset narrowly defined; like them, too, they are quite ready to tell owner-occupiers about poor standards of property or garden maintenance. Walkabouts, jointly with the council's environmental and city services people and the police, and sometimes with councillors, are used to pick up local issues.

Residents value the possibility of being near family, with Sunderland tenants having always expected that the housing available should be on estates they know near people they know. '*Offer them even a lovely 3-bed house, across the river – they won't gan there.*' There is a sort of quiet community spirit – for example, one of the little play-parks is maintained by Gentoo and the council, but it is 'policed' informally by local people, who are quick to tell kids off if there is broken glass or misbehaviour. There are few major problems raised, with partnership committee meetings very quiet and indeed Gentoo's earlier focus groups now discontinued. With the exception of occasional complaints about the hanging-out around the Hylton Castle pub, the rather tatty club and perhaps the shops, the problems are of the 'could be anywhere' variety: complaints about a children's home in one of the streets, wheelie-bins vanishing before every Bonfire Night because they are useful to transport wood (!), and the low-standard flats above the two groups of shops. The main incipient danger sensed by the ward member is in relation to the penetration of private renting: landlords who don't care, letting to 'transient' people with no engagement in the community, whose front gardens never get looked after; not necessarily problematic individually, but capable of adding up to a 'bad tooth' in the street.

The Future

In formal planning terms, Hylton Castle received little attention in the city's previous Unitary Development Plan (UDP), with the exception of some modest allocations for new housing development and some restructuring, most notably the blocks to the south of Cheltenham Road.

This reflects the point made at the outset, that estates of this type are not really on the radar since they do not show up in a needs-based set of priorities. There are a couple of limited opportunities to introduce a new and enhanced residential offer on a small number of redevelopment sites, and linking these to a rejuvenated park could offer an opportunity to make more of the green assets of the locality.

Clearly, the area will continue to offer a mix of social renting and owner-occupation. The Right-To-Buy has seen a greater mix of tenure evolving in the traditionally socially-rented areas; but such localities may well need support to function effectively within the mainstream market, since the market is not necessarily a stable equilibrium and the future penetration of private renting is difficult to predict with any certainty. And as noted, the problem may be that the two tenures could exist in mini-enclaves: with new developments failing to 'speak to', and integrate with, the wider existing setting.

On the other hand, estates like Hylton Castle do have the potential to provide a response to growing demand in both the social rented and intermediate housing markets. But as the list of issues suggests, this will need an emphasis not just on physical change (place-making, park upgrades, etc), but also urban management and liveability issues (including 'safer places' and education); and, also, 'selling' the benefits of change, through a programme of place-branding and marketing.

Aims

The Residential Futures study for Tyne & Wear rehearsed the question of why one would want to intervene in such neighbourhoods. Some of them are at the top of the social tenure 'market', and are thus playing a valuable role within the whole housing spectrum. Hylton Castle is quite sought-after within this sector. However, the aim would not be to detract from this, by fixing something that ain't broke. It would rather be to further diversify the tenure mix (a process already often underway), and to allow and encourage these localities to continue to evolve: moving towards thriving mixed-tenure communities, whose liveability and place character make them a desirable choice both for social rent and affordable owner-occupation.

A failure to manage this transition could mean that those who have bought their own homes will struggle to sell them on, if the locality were to slip slowly into stigmatization. It is noticeable that the RTB trend is not necessarily a one-way channel, automatically leading to enhanced image and stability. Gentoo have not actually been buying back (other than as 'mortgage rescue'), but they are aware that for some older people who bought on deep discounts, carrying on being an owner-occupier does not now necessarily look more attractive than being in a rented house which Decent Homes has brought up to a standard they cannot easily now afford as low-income owners. Just letting market forces shape these areas' futures could have long-term consequences for the viability of such neighbourhoods. A managed transition into the market looks to be necessary in order to ensure long-term viability.

Things To Do

This is likely to involve environmental upgrade, a focus on liveability concerns like education and ASB, better neighbourhood management and making the most of new developments.

The area's fabric is relatively stable, so the interventions that might be considered tend to focus more on improvements to the local environment – the public realm – and to the amenities and facilities provided within the wider area (including the arrangement, location and level of provision of the local centres).

Carefully-considered and focused intervention in key parts of the public realm could help to trigger changes in the perception of the locality, among both residents and the wider community. One example is the road environment. The main arteries, such as Ferryboat Lane and the Caithness/Cheadle/Cranleigh Road cross route, tend to function as distributor roads, dominated by cars, lorries and buses and offer a pretty unfriendly experience to the pedestrian. Changing the character of these routes would mean gradually introducing a palette of materials, planting and furniture to soften this sometimes harsh environment, and probably to limit speeds. Similarly, smaller more local interventions in specific sub-areas could start to transform the quality of the place and its liveability performance.

The green space also needs something of a rethink. The quantity, quality and utility of the public open spaces in Hylton Castle (and Town End Farm and Castletown, since some is shared) could be reviewed, with a view to rationalizing and revitalizing the most important spaces. These estates, like many of their period, are awash with 'amenity' open spaces woven into the wider development – possibly once upon a time laid-out according to a master plan, but some now little used, not 'owned' or cared for by anyone much, and tending, here as in many estates, to attract anti-social behaviour. These are supplemented by clearance sites like Corfu Road, and by very underused backland garage sites, as on Cheadle Road, so there is a *lot* of spare-looking land.

Some of these spaces could contribute far more to the neighbourhood, if developed for housing or community buildings. A lot of open spaces would remain, each given specific jobs and managed in a way that gets the most out of them: local play parks, play areas, wildlife havens, dog-walking areas, and so on. Gentoo staff seem a bit ambivalent about this (rather a feeling that it is just good to have more green space, whatever it is doing or not doing?), though they would be keen to get the garage plots sorted and into some sort of worthwhile use.

The third aspect of the public realm, after streets and parks, is the local centre. Chiswick Square, with its mix of uses, does contribute to what planners are pleased to call the 'vitality and amenity' of its area. But it is apparent that a redesign and refurbishment is needed. The characterless open space in front of the shops, for example, does little to enhance the sense of place or create an attractive bustling local centre. Better parking and bus facilities; community recycling; health facilities and so on might all be located in a re-designed Chiswick Square. They could be combined with new, attractive buildings, perhaps offering both a wider range of shops and services, and new housing.

Chapter 13, below, contains a brief discussion of '*Who* might do these things?'. In Hylton Castle, the presence of a dynamic player like the Gentoo group, alongside the local community and city council, does offer some prospect that a sense of purpose and a readiness to exploit potential might be brought to bear.

Don't Take It for Granted

However, that means somebody actually taking the issues seriously. Hylton Castle is in a way classic 'don't take it for granted' territory – a place that is easy to do nothing about while concentrating on the very rough (inner-city tower blocks) and the very nice (posh and pushy conservation areas). It was quite well done at the outset, if rather uninspiring; it is quite popular; some of its earlier problems seem to be behind it.

But it has lots of competition, and in an eventually-revived new house-building market will have more. Things could change, and as seen in Gateshead, one-off 'problem-solving' responses without an overall strategy can produce contradictory and unintended consequences. And, too, there is real potential, which ought to be deployed: underused land, a local centre that could do better, a housing mix which could be augmented not undermined.

As one of the later cottage estates, Hylton Castle is perhaps less 'cosy' than Tower Gardens or Carr Hill; but it illustrates many of the possibilities that corporation suburbia can offer.

Notes

1. Caption quoted from the Gateshead Housing Company's *The Gateshead Housing Company News*, October 2012.
2. Tenure figures are based on an email of 2 January 2013 from Michael Donachie, Head of Operations, Gentoo Sunderland.
3. Statement in Northumbria Police/Sunderland Partnership's *News from Your Neighbourhood*, November 2011.

Chapter 5

Radburnland:
The Later Post-War Suburbs

The third pairing examines two estates from the last, and very extensive, phase of
municipal house-building, in the years up to 1970 or so. They are Bromford, alongside
the M6 in Birmingham; and Orchard Park, on Hull's outer northwest boundary with
the East Riding of Yorkshire.

Bromford

The Bromford Estate is an eastern suburb of Birmingham. It is a 40-hectare post-war
estate, built in the mid-to-late 1960s on what had been the city's racecourse: hence the
street names paying tribute to Newmarket, Kempton Park, Hyperion and, inevitably,
Arkle. Sadly, the 'Racecourse' pub is now closed and boarded.

People moved in from inner-city areas like Handsworth, and as on many other
estates talked about it as a utopia by comparison, with green space, its modern houses
and flats and the parade of shops (though one of the first wave of tenants recalls that
for a couple of years there was only the 'Arkle Stores' corner shop – which *is* still there
– serving the whole estate).

According to the housing expert Brendan Nevin, '*The Bromford Estate was constructed
in the late 1960s and very early 1970s by Bryant's. They won most of the contracts to develop
high rise in the city*', with a history of deals and political cover resulting in many of those
associated with the procurement process ending up in prison. He adds that of the big
three estates in that wave, both Bromford and Castle Vale – unlike Chelmsley Wood
which was transferred to Solihull borough and became part of a more localized circuit
of lettings – '*disintegrated to some extent when considering the original form ... Bromford became
a battle ground over asylum seekers amidst a discussion about demolition a few years back*'.[1]

Bromford Today

Bromford consists predominantly of quite low-density low-rise housing, interspersed
with very prominent multi-storey blocks in two clusters, plus a few maisonette
blocks and some community facilities. Its layout is recognizably that of the post-war
years, heavily influenced by the 'Radburn' separation principles – though not applied

throughout. One small group, north of Bromford Drive at Reynoldstown Road, was built for sale from the outset – but otherwise, the estate is just about entirely a municipal product of its era.

Socially and economically, Bromford has seen more change over the last decade than at any time since it was built. First, it has grown: the 2001 Census recorded a total population, for the two census tracts which best 'fit' the estate, of just under 3,000, and it is now just above. Second, while the number of households did not grow as quickly, they are now on average larger than they were a decade ago. Both of these trends are shared with Birmingham as a whole. And, third, the people, who were 85 per cent 'white' (and 84 per cent British or Irish born) in 2001, are now far more mixed ethnically: the 'white' figure is 61 per cent, while the various 'black' groupings have gone from 7 per cent to 18 per cent, with the 'Asian' and 'mixed' categories rising from 9 per cent to 20 per cent. Four hundred and twenty-three people (14 per cent) are now recorded as born outside Europe compared to ninety-four, or 3 per cent in 2001.

The pattern of jobs that people do has also changed somewhat. They are now rather more concentrated than they were in the lower-paid occupations, with the census headings of elementary, machine operations, sales, caring and other service activities predominant. Fifty-nine per cent work in these fields (this is up from 52 per cent in 2001, and compares with 28 per cent for the West Midlands as a whole), with the proportions in the skilled and admin groups falling by a comparable amount. The two occupational groups which have dropped the most sharply are the 'process plant and machine operatives' and the 'skilled trades occupations' – not perhaps surprising in an East Birmingham that has lost two huge industrial plants (Alstom rail and LDV trucks) in the last decade.

Housing tenure has changed, but in an unexpected way, over the intercensal decade. In 2001, 55 per cent of the houses were owner-occupied. This actually fell, to 46 per cent, by 2011. The corresponding rises were in both the social-rent category (42 per cent up from 38 per cent) and in private renting (12 per cent up from 7 per cent). Within the estate, there is a big difference between the more easterly of the census tracts (55 per cent social) and the westerly (22 per cent social). The number of car-owning households has also fallen slightly: 55 per cent in 2011 (down from 57 per cent in 2001), in contrast to the city (64 per cent) and West Midlands (75 per cent) averages. Again, the more easterly part of the estate has markedly lower car-ownership than the western, another indication of where the changes and the incoming population have been concentrated.

The census 'output areas' which cover the estate show quite high deprivation: lowest at the western end, which is all houses not flats; but all in the 15 per cent 'most deprived' category (BCC, 2012b). Unemployment is high, at 17 per cent in Census 2011, rising to 22 per cent in the easterly sub-area: this is double Birmingham's citywide average of 11 per cent, itself well above the national level of 6 per cent. There are very high levels of benefit dependency (and so long queues at the Post Office): though as The Hub's community worker, a local resident, remarked '*in my road, most people work, there are 2-car families, and they've mostly bought their house*'.

The estate was wryly described in a study for the City Council as '*well-located, but not well connected...*': a lot of transport grinds by, but tends to cut it off from many of its neighbours. It is bounded to the north by an elevated section of the M6, the Birmingham–Derby mainline and the River Tame, by Bromford Lane (A4040) to the west, and by the Firs Estate and predominantly pre-war housing areas of Hodge Hill around Chipperfield Road to the south (Llewelyn-Davies, 2006). At its eastern extremity, it peters out into a no-man's land where more tower blocks used to stand, a rather intimidating jungle of brambles and cracked concrete pathways which just about link it to the Chester Road. Resident Mike Daniels, on his website, summarizes the effects: '*The Estate has the M6 motorway, a railway, planes over head and a busy main road, the drowning noise from the motorway is bad, but you seem to get used to it*'.[2]

This makes it something of a physical dead-end, certainly east of the Chipperfield Road turning. Another resident, speaking on the 'Bromford Pride' video, said: '*I call it the Alamo, there's no way out, there's only one road in and one road out ... and we're surrounded by a canal, and also the M6*'.[3] The isolation point comes up frequently in local people's perceptions.

Bromford is only about 6 km from Birmingham city centre, but that is 20–30 minutes on the 72 bus (3 buses per hour). Bus links north-south on the 'outer circle' (A4040 Bromford Lane) are good, with 8 buses per hour, but they don't serve the

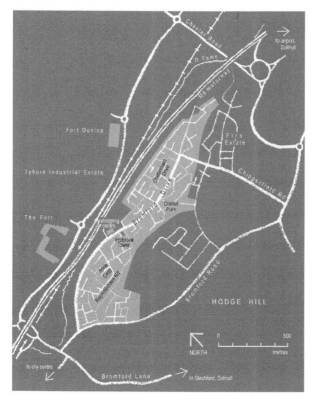

Figure 5.1. Bromford, Eastern Birmingham.

estate directly, so getting to the two nearest district centres – Stechford and Erdington – involves walking to the western end at Bromford Bridge, or changing there from the 72. Residents rely heavily on the bus services: car-ownership is relatively low as we have seen; there is no rail or metro station nearby, and walk journeys are often awkward – northwards for example, the M6/rail/river corridor is an impenetrable barrier for something like 2.5 km. Journey to work patterns reflect the suburban location. A low proportion of Bromford residents, compared to others in the eastern suburbs, work in central Birmingham; more travel to the Tyburn Road industrial area (Jaguar), Solihull (Land Rover), the Airport and NEC. It is part of the Birmingham–Solihull 'Eastern Corridor', and as much of its economic future may be tied up with Solihull's growth performance as with the city's.

The nearest shopping centre is Fox & Goose a mile or so to the south towards Stechford, where a 6,000 m² Tesco is now the major store. There is also a Sainsbury's at Castle Vale, to the north of the estate. Both are easily accessible by car, but again there is only very limited access by bus from within the estate itself – an hourly shopper bus in the middle of the day.

The small local shopping parade on the estate looks what it is: walk-in service facilities for poor people, in a battered little row which may not have had a coat of paint since Black Sabbath were last in the Top Ten (1970, since you ask; they were from Aston, actually, not Bromford). Residents with a car will bypass it to use the off-estate superstores; and anyway it has no convenient parking, despite the lashings of open land adjoining it. But it has a Post Office, small supermarket, chemists, optician, chippie and the surviving pub – of three originally on the estate – and close by are a small sports/community centre, a council housing office, a members' club, a community hall, a surgery, and the Tame Valley school. Other clusters of shops, at the top of Chipperfield Road or on the Firs Estate, are technically within walking distance for some locals, but not particularly handy for them.

What It's Like

The Bromford estate itself feels rather 'loose' as an urban structure. Arriving from the city (western) end, the road sweeps through openness, with the M6 viaduct as backdrop to the left and low terraces set well back to the right. It is strung out along the 2 km of Bromford Drive, with the neighbourhoods hanging off it to north and south in the form of Radburn closes and courts. It is probably fairly low down the 'hierarchy' of east Birmingham estates, along with the adjoining Firs Estate. There are no real sub-areas distinguished or distinguishable within it, though the earliest-built part at the western end around Arkle Croft is perhaps seen as the most settled and desirable.

It has some pleasant well-established and popular areas of housing (with gardens), with two big groups – around Reynoldstown Road/Arkle Croft and around Chillingholme Road/Cheltenham Drive – which are almost entirely houses not flats and which seem pretty stable, if sometimes a bit 'tired'. Many of the houses have the estate's (and the period's) trademark feature of side-hung tiling on the façade, and this

Figure 5.2. M6 viaduct as backdrop, gardens and greens interspersed in the housing.

adds a restrained but friendly touch of colour to the sequences of little terraces and pairs of semis.

Even here, the Radburn layout brings with it the customary counter-intuitive street-naming and house-numbering, with disorienting walkways and alleyways: calling to mind the dry recommendation in *Formes Urbaines*: '*se rappeler que généralement le numéro 7 d'une rue est situé entre le 5 et le 9 ... remarquer que la porte d'entrée d'un immeuble s'ouvre sur le trottoir et noter au passage l'extrême facilité qui consiste à garer sa voiture, marcher sur un trottoir, appuyer sur un bouton de sonnette...*' [remember that generally ... the number 7 of a street is located between numbers 5 and 9 ... notice that the entrance of a building opens onto the pavement, and notice how easy it is to park the car, to walk on the pavement and to ring a bell...] (Panerai *et al*., 1997; translation Samuels, 2004). The package also includes rear vehicular courts and lanes which are not overlooked, look tatty, and seem to contain most of the city's stock of disused sofas.

Back on the positive side, one of the attractions from the outset was obviously the generous amount of open space. As well as the quite wild and hilly copse known to the council by the catchy name of the 'Bromford South public open space' but to residents as 'Comet Park' (after a now-dead pub), there are other more open-aspect parks and green spaces, plus the pedestrian pathways and little greens which wind through the housing. Appealingly, the former paddock or parade-ring from the racecourse is picked out in the pathway round one of the little parks at the west end of the estate – though this being dear old downbeat Birmingham, you can barely perceive it, and there is not even a sign about it. Here and there, these spaces can look a bit pointless, and/or poorly maintained. Or they have been landscaped with humps to stop kids playing on them, as at Thirsk Croft.

But as an example of the best of what 'Radburn' was meant to be, and sometimes can be, it would be hard to beat the winding green that the Cheltenham Drive and Kilmore Croft houses face onto: an attractive and well-designed ensemble, framed by carefully-grouped homes in short terraces.

Figure 5.3. The 'Radburn' vision: here realized in the pleasant mature walk at the heart of the Bromford estate.

There are also, it is true, some poorly-used areas of open space, looking suspiciously like Space Left Over After Planning – as well as the gaps left by the disappearance of many of the tower blocks which used to dot the estate.

The Tower Blocks

The estate's image seems to be dominated by the history, and continuing presence, of the multi-storey blocks. Seven have gone, seven remain – a main group of five, and a pair straddling Bromford Drive by the shops. Two of the five are used as warden-service accommodation for the elderly, and together with the adjoining Ambridge House social club, seem well-thought-of. But even though half the blocks are now demolished – the most recent being the 'notorious' Bayley and Stoneycroft Towers which went in April 2011 – and even though much of the area is actually two-storey housing, it is the flats and their problems that are the essence of Bromford's public profile (Birmingham Mail, 2011; Shannahan, 2012; Chavtowns, 2005).

Figure 5.4. Bromford's image: tower block after tower block.

Of the two wardened blocks, the postwoman said *'they're carpeted and done up for the older people. But the others haven't been, they're more run down, most people aren't in work, there are some asylum seekers, some with a kid...'*. These other five were wryly described by the youth worker as

a lovely mix of folk with mental health problems, drug addicts, alcoholism or all three; with single parents, young families, single people who might be divorced, generally unemployed; yes, some asylum seekers – though some of them go into the houses or maisonettes. For families it must be horrendous. People are scared, in your flat and shut the door – the only communal space is the corridors and lifts which are awful and scary. So it's one of the worst things this country ever did. Of course for some people, they've lived there for ever and they love their flat – but the rest of the environment is awful.

The two tallest blocks (the Warstone and Holbrook pair) are scheduled for demolition – in 2014 and 2015. Some of the units are empty, and indeed one is obviously burnt-out.

The youth worker's feeling was that demolishing the 'big two' could help to transform the area. Of course, two hundred fewer people would worry the mini-market and affect the school's intake a bit, but the potential could be massive, for new housing and shops. But as he and others pointed out, the thing that has *not* happened in Bromford is re-use of sites: of the towers which have already gone, from good central sites at the Chipperfield Road turning, and at the far eastern end in the 'land that time forgot' – 3 to 4 hectares where five towers once stood, many years ago now; and where pubs and a children's home have gone as well. There are of course constraints which partially explain the inactivity, but it is part of both the reality and the image for Bromford.

Two others involved in the community felt that the demolition of the towers would be more symbolic in nature, with the problems deriving from housing allocation more than the physical form. And it does seem that the two blocks reserved for older people, coupled with their adjacent club at Ambridge Court, work as a little local community where people look out for each other and like the accommodation.

The issues which were historically associated with the worst blocks – notably drugs, and anti-social behaviour – were not raised very often in discussion. The impression was that the actions that had been taken, notably the demolitions, have taken out many of the things that people were happy to see go. A smallish number of people had been creating very big problems. According to the local Church of England vicar, '*If you talk to the police, the crime statistics are relatively low*'. There is an impression that while drugs are still a problem, residents now distinguish between a main issue of drugs 'coming on to the estate' (dealers from Alum Rock and Washwood Heath, selling to incomers who have been dumped into the blocks), and the more local cases of 'our own with problems', seen as a regrettable but to-be-coped-with part of Bromford life *per se*. Of course, any such lessening of the issues does not necessarily affect stigma: a point discussed further below.

Managing the Housing

Tenure over the whole ward is still – just – majority renting. The 2011 Census records 42 per cent social rent and 46 per cent owner-occupied. And of course, the almost-half of the council stock which has sold is predominantly houses, not flats. So it is a major fact of life for housing managers, and has been for years, that with the houses sold and not replaced, they are now far less able to meet demand for non-flat accommodation in the social sector. Private renting is much lower (12 per cent) than in the rest of Hodge Hill, immediately to the south, though as seen above this represents a sharp rise over the last 10 years.

No particular sub-areas are high or low on RTB within the stock of houses, reflecting the fact that within Bromford there is no marked differentiation between small localities. On the edge of, and just into the adjoining Firs estate, one grouping around a pleasant little green was mentioned where almost all the houses have been sold off, but no similar locations were identified on Bromford itself.

In the hierarchy of east Birmingham tenants' choices, and recognizing that there is far less choice than, say, a decade ago, 'The Bromford' seems to sit above the more inner-city Nechells but below the Bromford Lane/Round Road housing across the

M6 in Erdington – which is probably seen as less like a big council estate because of its less wide-open layout, its more traditional suburban format and the winding tree-lined roads. Bromford's layout, its towers and its clumps of maisonettes are all compared unfavourably with that mix. And since Castle Vale's transformation, it too is above Bromford in tenants' perceptions, with indeed a sense of envy at the scale of resources poured in there, but not here, to effect the turn-round. As between Firs and Bromford, a council officer observed that although there seemed little distinction, she had detected a slight sense that Firs residents are seen by Bromford people as *'thinking they're better than us, won't come down and use the community centre'*, and so on.

However the general officer view is that Bromford is reasonably stable – except for the high-rise blocks: where one contribution to the wish to move comes when singles or childless couples, who have been allocated a flat, then have kids. Of course at present anything lets, but the flats were never that desirable and in slacker market conditions demand would be quite likely to fall away. Yet as one of the housing managers noted, they are actually comparatively expensive to rent, with charges for lifts and concierges, and can cost more than a three-bed house.

The tower blocks are not just occupied by people who are at the bottom of the allocation heap. There are still some original occupants. But the flats are very often allocated to those classed as 'vulnerable'. And this connects to the quite prevalent feeling that the council is importing problems, especially drug-related ones, to Bromford. Anti-social behaviour, though less of a problem than hitherto, is still an issue: as the council's service integration head pointed out, *'we have got a "Safe Haven Project" now,* [joint police and city, working with young people] *but that has to be based on the stats, so there must still be something there'*.

As to whether Bromford presents particular management problems, local and district staff did not see any special difficulties, and seemed very positive. Bromford is certainly regarded as having good tenant involvement now, with a strong Housing Liaison Board and people coming forward to engage about the community centre. This includes not just long-standing residents *'passionate about the estate'*, but also newer people, including African residents, wanting to be on the committee. So even though there have been knock-backs, like the trashing of the newly-installed 'Comet Park' equipment, and the inability to get the clearance sites at the eastern end into use as allotments, the community has not given up.

The management of the wider environment does now seem to be on the city council's radar as well. At both officer and member level, there was – informally at least – acknowledgement that it is fair comment to point to the acres of occasionally-mown grass, the lack of care or character to many of the green spaces and little parks, and the way that too many of the roads and pathways look a bit crumbly and 'tired'. This could be seen as evidence of council departments – whether Parks, Housing or Highways – having higher priorities. However there is now a deliberate attempt to devolve responsibility and some budget to 'constituency' level (in this case Hodge Hill, a four-ward district, so about 120,000 people), with leadership by an officer whose explicit task is 'service integration' and an emphasis on structures for local engagement. On the ground this means things like '*district neighbourhood caretakers who now go round doing bits, so it does now look better*', walkabouts by multi-department groups, and allocation of a highway engineer into the area with a remit to review conditions and provision for pedestrians. Officers feel this is already starting to show benefits: the jury's out!

The Local Housing Market

As seen above, the housing was almost all, though not entirely, built by the city council. The Right-To-Buy has moved almost half the dwellings into private ownership, so this stock is what primarily makes up the current market. House prices on the Bromford estate (for a three-bedroom house) fall in the range £90–120,000, mostly at the lower end of that range. The average asking price was just over £104,000. The privately-built housing to the immediate south, up the slope of Chipperfield Road and the roads off it, showed asking prices (with one exception) for three-bedroom houses to be in the range £120,000–£138,000, averaging £125,500: a differential of some 20 per cent. However, it is noticeable that a few at least of the Bromford house prices almost converge with the bottom end of the Chipperfield Road range: with, for example, a three-bed semi in Wincanton Croft (Bromford) offered at £119,950 and one in Millington Road (500 metres to the south) at £120,000.[4]

What is also striking is the nomenclature. *No* house in the listings reviewed was described as being in Bromford, in the way that a home in Stechford or Yardley would be so located – and very few as being in the B36 postcode area. Houses offered in the private-build area immediately to the south are generally stated to be in Hodge Hill. Some residents on, for example, Chipperfield Road are very definitive about this distinction, but other – often younger – ones sometimes say 'the Chipperfield Road area' or even 'part of Bromford'. However in the property market, the estate's image is clearly something that sellers are very wary about: evidence of continuing stigma.

An estate agent, whose patch includes Bromford, asked who would buy a reasonable looking post-war three-bed semi on Bromford Drive, on display in his window, said '*local people, or an investor if they think they can get the rental return*'. He made no reference to the reputation of the estate; his view was that a good part of the market would be '*people who grew up there, coming back. A lot of it is simply a question of price – it is cheaper, and the further you go up the hill* [i.e. southwards into Hodge Hill] *the more the price goes up*'.

Private renting and investor interest does not seem to be particularly prevalent on the estate. In contrast, the area to the south, on and off Chipperfield Road, probably shows as many 'To Let' boards as 'For Sale'. This reflects the observation, from a city council officer and backed up by other people, that Bromford is not just physically slightly isolated: it is also not part of the east Birmingham 'trajectory' which has households – often ethnic-minority families – looking to move along an eastward axis as they move up the housing ladder, but still wanting to stay in the range of girls' schools, mosques and other community links and facilities. Hodge Hill and Shard End are part of this; Bromford is not. And within that circuit, private renting is an important part of the mix.

Residents: 'Bromford Pride'

The Bromford community was described as *'very quiet and undemanding'* by one city staffer. The local councillor, though, pointed out that on at least one occasion in the recent past, local people had got together, created a fuss at council 'tasking' meetings and in the media, and got at least part of their demands met. Ethnically, it remained for many years the white working-class suburb it started out as. A council staffer said *'fifteen years ago, I was the only brown face down there, but that's much less the case now'*. It is more diverse than ever before, with residents of West Indian or Pakistani/Indian extraction – as well as some more recent arrivals, notably Nigerian NHS workers mostly along Bromford Drive, and a few Somalis. But it *looks* noticeably less diverse than most of the rest of Birmingham – there are, for example, no *halal* shops, no Caribbean takeaways. And this impression is mainly because, as noted above, it is home to far fewer Asian-origin households than are nearby areas. As in Stechford to the south, it has a history as one of the city's Irish locations, but this is mostly a matter of heritage, religion and family links now, and not particularly evident. Bromford's story is like that of many estates across the country: it was the utopia, and now it is not really a place of choice. That change came about, in the view of at least some locals, with the switch in policy – no doubt done for good reasons – so that council renting became equivalent to need, rather than aspiration and the sifting of tenants. Now, *'aspirationally, if people could afford it, they'd move off without a breath. Especially young people – if you succeed you move out'*; and this community worker thought they were feeling *'this place is lost'*.

The views in the very interesting 'Bromford Pride' video nuance this somewhat. Almost all are from young people, generally 16–20, though there is a delightful moment where a deadpan 9 year-old, asked in the chippie what he thinks of Bromford, opines *'I'd give this area 7 out of 10'*. One guy says he is Bromford *'proud and born and bred, I'll die in this area'*, and another, asked if he will still be here in 5 years' time, replies *'yeah, definitely, definitely, like I say, I love Bromford, I'll still be here when I'm old and grey; I'd get buried in my back garden if I could…'*. A brother and sister give very different responses: she says *'still on The Bromford'* (they all call it 'The Bromford'); for him, it is *'myself, I'd like to get off the area, y'know what I mean, make something of my life, something better for my kids than what I've had – it is a nice place, but I mean it's not the best place to be'*.

The interviewees also discuss the stigma, or as they refer to it the reputation, of The Bromford. Some of it was attributed to the isolation – nobody actually comes here, but it does not stop them having attitudes to it. Also *'it's the negative press, and the police: if you speak to them, it's about the nicks they've got, it's always the bad, y'know, and not the good, and there's a lot of good here'*. But even with his pride, this respondent would move off: *'it's not the best place really, is it?'*.

The neighbourhood worker's commentary in discussing these attitudes was that people definitely think there is a stigma, but that in a funny way it is a badge of pride. Asked if that was a bit like East-enders in London – no, smaller, more isolated; but there is an identity and a 'Bromford pride'. The young people know the place is not all good, that it is tough, that there is a lack of jobs, but many will live here and bring up families here; it is not 'aspirational' but there remains a working-class attachment to the area especially via family and friends. As to whether there is a 'community': his view was that there is a core who know each other, went to school together, may even move off and come back, so there is undoubtedly community spirit amongst them. There is certainly a wariness about people you do not know (and indeed this is perceptible as one walks around), but strong networks of family and friendship. Once again, sister and brother disagreed, on the video: yes there is a community (her), no there is not (him)!

The landlady of the Bromford Bridge – the surviving pub of the three – who is not a local, but comes from Great Barr out towards Walsall, said that she had been very pleasantly surprised since taking over the previous summer. She had known the area to have a bad reputation, but *'our customers are very friendly, quiet, it's busy all day at the weekends, during the week it's OAPs during the day and then an after-work crowd. There's a lady who bought on Kempton Park Road for about £105,000 and is very pleased with the house and the area – she comes in the pub'*. This is a far from apocalyptic view of the area, from someone who might have been expected to see the rougher end of its daily life.

Mike Daniels, quoted earlier about *'the drowning noise from the motorway'* adds *'I did enjoy growing up here and have many good friends and old neighbours that I still care about, but it seems to me that Birmingham city council have forgot about it'*.

The Future?

The city council have not entirely 'forgot about it' but their responses are somewhat patchy. There is commentary above about the things that have *not* happened – notably, post-demolition, on sizeable chunks of vacant land. Not all of this is the council's fault, though. The land does suffer from particular constraints. Much of the estate is in the floodplain of the nearby River Tame, and the newly hyper-nervous Environment Agency (EA) seems to regard *any* development in the area as tantamount to melting ice caps. Layered on top of that is the 'safeguarding line' for the High Speed 2 rail line (HS2). This brings blight and uncertainty – but also, curiously, the prospect of flood defence works which could help resolve the development impasse.

But the council have hardly been faultless. There is a dual impression – of dithering, and of lack of attention. Long before the EA and HS2 surfaced as concerns, there seemed to be no clear line on what the future for Bromford, and its available sites, might be: use for employment land versus use for housing, do up the blocks as 'Decent Homes' versus pull them down, and so on. Even now, the area needs a positive and clear lead from the city, to push the EA into a reasonable position, to badger the Department for Transport into proper Dutch-style acoustic screening of the M6, and to secure commitments which avoid the danger that HS2 just freezes everything for 20 years.

The lack of attention also seems to extend to the estate environment. Two days of wandering about found just one bench in the whole area – pretty remarkable for an estate of some 3,000 souls. As remarked earlier, within the housing there is a tired and poorly-maintained feel to quite a few corners, even where residents themselves have clearly invested their own money and time in their homes. It is understandable that the management focus will historically have been on the problems, and in particular on the 'multis'. But once again, the danger is that, in rather taking the rest for granted, and not having a coherent total approach, the *potential* is overlooked and let drift.

There was indeed some criticism of the local authority: its 'silo' nature where departments do not seem to talk to each other, its tendency to swallow up concerned residents in process ('meetingitis', said one) rather than genuine engagement; the perceived unfairness and bad outcomes of housing allocation. This is difficult to judge from the outside. But the feel on the ground is sometimes of a rather forgotten place. The council's new and more integrated service approach may hold out hope for change on that front at least.

Well, what future might one envisage for this estate, with its tantalizing, frustrating mix of quality and grim disconnection? The starting-point would probably *not* be the city council's key planning document, the Core Strategy, which plumbs depths of leaden abstract-noun dullness in what it has to say about Bromford. Paragraph 8.128 says that 'The Bromford Housing estate is an area with potential for significant change to provide new development opportunities while at the same time overcoming problems of poor residential environments'. According to Policy E15, 'Within the remaining residential areas of the Bromford Housing estate the emphasis will be on the improvement of the housing stock, environment and local amenities including the provision of enhanced community facilities'. How will this be done? 'New housing development opportunities will be identified through stock assessments and the review of the SHLAA' and 'Further detailed planning and development guidance will be prepared as necessary to facilitate development opportunities' (Birmingham City Council, 2012*a*). Oh dear.

Speaking at Patrick Abercrombie's memorial service in 1957, Clough Williams-Ellis said 'he gave wings to planning, never letting its ultimate end – more happiness for more people – be obscured by its solemn technical processes…' (CPRE, 2012). Almost 50 years on, sadly, Birmingham's planners seem mired in the sort of administrative solemnity that Williams-Ellis meant. What on earth are Bromford's residents to make of it, as a plan or vision for their neighbourhood's future?

So?…

So what we now have is a neighbourhood, predominantly local-authority-built, where the fact that many tenants have chosen to exercise the Right-To-Buy, and in particular to buy the *houses*, means that the renting households are increasingly concentrated in flats. There are still a few problems of anti-social behaviour, the estate remains quite stigmatized, and local people are very aware of that. Yet Bromford is apparently a satisfactory home to many families; it is adjacent to relatively good quality housing areas (to the south); and there is a functioning local housing market. In the view of the council officer quoted earlier '*if you said "what's the role of Bromford?" it's probably affordable mixed market – but there's not enough family stock, there are still too many 2-beds and maisonettes'.* The fact that even formerly unpopular accommodation is letting reflects the tightness of the current (social) 'market', not suitability for the future. These are pointers to what, if the constraints can be lifted, the area's potential actually is.

Calls to pull down tower blocks are often an easy shout and a knee-jerk response to the architecture and to the results of allocations policies; not always to the actual attributes of specific blocks in specific places. But in this specific place and with these specific blocks, it looks like Bromford's future would indeed be very much more stable if it was recast as a more or less completely low-rise estate. This would recognize its quite peripheral 'suburban' location, and it would respect the choices of those who have actually chosen to live here: going with that flow. It would mean fewer 'units' – but more potential. Some of the tensions in our current housing policies and approaches are very clearly being played out here.

Orchard Park

Orchard Park, on the northern outskirts of the city of Hull, is the last of the six special study areas, the most recently built, and the one with the most uncertain future.

The wider area of north Hull, within which Orchard Park sits, is a fairly distinct suburban district of the city between the University of Hull to the south, the River Hull to the east, and open land (part of East Riding) to the north and west. It is made up of several separate sub-areas: Orchard Park is its north-western-most part.

Built very rapidly in the 1960s and 1970s to keep pace with the city's slum clearance programmes, the Orchard Park estate was produced mainly by modern 'system'

Figure 5.5. Tight-packed rows, on the Hull/East Riding boundary. (*Photo:* Urbed)

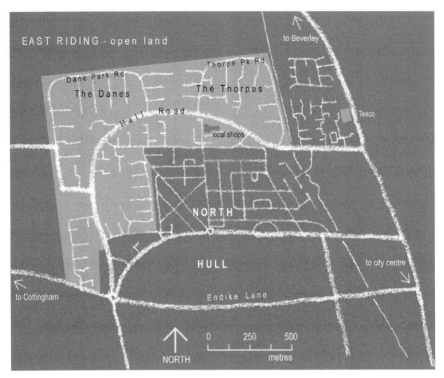

Figure 5.6. Orchard Park and its city context.

methods of construction. As in Bromford, the suburban housing mix was interspersed with tower-blocks. The authors of the Pevsner guide to the city describe how here and at Ings Road in east Hull 'The wide open layout of the immediate post-war estates was abandoned in favour of a tighter development based on the Radburn principle of separating vehicles and pedestrians by providing roads at the rear of the houses and footpaths at the front… The Orchard Park estate took the form of four closely linked "villages" of traditional houses with a twenty-storey block as the focal point for each'. They quote Alison Ravetz's critique of Radburn layouts: 'unfamiliar geometries, unclear distinctions between public and private space, and networks of public footpaths that encroached on public privacy' (Neave and Neave, 2010).

And certainly Orchard Park's version of Radburn, with its succession of parking yards and pathways rather than ordinary streets, and its awkward jumble of housing blocks, fits that description. In contrast to Bromford's interpretation of Radburn, there is – in the The Danes and The Thorpes at least – no 'shared green space' benefit as the upside of the layout: it is almost all downside. But in a way it seems unfair to associate America's original Radburn with this scheme: it is so bastardized a version, and so badly done, that the concept's originators would not even recognize it.

Socially, Orchard Park is a mainly working-class outer suburb which houses families on low incomes: income levels are indeed among the lowest in Hull, which in turn are low by regional and national comparison. As an indicator of how much money is(n't) around: you can tender a fiver in the 'Pint & Pot' and get two pints of Fosters, which must be a Northern Hemisphere record – though your choice of eating might be restricted to the last packet of BBQ Hulahoops on the premises. The ward's residents compete in the wider Hull and East Riding labour market – they do not have any particular local work that they specialize in. The major employment axis for them lies to the south, with 1,295 (37 per cent) of working residents commuting along a corridor ending in the city centre; 589 (17 per cent) people work within the ward itself (Hull City Council, 2010a). The distance to the city centre is not great (about 6 km) but the bus journey is the thick end of half an hour whichever trundling route is used.

Over the decade between the 2001 and the 2011 Census counts, the total population, at just over 4,600, hardly changed, though the household size rose slightly, presumably reflecting increasing pressure at the bottom end of the market rather than the trend to smaller households more generally (including in the city of Hull as a whole). Population characteristics did not change much either: a small fall from the previous 99 per cent 'white' (to 94 per cent) – but this still only meant that the 'non-white' people rose from 33 to 263 in the total; and still 93 per cent British or Irish born (also 99 per cent in 2001). The two groups which accounted for almost all the increase were those born in the EU 'Accession' countries and those from outside Europe, and indeed the city as a whole is home to over 8,000 East Europeans, often Poles and Lithuanians working in the agri-businesses of the East Riding hinterland. Perhaps because of the estate's homogeneity, the people you meet are generally chatty and confident, in contrast to the rather unsure feeling in some other localities where eye contact is avoided and interaction kept to a minimum.

The Census figures also illustrate another aspect where Orchard Park has seen less change than elsewhere: housing tenure. Social housing still accounts for over 68 per cent of the stock (75 per cent in 2001); so the proportion of homes that are now owner-occupied has risen from 17 per cent to 23 per cent – about a hundred more than in 2001. Private renting has hardly changed, with an increase of just ten homes in this sector taking the proportion to 9 per cent. The figures for car-owning households underline the impression of poverty: 40 per cent – in an outer suburban location – in 2011 (up from 37 per cent in 2001), well below the city's 59 per cent and the Yorkshire & Humber region's 72 per cent. It has, however, retained one of Britain's greatest concentrations of kids on chopper bikes.

The jobs that people do are very heavily concentrated in lower-paid occupations, with 71 per cent working in the Census categories covering elementary, machine operations, sales, caring and other service activities. The national average in these occupations is 40 per cent. Not surprisingly, the proportions in the skilled and admin groups (18 per cent compared with 23 per cent nationally) and in the three best-paid groups (12 per cent compared with 36 per cent) are strikingly lower. Unemployment is very high. The Census statistics for those 'unemployed as percentage of the economically active', where the England & Wales average was 6 per cent in 2011 (7 per cent in the region; 12 per cent in city of Hull), shows an average for the three Orchard

Park census tracts of 27 per cent, with one of them touching 30 per cent. This is much the worst position of any of the suburbs studied here.

Choice and Rejection

Deprived households are those with the least choice in the housing market, and Orchard Park shows evidence of high levels of deprivation: the ward is the third most deprived in Hull, and the eightieth nationally. Indeed parts of it fall within the top 5 per cent most deprived areas in the country, with a neighbourhood called The Danes falling within the top 1 per cent. This is exacerbated for residents by high levels of crime and anti-social behaviour. Despite generally falling crime levels, in 2008 Orchard Park had the second highest number (1,684) of reported crimes amongst all Hull wards – only Myton/the city centre was higher. It had, too, the third highest rate per head of population. The area's complex Radburn-type layout, with poor overlooking and too many dead spaces, tends to make this worse because it is difficult to police.

Orchard Park, not surprisingly, is not an area of choice. The demand for homes remains low, in comparison with other areas, with low numbers of 'bids' for tenancies per property, longer than average re-let times, and a lower than average proportion of homes where people have exercised the Right-To-Buy.

It has, too, a record of rejection and empty property from the time when people *had* more choice. Of course, in the current very tight social housing 'market', vacant properties are now much less numerous than formerly. But the empty homes record has historically been an indicator of lack of popularity. At the point in the housing market when households *did* have more real choice of where to live (2001–2003), Orchard Park – and especially The Danes and The Thorpes – performed remarkably poorly. By 2001, the estate was 26 per cent vacant: the highest in Hull. Reported re-let times were 322 days; this was three times as bad as any other estate. Even as recently as 2010, The Danes had sixteen voids out of 451 properties – and this despite earlier demolitions which had already reduced the stock.

This is a picture of a locality that is not attractive enough in the long term to bring people in and keep them there by choice: it was quite simply some of the least popular housing in Hull.

Predictably, Orchard Park suffers from a poor image and reputation. At the most obvious level, what people will pay for property provides something of a benchmark: Orchard Park's average house price over the 2 years to the third quarter of 2008 was £56,000, compared to a city average of £89,000 and the adjoining areas to the east of £101–106,000. 'Satisfaction with neighbourhood' as surveyed by the council shows low levels: 57 per cent in the ward, compared with 72 per cent citywide (and 85 per cent in nearby Beverley Ward).

As with many estates, these patterns tend to be self-reinforcing – people with choice reject the area because of its image, and this further worsens things in a spiral of decline (Hull City Council, 2010*b*). Residents are acutely aware of the stigma, of course: one told the Urbed planning team: 'My vision for Orchard Park is that it comes in line with all the other communities in Hull and it's not singled out, when my son's 18 and goes for a job he isn't discriminated against because his postcode is HU6' (Urbed, 2006).

Unattractive Housing, in an Unattractive Environment

So this late-period version of 'corporation suburbia' is in trouble. A lot of that, clearly, is to do with it being an outer council-built suburb in one of England's poorest cities. But some of it is because of what it *is*.

Not just the housing. In many parts of Orchard Park, the quality of the environment is poor. Rear parking yards are difficult to maintain to a high standard. The overall layout has produced a lot of shapeless underused space which has no clear 'ownership', as well as a locality with no recognizable shape or sense of place. A walking trip is a long plod through nothing very much, and bus-stops on the main loop road (Hall Road) feel as though they are in the middle of nowhere. And yet right across Orchard Park Road, in streets like 40th Avenue, the earlier North Hull cottage estate – far more conventional in layout and house design, far more coherent, far more stable – shows a model which was deliberately ignored in the brave new world of the 1960s.

The New Labour years did produce some extra services: a very well-run Health Centre, a sparkling new Academy named (Ferens) after a great Hull benefactor, and a huge Tesco, though all are at the Beverley Road end so about 15 minutes walk from the middle of the estate. The in-estate 'shopping centre' on the other hand is an ugly run-down half-empty cluster, where the best that can be said is first, it still has a post-office, and second, the shop that until recently actually sold golliwogs has mercifully closed. The green space too: the estate is on the edge of Hull, adjoining open East Riding land towards Cottingham in the west and towards Beverley in the north, yet it is actually short of high-quality, well-used parks and green spaces within the residential area itself.

Figure 5.7. The 'downside' of Radburn – grim unsupervised rear courts environment.

Figure 5.8. Boxy little rows, at 90° to the roadway, with dull 'amenity spaces' in front.

So although there is a lot of countryside and open 'urban fringe' land close at hand, the neighbourhood spaces (and the council's mapping shows at least eight of them) for families and small children are dull and uncared-for. They were also almost all graded very poorly in the open space assessment carried out for the city in the last few years.

And then the housing itself: frankly unattractive – boxy little rows running off at an angle to the sweeping over-designed through-roads, with gaps here and there where piecemeal demolition has been tried, as a way of picking off particular problem blocks.

The physical state of the property is also an issue. The multi-storey blocks are being emptied, with all the 20-storey ones to be demolished; and the houses, despite some improvements, still do not meet modern energy-saving standards. The council's preferred strategy was for substantial clearance and redevelopment, and that would still be the case if access to 'Housing PFI (Private Finance Initiative)' money had not been withdrawn.

The Future

Residents' hopes and fears for the future are a touching mix of the positive and the negative. Mary Wallace, speaking to the Urbed team, insisted that: *'The children of this area have great dreams, they want to be architects, doctors and all sorts of things … there is a great desire in this area from all ages to see people from Orchard Park make something of themselves, to go and be great at something'*.

Important too, to recognize that for many people the estate may not be perfect but it is a reasonable place to live and bring up kids, or to find a flat or bungalow in the area you have lived in for most of your adult life, and where many of your family and friends may still be close by. A government study of problem estates included Orchard Park as long ago as 1980, but as Alison Ravetz points out, even then tenants were looking back on a golden age when it 'used to be lovely' (Ravetz, 2001).

Other people expressed worries to Urbed about the likely track that the estate is now on: 'What I don't want is the slow decline and decimation of Orchard Park. I think the danger with the proposal to knock down the flats … it feels like a managed decline of the area' or 'Where do we go from here? In 15 years' time it won't be worth living round here. It's a shame really'. And 'I dread to think what it will be like in a few more years unless something happens' (Urbed, 2006).

The future, though, is indeed very difficult to forecast with confidence. Residents have twice in 5 years given broad support for extensive change: first for the 'keyhole surgery' scheme which Urbed worked up with resident groups in 2006, and then for the more sweeping clear-and-rebuild ideas of URS/Scott Wilson at the core of the PFI scheme in 2010. The first may not have been fundable – complex, and probably not creating enough new value; the second fell once the PFI money was withdrawn by the incoming coalition government.

But radical change is probably going to be the answer in the end. Unlike many parts of corporation suburbia, it is hard to see what features Orchard Park has that would enable it to grow and be nurtured 'organically', into a successful popular suburb – and in Hull and the East Riding, there is no shortage of other places that people would choose first, and could afford. The city council, though, cannot just leave it: for one thing, that would be unfair on those living in what is, and is likely to remain, a problematic neighbourhood. And it is also actually unfair on the rest of Hull: this is a city council asset, but one which is wasting and one which is costing money.

So at present they are engaged in a process of upgrading and adjustment which should at least hold things stable; taking down all the towers except two medium-rise ones, working with RSLs to develop new houses for shared-ownership and rent, and building new one- and two-bed council homes. Money is being assembled from a cocktail of sources such as the 'Green Deal' and 'New Homes Bonus' to both build new and to repair some of the faults in the external environment as originally designed. It's a heroic effort.

Orchard Park, created at the tail-end of the long years of estate-building, and at the outer edge of its city as that city started to run out of economic steam, was probably always an 'estate too far'. That does not mean that it has no future: but it places it at the 'problem', rather than the 'potential', end of the corporation suburb spectrum.

Notes

1. Personal communication from Brendan Nevin 1 February 2013; see also Power and Houghton (2007).
2. Mike Daniels makes this observation on his *bromford-bridge.pwp.blueyonder.co.uk* site.
3. The *Bromford Pride* video, from Solar Pictures UK, was accessed via www.youtube.com, 10 February 2013.
4. Price comparisons are mainly from Mouseprice Birmingham pages on www.mouseprice.com.

Chapter 6

Threads

Places to Celebrate, Places to Nurture

Celebrating the estates of corporation suburbia is not perhaps the most fashionable of causes. Yet looking at the total achievement, and at the particular localities in the case studies, the first thing to say is that this is a thing that Britain did a lot of, and in many places did very well. They are a variant of the widely-admired garden city concept, and share many of that idea's strengths and attractiveness.

Rod Hackney, in his introduction to *Just Like the Country* observed that the tenants' tributes to their inter-war estates offer a 'testimony to the best that state-provided rented housing can be'. That booklet also contains personal testimonies to what a difference to lives the new housing really made. An endearing example is May Millbank's memory of moving from Kings Cross to the Watling Estate in Edgware in 1937:

As we were brought into the house we thought 'Is this all ours?'…We looked out of the window and my brother, who was two years younger than me said 'What's that over there?' He couldn't make out what the green was or what the flowers in the garden were and I was glad he asked because I wasn't sure if the flowers were also called grass. (Rubinstein, 1991)

The social achievement should not be minimized. In Alison Ravetz's formulation, it is 'clear that, whatever later faults appeared, their new homes did at first lift people from substandard housing and degrading slums, enabling them to live dignified and modern lives on something like a par with the middle classes' (Ravetz, 2001). And this is particularly true of the cottage estates compared with, say, the schemes dominated by flats.

Some of the Threads

Looking forward rather than back, it is their *potential* that needs to be stressed – not just the problems: which undoubtedly exist for many, but are not their whole or defining characteristic. The case studies show that within a pattern of many common features there is also a diversity of situations.

Looking at the six places, and working north to south, starts with Deckham and Carr Hill, on Tyneside. This is generally good-quality housing, though some parts are rather bleak and have smaller houses, and it perhaps gives a feeling of a lot of the same over quite a wide area. Some of it is quite poor, in a not very prosperous region, and there are many competing locations attracting the mortgage money of its potential residents. But it looks to have a lot of potential, for quite a range of people.

Sunderland's Hylton Castle, too, has reasonable quality though in a looser layout and a more peripheral location. It has suffered from some stigma, because of a (not really justified) association with crime/ASB in a neighbouring area. Its physical and social stability would benefit from positive management – and from rethinking its open space asset to stress quality rather than quantity.

Along the east coast, Orchard Park on the outskirts of Hull has less going for it than any of the other five. Poorly designed and laid-out, it is both problematic and stigmatized. Again, it has too much pointless open space, and again, any resident with buying power has plenty of options in the city-region's housing market.

Bromford in the Midlands, nestling cosily under the M6 elevated section, is an intriguing mixture: some pleasant and popular family housing, but stigma because of its generally-problematic tower blocks. There have been headaches over ASB, and the locality does feel a bit isolated; but there is nonetheless real potential.

Down in London, Tower Gardens has considerable charm and popularity, though its house prices are still, somewhat surprisingly, below those in neighbouring streets for properties which are, superficially, less attractive. There are, once more, concerns about resident behaviour and a need for management; and also questions about long-term stability if the effect of the Right-To-Buy is to unduly increase the slide into the private rented sector.

Becontree's size means that it is not all one place with one set of patterns to be picked out. At the same time, as Chapter 3 notes, within that, there is really only one part of it (Gale Street) which can be said to have a definable *area* identity: on an even larger scale than Deckham, it does go on and on. As in the other London case study, there are questions about the penetration and impact of private renting. But there is also another interesting market pattern emerging, which is that the area is starting to be of interest to new, ethnically-defined, groups; an indication that unlike in some of the North's suburbs, there are far fewer market alternatives around for the would-be home-owner.

Thus there are some common (and often obvious) patterns, though marked differences too. Understanding them may help in exploring the potential of the estates in future.

But Would You Live There?

This is to look at the estates in a fairly analytical way. Perhaps, though, one should also ask the title question from David Rudlin's report for the Urban Task Force about city living: 'But would you live there?' (MORI *et al.*, 1999). Architects and planners are famous for their keenness to design brand-new places for other people to live in, while themselves renovating a seventeenth-century cottage 20 miles away … but it *is* something of a test for any urban environment to ask that question.

Personally, on this test, the six estates in the case studies form a sort of continuum.

It shades from the clear 'yes' of North London's Tower Gardens to the categorical 'no' for Orchard Park in Hull. The continuum passes through Becontree's pleasant, stable, handsome Wykeham Green, off Gale Street near Becontree station; on through the better parts of Gateshead's Carr Hill/Sheriff Hill development, and the unexciting but quite satisfactory Hylton Castle in outer Sunderland, to Cheltenham Drive's 'Radburn' green in Birmingham; then perhaps to the duller less well-looked-after parts of Becontree and Bromford; then the rather cramped and harsh Deckham Hall in Gateshead. And finally, poor old Orchard Park.

Why? What is one reacting to? It is partly to estates, or parts of them that feel stable and cared-for; also to intimacy and scale, and thus to the design *per se*; and to whether or not the place feels isolated, either in the sense of a long way out, or just being nowhere near shops, social facilities and so on. To this, one would no doubt add, if a household with children, the schools and their performance.

This does give an insight, even if a highly personal one, to the sorts of choices people are actually making about whether or not to move to – or stay in – such areas. On the other hand, it is important to remember that one should not be writing areas off simply because *we* do not like them; or if it feels a bit like the end of the known world, as might be the reaction on a grey November afternoon in Hylton Castle or Bromford.

People do like a lot of these places, and they think they are broadly OK even if they criticize certain aspects. Deckham and Carr Hill, Bromford and Hylton Castle are full of residents for whom these places do 'work'. The question is, can they work better, and move from 'problem' to 'potential', from stigmatized to area of choice?

Different Places, Different Contexts

In trying to assess what is chosen and what is not, it is apparent that some things must be dependent on the context, and some estate-specific. Looking at the six estates, and at other locations considered in later parts of this book, a number of common themes do emerge; so do some things which tend to differentiate areas from each other. Common ground first.

Under the broad heading of design issues, it seems to be common ground that success is less likely if (as is often the case in post-war estates) the cottage estate format has, mixed in with it, troublesome forms such as deck-access slabs or tower-blocks: like the multi-storeys in Bromford, and the towers at Castle Green in Becontree. This can also apply where there are too many and/or too concentrated maisonettes or walk-up flats in the mix: as at Deckham Hall, Walker in Newcastle's East End, or Craigmillar (Edinburgh); or indeed in Inner London walk-up tenements in those dim and distant days of the 'difficult to let' estates… But on the other hand, the Brighton estate (Craven Vale), described in Chapter 8, 'works' (and it never did not); yet it includes a high proportion of walk-up flat blocks. So the form *per se* may be problematic, but is not enough of an explanation.

A sense of place seems to help in conveying and reinforcing stability and liveability:

weak in larger estates like Becontree and some of Deckham; strong in Tower Gardens, in part of Bromford, and indeed in one or two more distinctive bits within Deckham/ Carr Hill and Becontree themselves. Connected to this is the need to rethink the green spaces, to stress quality not quantity and give the area more 'shape' (Hylton Castle, Orchard Park). Also on the physical-form front: most of these estates have feeble local centres which do little for them or even tend to drag them down (Hylton Castle, Bromford, Deckham; and also the Rochdale, Kirkby and Hull/Bricknell case studies in 'Residential Futures').

Urban management comes up repeatedly. It was raised 'in terms', as the barristers say, in relation to Tower Gardens and Hylton Castle, and it covers a range of things on all the estates: failure to maintain the physical condition (raised in Deckham, though now being tackled by an explicit neighbourhood management initiative); managing resident behaviour (Tower Gardens); crime rates (Hylton Castle, and Wythenshawe in Chapter 8 below) and ASB (Bromford). This connects of course to the very prevalent issue of stigma, even for ostensibly quite pleasant and good-quality areas in Bromford and Tower Gardens.

A shared issue, though with variable impact across the regions, is the increasing penetration of the Private Rented Sector in the post-Right-To-Buy era. Not necessarily problematic in itself, and indeed potentially opening these neighbourhoods up to new choices: but with concerns about the impact on area stability in Tottenham and Dagenham, and with unanswered questions about what it implies for the future in Gateshead and Birmingham.

All this discussion assumes that the corporation suburbs are on the radar of the local authority. But councils are overrun with competing priorities. And these estates are not always clamouring for urgent attention. The Northern Way studies (Urban Studio, 2009d) looked, for example, at Mereside, a council-built estate on the outskirts of Blackpool: decent well-built houses, good layout, successful local schools, but poorish, with feeble 'liveability' performance and a sense of stigmatization within the hierarchy of Blackpool's housing areas. The studies identified a menu of things to be done – to the local centre, to the parks and open space, and so on; and suggested what sort of partnership might do them. But Mereside is not in crisis. It could probably be left alone, without disaster – though with (the oft-repeated theme) underachieved potential. Blackpool and its regeneration partners have as their priority the ReBlackpool initiative, focused on the town centre, resort core and ailing B&B/private-rented sector. This is fine – but as is the case all over the country, it can tend to mean that the estates miss out on the attention that could genuinely benefit them, and that the overall 'residential offer' is not considered in the round.

There is, too, a more general point: the need for public agencies to think strategically about the corporation suburbs. Raised explicitly in the Sunderland example, which points to the existence of an 'A19 corridor' of similar estates, it also relates to Gateshead/Tyneside (who has the strategic role, post Housing Market Renewal?), and to Bromford: what is the strategic context beyond 'problem-solving demolitions'?

Key Differences

Looking at what differentiates the estates and their prospects, it is tempting to point to their age: the older the better! But actually this is code for their layout, and sometimes the house designs. The suggested 'continuum' from Tower Gardens to Orchard Park is, amongst other things, a continuum from legible urban streets and Arts & Crafts house style to incomprehensible layouts and cheap-as-chips construction, as well as from 1905 to 1965.

It is clear that the design approach weakened after the Second World War. There is generally less coherence when compared with pre-war building, as the garden city tradition did battle with the Modern Movement. And as seen explicitly in the example of Wythenshawe (Chapter 8) there were marked design changes, none of which helped: to the houses themselves, to the choice of open-plan fronts versus gardens, to the original planned density, and to the introduction of flats, whether walk-ups or tower blocks (Hebbert and Hopkins, 2012).

Clearly the location has also made a difference to trajectory and prospects. Estates may be on a city's outer edge, or 'embedded' like Tower Gardens. These are not better or worse locations, but they make for different roles. At a larger scale, the regional 'North' versus 'South' difference is shorthand for weak versus strong labour markets and housing markets, within which these estates are part of the 'residential offer'.

In particular, there are big differences in the strength of the local/sub-regional housing markets in terms of the competition which the cottage estates face. What Deckham/Carr Hill and Orchard Park can offer has to compete with much more affordable modern housing for sale than is the case for Becontree and Tower Gardens. Here, the very constrained London and Southeast housing market makes what they have much more competitive. Indeed in Becontree this seems to be encouraging 'new' groups of purchasers to explore the area as a possibility.

House size, too, affects how different sub-areas perform. Within Gateshead, Deckham Hall's homes are in general smaller (and on smaller plots) than their neighbours to the South, so that they appeal less to families. Similarly, the two-bedroom houses in Becontree and Bromford are seen to act as a constraint both on incomers' choices and (in London anyway) on the private rental market.

Other differences, estate to estate, can be seen in relation to the effects of RTB – worries about it leading to instability in Becontree, or about an accentuation of sub-area differences in Wythenshawe; and while it may be reinforcing stability in Brighton's Craven Vale (see Chapter 8), it could also be closing off any future role other than open-market-for-sale there. Similarly, there are variations in attitudes to the municipally-built suburbs versus their privately-built counterparts: people's view of the gradation of Sunderland's suburbs, for example, seems much 'flatter' than that in East London around Becontree. Importantly, too – though it is a bit late to do anything about it – the estates' histories: notably, a key variable seems to have been the extent to which they were the destination for slum clearance moves, versus being the housing of choice for the 'aristocracy of labour' between the wars.

One final aspect of difference between the places is to do with local people's support for radical change. In Orchard Park, this was established, as a result of Hull City Council's successive rounds of consultation on their redevelopment plans. In Gateshead and Birmingham, much less extensive proposals were generally welcomed – often because they were seen as removing problematic blocks or groupings. In the other three case-study areas, big physical changes – unlikely anyway – would probably meet with opposition.

It Can Work!

A key thread from all this is that corporation suburbia often 'works' – but it could work better, and sometimes it plainly does not. Many of these six case-study estates do 'work': their design has stood the test of time, people are satisfied with the houses and the area, and the places are well integrated into their surrounding context. Looking at the six, and with the exception of Orchard Park, they all have potential *as they are*.

So this chunk of British suburbia is an asset, actual or potential, which should be celebrated, admired, promoted, 'exploited' – for people who live there, and people who might in future. And although the pre-war estates are the best expression of the garden city/garden suburb ethos now being 'rediscovered', their post-war successors have many of these attributes too. We do need to get the most out of what we have; recognizing and nurturing the value and attractiveness that can still be there for the taking.

Making a Difference – Without Spending Half the GNP

Nurturing corporation suburbia is indeed an important priority. Policy and intervention could make a difference. Each estate – not just the six, but across the country – will need different degrees and types of support, of action, and of change. The great attraction, though, is that the need is not, usually, for 'big-bang' intervention or policy which is radical and inevitably costly.

We can make much more of the asset represented by the cottage estates via initiatives which are rather more low-key: the sort of 'TLC' measures suggested in the *Residential Futures* studies (Urban Studio, 2009c) and in Chapter 13 below. Things like local upgrading, small targeted grants to improve the quality of neighbourhood facilities, work on image and stigma, employment access, infill housing, and so on; each package specific to each estate's needs and potential.

Some, of course, may need more and different intervention, not just 'TLC'. In places like Orchard Park, the balance between the cost of the effort and the return in terms of released potential looks very different. For many of the estates, yes, a fairly low level of intervention could bring rewards, if intelligently handled. But in some cases the investment case will have to be based on a more 'problem-oriented' approach. That will mean, in the end and once the money is there again, more intervention of a root-and-branch nature to release the potential in a more radical way.

The Overall Message: Value, with More to be Released

In general, though, the message from the cottage estates is about the potential release of value through quite low-key investment. A country with a long-run housing shortage, and recurrent difficulty in working out how to fund and deliver new housing development, needs to take advantage of the stock it already has, and get the most out of it in every sense.

The following chapters shift the focus from the past, and the place-specific present, to some of the general patterns affecting corporation suburbia. They look at what the estates' role now is in the housing market; how perceptions of this stock affect its performance; and then on into the future: what potentials might be locked up in such an extensive 'asset'.

Chapter 7

Market Patterns and Roles

Changing Markets, Changing Roles

This important and distinctive part of the country's housing has undergone a lot of change over the last thirty years. The change has been not so much physical – the houses and their layout – as organizational and social. The prime mover was of course the Right-To-Buy, which has meant that this housing, which was almost entirely publicly-owned in 1970, is now about 50 per cent owner-occupied or let privately. It is important to note that, as Jones and Murie's study of RTB stresses, well over 250,000 had already been sold by 1979; that is, RTB did not *start* the sell-off (Jones and Murie 2005; Hills 2007).

So the corporation estates are now involved in the private market. Indeed, they are involved in two private markets: the owner-occupied sector, and the private-rented sector (PRS) – much smaller, but quite dynamic. They are actually also part of a third 'market': a social housing market, where the access to the accommodation is not just controlled by price (rental or sale value) but by other controls which the social housing providers operate, ranging from 'points' to priority systems. This operates like an economic market in at least one important way: that is, when demand goes down (as it did generally during the 1990s) the 'price' (in terms of ease of access – say, the points needed for a tenancy) goes down too; and when it goes up (which it has done since about 2002 as it has got harder to buy or rent private housing), that 'price' goes up too: a council tenancy, especially on a popular cottage estate, is harder to get now than at any time in living memory.

As a result, we now have a million and a half homes on these estates which are part of the mainstream housing-for-sale market. This chapter explores how these 'markets' are affecting the cottage estates: how far they are now completely embedded in that market, what part in the market they play, and what that might mean for the future of corporation suburbia. It draws heavily on the key work on the topic – Jones and Murie's *The Right To Buy*. And it starts with their set of probing questions on the issue:

Even after 25 years of the Right to Buy it is not clear to what extent this distinctive part of the housing market will be fully absorbed into the market. Will former council properties always be distinguishable? And compared with other properties of the same size and type, will they command a different price? Will the fact that a property is on a former council estate always be an attribute that affects its marketability and price? (Jones and Murie, 2005)

What is happening to these estates? – the preferred stock in the council-built range. These housing estates make up a huge set of assets. They are not necessarily all heading in the same direction: some are quite troubled, some are secure, stable and settled. Overall, though, the cottage estates were and are the ones that people preferred. This is not just a question of impressions; it can be seen in the figures. The preferences are reflected in lower average rates for turnover of tenants, and in higher proportions of property sold (and indeed sold on a second time). Jones and Murie use Birmingham statistics to show 'that sales and resales are linked inversely to turnover in council estates … the likely causal relationship is that low turnover estates lead to high sales … they seem to have reduced turnover in the already low turnover desirable estates in the short to medium term…'. They add though that as resales have increased so has turnover, and their judgement is that there will have been little effect on 'the pecking order of the stability of communities' (Jones and Murie, 2005).

'Convergence': Becoming Part of the Market

The question about if, and how much, the estates are 'converging' to become part of the wider market is partly about how much of an estate has been sold, and partly about its relative house prices. Jones and Murie (2005) refer to their own earlier (1999) work in Glasgow, where the proportion of properties sold between 1980 and 1995 varied from 33 per cent in Anniesland – good quality, close in to the city, mostly family houses from the 1920s – down to 4 per cent in the enormous post-war estate out at Castlemilk in the south. Similarly they found that 'In popular areas of Edinburgh such as Saughtonhall or Corstorphine and the suburban areas of Currie or Balerno, sales amounted to 82 per cent of the 1980 stock. In contrast, sales in the large estates of Wester Hailes, Niddrie and Craigmillar were less than 3 per cent of the stock'. It is obvious that where there have been very large switches (Anniesland, Balerno, and so on), the likelihood of the ex-council properties 'merging' into the wider stock is that much higher.

The price trends, too, showed a lot of convergence in that the most important factor seemed to be how neighbouring areas were seen and priced. So what happened to each estate's prices varied – they 'converged' with the market, but 'diverged' from each other. Murie concluded in a separate study that 'sale prices of council properties in the twelve estates in Birmingham have diverged over time … the most obvious explanation of the emerging pattern is that the estates begin to be absorbed into the surrounding market. If the estate is next to a low-value area, the appreciation in values is much less than where adjoining areas are relatively high value' (Murie, 2008).

So What *is* the Differential, Now?

So there has definitely been convergence. But there are definitely still differentials, too, and they vary from place to place. Having looked at Birmingham, Leeds and London, the RTB study concluded that 'Right to Buy resales are embedded in the housing market primarily as larger homes for younger families to trade up to or as 'starter' homes for new households. In some places resales are 25 per cent cheaper than equivalent mainstream housing nearby but the differential can be much lower, almost disappearing dependent on house types and market pressures' (Jones and Murie, 2005). The results from that survey work are summarized in table 7.1.

Table 7.1. Summary of survey of differentials and explanations. (*Source*: After Jones and Murie)

	Ex Council	*Mainstream*	*Diff.*	*Comment*	*RTB as % Market*
Birmingham	70k–110k	<90k–120k	≥5%	Key attraction	–
Kings Heath			–	= cheaper than	10%
Selly Oak			–30%	equivalent	20%
Bearwood		–		mainstream	25–30%
Leeds	–	–	–		–
Morley	50k ter., 60-80k semi	100k	25%		5–10%
Moortown	70–90k semi	120k	25%		10–15%
Havering (Harold Wood, Gidea Park/ Collier Row)	140k house 115k flat	115–200k		Ex-council to bottom of range; seen as being of good quality	?
Camden	100–170k one-bed flat 170–250k three-bed flat	180–210k one-bed purpose built 200–230k one-bed hi-spec or period conv.		Big variation depending on precise area	?
Lambeth	–	–	–	–	–
Vaux/Wat/Kenn	130–170k one-bed 210–260k two-bed flat	Little or no discount, because of high demand	0	Ex-council now quite well integrated into market in central area; less so elsewhere, with some areas still no sales	
Brixton	140k two-bed	Some discount	?		

Almost a decade later, in the two areas of London estates described in Chapter 3 above, these differences and variations seemed to more or less persist. Observations for Tower Gardens in Tottenham are based on a small sample from Rightmove and agents' websites, and for Becontree/Dagenham primarily on Rightmove, plus an estate agency at Heathway, giving approximately sixty observations.

For Tower Gardens (N17), both two-bedroom and three-bedroom houses show prices about 25 per cent less than in the area (in the Wood Green postcode, N22) of non-council-built property immediately to the west. This despite the attractiveness of the houses and streets in Tower Gardens compared with the unprepossessing Edwardian streets nearby. Other non-ex-council property outside the estate (but still in N17) seems to be about 10 per cent more expensive (three-bedroom). For two-bedroom houses, the comparison is with other ex-council homes, built later and not in the Conservation Area; in this case the prices are about the same. So just *being* ex-council still seems to have a small but persistent effect on the prices.

In Becontree, houses in the LCC-built areas at the western (Barking) end, off Longbridge Road and Becontree Avenue, are up to 20 per cent cheaper than their privately-built equivalents nearby, on the Faircross and Leftley estates and back in towards the town centre. Further north, in Chadwell Heath, a like-for-like comparison suggests more like a 10 per cent differential (£210,000 rather than £230,000) for a semi. Houses in the centre of the vast estate (around Green Lane, Wood Lane and Heathway) generally average lower prices again, between £173,000 and £199,000. But one or two favoured groups of semis near the Tube at Upney and Becontree fetch up to £250,000, though this is unusual. In the favoured Wykeham Green/Gale Street (south) locality, which was always intended for higher-rent or sale, sales at up to £275,000 have been made. But even here the impression is that, off the estate, these attractive high quality '1930s modern' homes would have fetched substantially more. Again, the message is of local markets which have settled down to a consistent pattern of noticeable, but only occasionally sharp, differentials.

Up in the North East, Gateshead's estates show sharper gradation and more differentiation from their surrounding non-municipal neighbours. The least attractive part (Deckham Hall) averages £60,000: the most 'garden-suburb' locality (Sheriff Hill/Carr Hill) £71,000: and one small grouping (the late-period Hodkin Gardens) £103,000. Comparable non-council-built homes in adjacent areas average about £117,000. So the price differentials vary widely, with the sub-areas being respectively 49 per cent, 39 per cent and 12 per cent cheaper than the surroundings. As Chapter 4 notes, this must reflect *inter alia* the reality that the wide range of alternative property available, including new-build, means that 'incomer' young couples just do not need to include ex-council property on an estate in their house search patterns.

In Sunderland, too, the market information shows strong differentiation. Hylton Castle's semis never achieve £100,000, averaging about £88,000, while privately-built infill within the area averages over £130,000; the differential is about 34 per cent. A much smaller differential (12 per cent) exists between these Hylton Castle private schemes and the ex-council sales in nearby Castletown, and Chapter 4 suggests that this may be because the Castletown houses are not in such a big sweep of municipal building, being grouped and interspersed on a smaller scale. At the same time, though, the price difference between Hylton Castle and 'Hylton Manor' a hundred metres to the south is enormous. Here, three-bedroom houses on similar size plots – but on a clearly private-sector (and more recent) estate – fetch about double the average for their ex-council equivalents.

The situation in the Birmingham case-study area, Bromford, is slightly different. Overall, there is again a differential of some 20 per cent with the nearby privately-built stock in Hodge Hill. House prices on the estate (for a three-bedroom house) fall in the range £90–120,000, mostly at the lower end of that range, and with an average asking price in early 2013 of just over £104,000. The privately-built housing to the immediate south showed asking prices (with one exception) for three-bedroom houses to be in the range £120,000 to £138,000, averaging £125,500. But within the average, there is some convergence. A few at least of the Bromford house prices almost overlap with the bottom end of the Chipperfield Road range: as in Chapter 5's examples, of a three-bed semi in Bromford at £119,950 and one in the southern area at £120,000.

The 'Place in the Market'

So, at these prices and comparisons, what role do these estates seem to be playing in the housing market? In the early days of the Right-To-Buy, it was sometimes assumed that because ex-council homes would be coming onto the market at much lower prices (given the deep discounts on the initial purchase price for sitting tenants), they would therefore slot in as a new bottom-end to house purchase in the range of properties on offer. But that was soon not the case. Jones and Murie found that while the initial transactions were carried out at very low prices, this was because of the entitlement to discount. The properties were actually more likely to be the more attractive, better quality, larger houses with gardens. And so when they were sold on, they found a different slot, above the bottom end of the range: not slotting into the lowest price range, and instead entering the market at a higher level. They also note that in some market conditions this meant that properties that might have been alternatives at the lower end, such as flats and small pre-1919 terraces, actually saw prices fall.

And as they say, the market role does differ from region to region:

in the north of England where house prices were generally much lower, former council houses were more likely to be accessible to first time buyers and to be bought by households with very similar characteristics to those who had previously sought to rent council houses... In the higher house price areas of the south of England, the size and quality of council housing meant that it was resold at prices that were well beyond the reach of first-time buyers. (Jones and Murie, 2005)

Judging by the property agent's remark about ex-council housing in Corbridge, in the Tyne Valley (see Chapter 4) this is not so much a purely 'regional' characteristic as a 'prosperous sub-market' one. Homes at over £200,000 are not first-time buyer material in the North East, for sure.

Who is Involved?

As to the households who these estates are now serving: obviously the three decades or so of the sale of council houses has, on these generally-more-popular estates, made quite a lot of difference to the sorts of households who live there (bearing in mind, of course, that even in the places most affected, there are still a lot of tenants renting as before). *The Right to Buy* summarizes who was involved in the change: 'During the early years of the Right to Buy a profile of a typical buyer emerged... This was a household in work, in the middle of the family life cycle, with two or more adults and with one or more earners in white-collar, skilled or semi-skilled occupations... Kerr's study (1988) in England and Wales found that buyers' incomes were on average about double those of tenants'.

But as the numbers increased, the people involved changed – and so it seems did their attitudes to why they were buying, how long they planned to stay and why:

younger households became more strongly represented… For this group the Right to Buy offered a different opportunity – that of providing the asset base to enable residential movement … the damaged reputation of council housing, poor services and facilities on estates and the relatively limited opportunities to move to better housing within the council sector were also likely to be a significant influence. (Jones and Murie, 2005)

And location – the estate itself, rather than the home – seemed to be important in this. 'New buyers in the Jones and Murie (1999) study indicated a stronger preference for moving from their present address in the near future than was reported in the previous [Kerr, 1988] study'. The analysis suggested that if all the factors about location were combined, these were much more significant than concerns about gardens, size of property or internal dwelling arrangements and improvements.

The other striking feature of the RTB sales, and their onward resales, has been how comprehensively this has moved from the simple model of sitting tenants buying at a discount and nothing else changing: 'the previous tenure of purchasers of former council homes was still most likely to be owner-occupation… The only major study providing robust data for England indicated that 51 per cent of council properties were bought by households that were already owner-occupiers (Forrest *et al.*, 1995) … they provided opportunities to trade up in terms of size, space and quality' (Jones and Murie, 2005). And they give a London region example from the Mole Valley area around Leatherhead, where the pattern is for RTB resales to be bought by first-time buyers moving from South London. This reflects the general pattern that in areas of high housing demand, a much higher proportion of households buying ex-council homes were headed by professional or managerial staff (and were already home-owners).

Using Atkinson and Kintrea's work from 1998 and 2000, the RTB study suggests a 'typology' of the residents who live in adjoining estates where there is now a mix of sales and rentals:

◆ 'metropolitan' owner: purchased in the area because the housing was affordable; contacts with other residents very limited; likely to move elsewhere relatively quickly (The 'Outsider');

◆ 'would-be-local' owner: bought in the area because they had some local connection such as relatives nearby or they were brought up in the area; like to move eventually to larger accommodation in the area ('The foot soldiers for social inclusion');

◆ 'stalwart of the community' tenant ('Estate focused but not excluded');

◆ 'disconnected local' tenant ('Socially excluded').

Ethnicity

The 'who lives here?' question also has an ethnic dimension. Murie's analysis of the changes on Birmingham estates between the 1991 and 2001 Censuses looks at this, and draws some quite sharp conclusions. Looking at the proportion of 'white' and 'non-white' on the estates at the two dates, he shows that, while the 'white' proportion on Birmingham estates as a whole fell by an average of 8 per cent, on the cottage estates where the RTB was generally most taken up (such as Falcon Lodge, Kingstanding, Pineapple and Shard End), the change ranged between nil and 5 per cent; whereas in 'inner' Ward End it fell by 21 per cent; see table 7.2. His conclusion is that selling off council housing did nothing to change patterns of ethnic separation or to accelerate ethnic-minority access to this quite sought-after stock: 'These data fit with a polarization of segregation thesis. They also fit with a view that the effect of privatization in these areas has not introduced greater mix or reduced the trend to segregation' (Murie, 2008).

Table 7.2. Birmingham estates, intercensal change. (*Source*: After Murie, 2008)

	% White 1991	% White 2001	Difference
Birmingham	78	70	−8
Shard End	95	90	−5
Kingstanding	94	91	−3
Falcon Lodge	98	96	−2
Pineapple	91	91	0
(Ward End)	(69)	(48)	(−21)

'Stabilized'?

Also connected to the changes that the Right-To-Buy helped bring about is the issue of stability or instability. A quite widely held view in the early days was that, because owner-occupation is associated with commitment to property and area, an increase in the proportion of owners would tend to make estates more stable. The process seems to have been more complex:

In the more desirable estates… Prior to the Right to Buy these neighbourhoods were seen as stable with concentrations of older tenants and little or no turnover … the initial group of purchasers did not generally buy with a speculative intent but intended to stay in their home for the rest of their lives … this changed in the 1990s as resales began … as homes for households in the pre-child and child-bearing stages of the family cycle it is likely that these estates are subject to regular turnover of sales… Turnover is therefore higher than in the pre-Right to Buy era but may not be as high as in the remaining council owned stock. (Jones and Murie, 2005)

So the social composition of these estates with the Right-to-Buy has undoubtedly changed a lot. It was intended to do this – and the two authors are in no doubt that it has indeed had redistributive effects, and that it has changed patterns of opportunity for the households who responded. But the changes have not increased 'stability' on the already-stable estates; they are helping bring about further and sometimes unpredictable change on many estates; and they are not much help to remaining tenants. Jones and Murie conclude that:

[any] arguments in favour of the Right to Buy based on social mix are misplaced. The Right to Buy is not impinging strongly on the life of council tenants except in reducing their housing opportunities… Right to Buy resales have also not stabilized the more desirable neighbourhoods, especially where resales act as starter homes and form part of the segment of the housing market with the highest turnover. (Jones and Murie, 2005)

Private Rental on the Cottage Estates

The other element in the 'traded' housing market which now features on many estates, is the private rented sector. This is an important element in London, where the market has clearly been so buoyant that RTB buyers have, in as little as three years, been able to remortgage so that they could let out the original home and move to a new address. Nor is it negligible in the other towns and cities either. Murie's figures for the Birmingham estates show a significant shift to private renting once property had been out of the social sector for some while (Murie, 2008).

Table 7.3. Birmingham estates: tenure changes including PRS. (*Source*: After Murie, 2008)

Estate	Out of social tenure	Into owner occupation	Into Private Rented Sector	PRS as % of all private sector growth
Shard End	−591	+383	+132	26%
Kingstanding	−1642	+1355	+407	23%
Falcon Lodge	−515	+545	+107	16%
Pineapple	−93	+67	+30	31%

Jones and Murie (2005) comment on the characteristics of the households in the re-lets they surveyed: primarily young people, non-family households, thus very different to the RTB purchasers themselves; and they comment that outside London they are generally on low incomes.

Murie's judgement is that 'It is reasonable to hypothesize that as the resale process works through, over a period of thirty or more years, the worst estates may see the decline of home ownership down to a very low or even zero level …while the best estates will remain mixed tenure, but the mixed tenure will include private renting as well as social renting' (Murie, 2008). As the detailed 2011 Census figures emerge, they are underlining that the 2001 situation these authors analysed was not a stable equilibrium, but a snapshot in the middle of a very dynamic process.

Rentals in the private rented sector reflect the very tight conditions in the two parallel 'markets': owner-occupation via mortgage, and social tenancies via application and qualification processes. The situation in Becontree (late 2011) illustrates how the cost of renting a three-bedroom ex-council home in the PRS is converging with that for privately-built houses, though with a differential still in evidence. A mid-terrace private rental at the east end of Dagenham cost about £850/month in ex-council property and an average of £938/month in non-council built: a 10 per cent differential. On the majority of the estate, private rentals (again, from agents' websites and Rightmove) averaged £945/month for a council-built end-terrace compared with £1,083 for a non-council-built one in Beacontree Heath – a difference of about 15 per cent. Council rents in the borough's remaining stock, by way of comparison, are approximately £500/month (including service charges) for a three-bedroom 'parlour' house (see www.lbbd.gov.uk, 2013).

What's Happening to the Houses?

As well as these long-run patterns of change, what is happening to the houses on the cottage estates? Obviously, many have been and are being sold on in the 'normal' way of the market: the mid-1990s study by Forrest and colleagues found that 95 per cent of resales in England & Wales by that time had been semis and detached houses: though of course in London flats were, and are, also readily marketable (Forrest *et al.*, 1995). And as shown, quite a high proportion, in some areas at least, are drifting into private renting – though there is little external evidence of actual conversions into more, but smaller, units.

The physical changes are indeed not very extensive. Personalization of the rather standardized 'neo-Georgian' product of course formed early and visible evidence of the former tenants' wish to show that they could now do what they liked with their doors, façades and windows. Some, but not many, owners have added or expanded porches, bays or side extensions.

Figure 7.1. The familiar signature of the Right-To -Buy (Becontree).

However, a trip round Becontree, for example, gives the impression of a *lot* less scaffolding than in middle-class inner London, say; and no comparable changes to the intensification and on-plot expansion evident in some privately-built outer London areas such as Stanmore or Hounslow. This perhaps suggests that even during the pre-2007 boom years these estates were not the focus of a lot of investment of households' own money in expanding or modifying their property in any major way. These big East London estates are not of course awash with spare cash – but they did and do have a lot of working families in reasonably well-paid jobs, and the relatively slow pace of change is therefore something of a surprise.

The three tenures – owner-occupation, social rent, private rent – are broadly recognizable as a hierarchy, in that order, of well-kept-ness of, and expenditure on, gardens, fronts and façades: with of course variation and exceptions in each category. Unlike in the inner city, it is less easy to distinguish where a landlord might be absentee or local, individual/'involuntary', or a company.

Outside the homes, the public realm – roads and streets, open spaces, local public buildings, shopping parades – looks much as it always has. Not surprising, perhaps: but it does mean that many streets and areas still have the indefinably flat and worn-down appearance of the traditional council estate: Lynsey Hanley again: 'that sometimes glaring, sometimes solid, sometimes flimsy - but somehow always uniform – look of municipal housing' (Hanley, 2007).

In Summary

Going back to the questions at the start of this chapter, about the extent to which this distinctive part of the housing market will be fully absorbed into the wider market: there clearly *has* been 'convergence', and the most popular cottage estates are more like their non-council-built neighbours than ever before. Yet a differential, even if small, still exists just about everywhere. This is not necessarily because the former council properties themselves are and will always be distinguishable. But the fact that a property is *on* a former council estate is still an attribute that affects its marketability and price. The estates' role in the marketplace has changed, and is still changing. The direction and the strength of the change varies from place to place, and it is not always just towards more integration, or greater stability, or a settled mix. A lot of what is involved is to do with attitudes and image, and that is the subject of the next chapter.

Chapter 8

Attitudes

Long-Run, Familiar, Taken for Granted?

It is apparent from its visibility in the marketplace that a differential still exists, and that it affects even the most attractive of the estates. This reflects a familiar set of attitudes – so familiar to most British people that they are not analysed that frequently.

There can be few British people unable to recognize what is or is not a council estate. What they are reacting to, subliminally as much as consciously, helps to account for patterns of estate history and in particular the fatal divergence between architectural intention and lived experience. (Ravetz, 2001)

The aim here is to unpick some of these attitudes and reactions, to see why the patterns are so long-term, and perhaps to consider if there are any ways of overcoming them.

The 'Estate' Label as Stigma

The starting-point for thinking about attitudes to (ex-)council estates is the role of tenure *per se*. The LSE London team who led the 'Social Housing in Europe' comparative study close their chapter on England with a curt summary of the position now:

Overall, social housing has moved from a tenure of choice to one where those in the tenure are mainly getting a good deal, but where social housing is often seen by many as inferior to private provision, especially owner-occupation. (Whitehead, 2007)

So council/social tenancy itself is viewed as less desirable. This is coupled with attitudes to 'estates' and 'council estates' which are long-established and pervasive. There is a whole familiar baggage of 'my old man's a dustman, 'e lives in a council flat' (Donegan, 1960); of separation and stigma epitomized in its pure and famous form by the Cutteslowe wall in Oxford (Oliver *et al.*, 1981); and to quote Lynsey Hanley on attitudes to estate residents: they will 'only go and have more babies, smoke more fags, fry more chips and set fire to the whole damn place when the lit match hits their shellsuit' (Hanley 2007); and later in this chapter is a sample of current manifestations of the continued appearance of the package she caricatures – or describes.

Yet 'estate' itself, as a term, seems to have carried rather less stigma in the 1930s. It is true that Mabel Wallis, living on the Castelnau estate, recalled that when her mother had to go and see the Headmistress about jobs when leaving Barnes Central School: 'She said to my mother "Oh, that's alright, she's only an estate girl, put her in service"' (Rubinstein, 1991).

Figure 8.1. Castelnau: 'only an estate girl, put her in service'. (*Photo:* CC Patche99z)

But the word still had a non-council life of its own. A page from an advertising spread in the *Evening News* in 1936, reproduced in *Dunroamin*, offers a 'rural estate' in Perivale, 'Morrell's Chelsfield Estate' in suburban Kent, the Oakcroft Estate 'the pleasant estate', and so on. On another page, Hilbery Chaplin Ltd were pleased to describe themselves as 'London's Leading Estate Developers'; and 'estates' in Teddington, Hayes and NW London are all proudly shown (Oliver *et al.*, 1981). In 1924 the Metropolitan Railway's promotion of sites along its route through 'Metroland' carried the same message – and 'estate' labels (Green, 2004).

Now, however, it tends to just be shorthand for 'council estate', and is less used for private housing, except perhaps for new-build during the process of approval and construction. Lynsey Hanley's choice of book title is testimony to that shift, and as she says 'it was their very estate-ness – the fact that they were built for a specific purpose rather than growing organically within an existing community – that would, at least in part, cause estate dwellers so many problems' (Hanley, 2007) As seen in Chapter 2, John Hills's analysis concurs in seeing the estate format as tending to reinforce both polarization and stereotypes.

Figure 8.2. From *Dunroamin*: the estate label in interwar marketing.

So is This now about Who *should* be Living There?

Behind the changing attitudes lie, to some extent, ambivalent and shifting attitudes to who social renting is or should be *for*. Glen Bramley's review for the 2011 British Social Attitudes report points out that:

Subsidised social housing has for most of the past half-century been the principal provider of longer-term decent quality housing for people who cannot afford to buy on the open market... we posed a further question inviting people to say which of four possible factors on a list should be treated as a priority in deciding who should be allocated housing rented from a local authority or housing association. This found that the strongest support (30%) is for people 'living in overcrowded accommodation... Close behind comes 'being on a very low income' (28%) with an implied suggestion that social housing should primarily provide a 'safety net' for the poor. However, nearly as many respondents (26%) select 'not being able to afford to buy or rent independently', suggesting a much wider range of eligibility for social housing. The fourth factor, 'being a key worker such as a nurse or a teacher', is supported by fewer people (14%). (Bramley, 2011)

So we are not all agreed about purpose or entitlement, and we are a long way on from the aspirational moves out to Wythenshawe, Becontree or Kingstanding during the mid-twentieth-century prime of the council estates.

The Evidence on the Ground

We saw in Chapter 2 that stylistic differences were important signifiers of the social differences. *Dunroamin*'s chapter on 'Private enterprise housing and the council estate' explores exactly this frontier, largely in the inter-war years. It points to effects on layout: 'The Dunroaminer's economic need to protect his environment's social status implied a requirement for the estate layout to discourage activities with lower-class connotations, such as children playing in the street... This further boosted the popularity of the cul-de-sac layout...'. And, as quoted earlier, the houses' appearance had to differ too: '...bought just because its exterior is so different from the decent exterior of the council house'. The authors of *Dunroamin* distinguish between attitudes driven by a 'community' ethic and an 'individualist' ethic. They point out that the two estate forms were really very similar – so the real differences were in the 'values' which the relatively minor physical evidence was carrying as a psychological 'load': 'the vision of the free individual as against that of the egalitarian community' (Oliver *et al.*, 1981).

London's early twentieth-century expansion showed this similarity/difference paradox well. Alan Jackson, in his *Semi-Detached London* describes the first council cottage estates, as in Tooting, Tottenham and Old Oak:

These suburban estates of the LCC and other local authorities did not differ greatly from those of private enterprise. Their occupants were for the most part commuters to central London, especially in the early years; their streets, when new, looked much the same; and the houses, though plainer in design, both inside and out, were of the same general pattern. But the passage of time brought a widening difference. On the whole, the gardens received less care and attention, fewer trees and shrubs were planted, and the streets and house surrounds were frequently left untidy and unkempt. (Jackson, 1991)

And here, as so often, he is getting into the territory of commentary on behavioural difference, which we look at below.

The Threat of Proximity and the Social Distinctions

Life on the social and stylistic frontier was, as ever, tense. An Eltham housewife is quoted as feeling that 'she "always felt that she had her own bit of country on that council estate"...'; but there was also frequently the feeling that the council estate was a working-class intrusion into the (actual or aspirant) middle-class suburbs: someone on the Mottingham Estate in the late 1930s recalled that people would say to them '"oh, so you're from the estate?" as if you were from a leper colony' (White, 2008).

Alan Jackson records that in the 1930s 'An Ilford chartered surveyor contributed the information that certain houses fetched an average of £920 at Ilford, but those similar in date and design on the edge of the LCC estate at Goodmayes realised only £726'. And a Chigwell resident is quoted as exclaiming to LCC officials and the Inspector at a CPO Inquiry: '*You have ruined my home! Do any of you gentlemen live near an LCC estate?*'. Jackson comments that 'Such devaluation of overlooking property was no doubt inevitable, but once the newcomers arrived, social fears were soon seen to be exaggerated…'. And he notes drily that '…the LCC's "out-county" tenants of the period were confined to the better-paid and in general, the more presentable members of the lower orders; some were even civil servants' (Jackson, 1991).

That dimension – the fact that the new municipal estates were by no means dumping-grounds for the poor and unwashed – was not confined to London. In Liverpool's inter-war Norris Green, too, the attractive semis and terraced family homes were popular with a wide range of households. 'Not surprisingly, the demand for the new houses was overwhelming and the Corporation was able to be highly selective in choosing its new suburban tenants … the expectation of allocation to predominantly "working class" tenants was confounded by the reality. Analysis of the 1919 cohort revealed that almost half of all houses, and mainly the parlour type, were allocated to non-manual workers… Criteria for access were restated in the mid-1930s in order to select tenants with safer, skilled jobs who could afford the rents' (Turkington, 1998).

The LCC's Becontree Tenants Handbook 1933 set out the basis for considering applications: in order received; a preference to London County residents but no exclusion of those from elsewhere, married sons of tenants, and married daughters if their husbands worked in London. Lilian Badger, a pre-war resident whose father was a tram conductor, is very clear: 'In those days you weren't allowed a house unless you could show you had a regular pay packet, and people like firemen, postmen, bus and tram men got priority, because they had that'. Across London, on the Roehampton Estate, this became part of the lore; locals 'gave us the name "Uniform Town" because we had bus drivers, policemen, tram drivers and postmen living on the estate. When we walked up into the village one of the locals would say "Hello, here comes Uniform Town. It was all in good fun"' (Rubinstein, 1991).

As Jackson says of the inter-war years 'In London, as elsewhere, the council houses erected in quantity in the twenties proved beyond the means of all but the most highly paid workers, despite the fact that post-1919 local authority rents were failing in general to recoup full costs' (Jackson, 1991).

Council housing was always a continuum, though. There was always a hierarchy, different in each town or city. The range was a product of a mixture of things. Partly it was conflicting aims (clearing the slums, creating 'respectable' suburbs, keeping costs down). Partly it was the variation in subsidy over the years, which caused changes in types and quality of housing to the point where people blamed the councils for deliberately lowering standards for later tenants (Ravetz, 2001); and where a 1927 letter quoted in *Just Like the Country* could bemoan the layout with 'the smallest cheapest houses placed cheek by jowl with better type brick houses. Thus the respectable mechanic has to live side by side with people from the slums' (Rubinstein, 1991). And it also reflected the fact that housing management practice and design were on separate tracks (Ravetz remarks that 'neither the Dudley nor Parker Morris Report, dominated as they were by design prescriptions for how people should live, really discussed the management implications of their proposed designs').

So being a council tenant therefore by no means meant an automatic association with poverty, or carried that sort of stigma. But at the same time, of course, many estates in the continuum *were* markedly poorer, or seen as 'rougher', and placed in the local hierarchy accordingly.

After the War…

And this pattern lasted well into the post-war period. Chapter 1's Introduction has already mentioned 1950s Lancashire, where people on the council estates might have been *poorer*, or more working-class, than those in the private semis nearby, but not poorer than households in the towns' older and often privately-rented property. And where there was no particular association of these corporation suburbs with ASB, crime, bad lads, whatever; so stigma was not really an issue for them. 'Council tenant' was a label, no doubt, but not then a crucial one among the myriad distinctions of the English class structure.

Interestingly, a review of the inter-war suburbs from the early 1970s seems to place the working-class suburbs and their residents in a continuum with other parts of, and people in, suburbia, rather than across a social divide: 'The bowler-hatted catcher of the 8-15, so often the stereotype suburban dweller, is no more 'typical' of suburbs in general than the skilled machinist driving about two and a half miles to the local factory, or the working wife setting off for her job in the nearby office or shopping centre' (Cowan, 1973).

An American academic interviewed, who grew up in a Manchester area council estate, built in the early 1950s, was 5 when his family moved there, in 1952. They moved from Old Trafford, a flat off Princess Avenue, by the railway. Their bit was 'a very small "estate", 20 units I believe (I can still remember all of the occupants on our side and the Moss Road side … those on Derbyshire Lane I'm less sure of)'. Was it in any sense stigmatized at the time? 'Then, yes, I'd say it was. I did have some mates from the Council houses, but most of the kids we knew were from the rest of Radstock Road … "rich kids" we called 'em … since their parents owned their homes. They weren't fancy homes, semi-detached mostly, but upstage compared to ours. Not sure if the other kids "looked down" on us … but I certainly felt "underprivileged" compared to them'. But there was and is also a much larger, and somewhat older, estate further down Moss Road, close to the entrance to the Metro-Vicks works and Trafford Park Industrial Estate. 'They were visibly less well-off than us … and mostly Irish Catholic kids (with holes in their pants and leaky shoes) … they had to pass us and then walk on a lot further to their Catlick school – past our Proddy-dog school on their way.'

As to whether it is stigmatized now, and if so when that happened:

much later, after the Right-to-Buy period, the estate came to be occupied by what seemed to me to be more marginal families (including some people 'of color' … it was always lily-white when we lived there!). I think today it might be more stigmatized … we went back a couple of years ago and met-up with some old friends. Almost all of the people we knew back in the day were gone now … with just a couple of hold-outs. It looked very shabby and sad … gardens gone to seed and dubious-looking characters living in some of the units!

On the interesting issue about whether the offspring of more aspirant families might have reckoned to stay on the estate, or always assumed they had to get on and out: this is of course intertwined with the 'leaving the provinces completely' dimension.

We *did* all leave … not just the estate, but Manchester altogether. I think we saw ourselves as 'upwardly mobile'… I was actually the first kid on the estate to go to Grammar School (and then on to Uni) … and my oldest sister went to Nursing School, which is like going to Uni – although it was at Manchester Royal, so still local. My other two sisters left to pursue careers elsewhere and have never returned… My parents never could afford to buy, and my sister and I decided it wasn't a good enough investment for us to buy the house.

But:

the 'wanting away' (which I never felt … even though I knew I would leave) wasn't related to a perception of the area as 'high crime' or having lots of problems. There weren't many anti-social problems then anyway: no drugs that I knew of … though plenty of alcoholism and drunkenness on the streets, but that seemed 'normal' to me (there were two working men's clubs adjacent to the estate, so we often saw drunks staggering home: our next door neighbor was one of the worst cases … we often saw him passed out in the bushes, and he died early – of alcoholism). The streets were safe then … probably not the case now, but I've no idea.

A similar story from an interview about post-war South Wales, perhaps a few years later: on the 'Beddau Garden Village', built as Homes Fit for Heroes in 1921, as an extension of 300 homes next to a hamlet and linked to Tynant with its 400 miners' terrace houses owned by the coal company, which had been built in 1900–1905; with more council homes added after the war and then some 500 private homes in the 1970s – essentially a mining village in a semi-rural setting.

Was it in any sense stigmatized at the time? 'Beddau meant "quite rough", because even within the working class there were some divisions and the sense that Beddau was dominated by council housing gave it a reputation outside.' But 'there was little discernible difference between people in the council homes and miners' cottages (many of them in ownership by the 1960s) – there was not much stigma. We were a fully-employed working class with a tiny underclass and an even smaller middle class'.

Do you think it is now?

There is more stigma now than before. Many reasons. The growth of cheap home ownership around Beddau drained the council housing of its mixed community. And increasing worklessness amongst an unskilled population, when the mining went, has brought a divide within the working class if you like. I was unaware of such differences growing up … though all were relatively poor in UK terms there were not the great divides we now see in Beddau. Now the area [as a whole, not just the estate] is split between a public-sector-employed 'middle class', a few industrial workers, and a swathe of workless benefit recipients without skills or cars to access the jobs which exist.

Again looking at the attitudes of those articulate, self-educated, possibly aspirational families and their kids, and their expectations about 'staying or going':

It was honestly never discussed. Most of my comprehensive-school cohort *didn't* go to university (5 per cent). I don't think we assumed we would stay on the estate. I think most assumed they would stay within a 5-mile radius and certainly not go to Cardiff, let alone leave South Wales … my family had no notion of university, and despite my high grades I made no assumptions about going to university. However, I guess it's now pretty certain that anyone who could leave would, given income/mortgage etc.

As in Manchester, the behavioural aspects seem not to have been an issue.

Not at all. There were plenty of fights on a Friday night outside the pub and you had to be able to use your fists. But this was still a working and Protestant community in a village where people largely knew each other. It had constraints… It had few underclass types: worklessness with its lack of socialization hit us after the Miners' Strike and when the pit closed.

So the problem was not the tenure per se: though now, social housing's residualization has made it into a problem. And while the Right-To-Buy seemed for a while to stabilize the social capital of Beddau as aspirational folk stayed in their bought council-built homes, now they or their families are renting them out to workless people and the social capital actually depletes.

The lack of well-paid jobs for unskilled people is the main crisis. These homes used to be occupied by a mix of well-paid working class people who might have read books, but they didn't need exams to get a job. They do now. So they don't get jobs. My cousin has been workless now for 35 years; trapped at home, smoking, drinking. The death of a proud working class is very real to me.

Also from this 1950s–1960s 'cohort', a woman who grew up on Preston's Ribbleton estate, and lived there till she was 17, recalls it as:

pretty close to countryside, we had large gardens and smallish green spaces to play on. We always played out in the streets as there was less traffic. [She has] no recollection of any stigma attached to the estate. The families in our street were very mixed, from a very large and probably very poor Catholic family whose children always seemed to have lice, to the family opposite them with two daughters and a school-teacher father. Behaviour problems weren't an issue… There was a very clear distinction between respectable families and non-respectable ones, but class or income didn't seem to be the issue, rather the behaviour.

With some streets seen as more 'respectable' than others, '*I was aware of other houses, and the people in them, being "posher": they were the semi-detached houses really.*' But there was no sense that other non-council stock (like the small terraces) was seen as better.

Once more, she has no recollection of having '*any idea that I would move on or out, until I was about 16. Even then it had nothing to do with where I lived, more about education. I don't think I had any idea about moving to a "better" place, though I think my mother may have done.*' But then '*she always said she wanted to move because she could see her mother's ghost in the house!*'.

As to later changes: '*I think the estate started to get stigmatized some time after I left. I certainly recall people telling me I "wouldn't recognize it". Then the issue was around anti-social behaviour, but that would have been at least a decade or so later…*'

Meanwhile, in the South

A final recollection comes from the South, and slightly later. Brighton's Craven Vale – or sometimes the 'Queensway' – estate lies along the side of quite a steep valley which slopes down to the sea and to Kemp Town, about 2 km east of the town centre and the Palace Pier. It was built in 1953–1956 by the corporation, between the quite well-to-do Queen's Park area and the racecourse celebrated in Graham Greene's *Brighton Rock*.

It is laid out in a sort of cottage-estate format, though only eighty-five of the homes are actually houses or bungalows; the other 252 are flats or maisonettes in similar-looking brick-built three-storey walk-up blocks. It is 'as-built': sixty years later there has been no redevelopment, and properties are all in a good state of repair, with surrounding grassed areas tended carefully by the council.[1]

Craven Vale has always been popular with council tenants, and now with private owners (about 45 per cent of the total). Around 60 per cent of the houses have been sold off to sitting tenants, and around 40 per cent of the flats and maisonettes.

Several original and long-term residents told the Community Association that none of them had ever felt any stigma being attached to their properties or the estate, either when they moved in, or now. They arrived in the 1950s from a variety of places, often from prefabs in outlying Woodingdean or from private-renting in central Brighton: the latter having indeed attracted some stigma, as small back-to-backs with poor facilities. All had been very pleased to be re-housed in Craven Vale.

Youngsters who grew up on the estate similarly told the Association that they had never felt any discrimination at their schools on account of living in Craven Vale, and none ever felt that they had to move away from the area once they had completed their education. According to one former resident (son of a copper):

When I was growing up there in the 1960s was no sense of stigma attached to the estate, and I don't think there is much now… The estate felt predominantly working-class and I was certainly conscious of the more mixed-class base of the infant and junior school I attended nearer to Queen's Park. It did feel that we were slightly apart though in social terms, with my Dad being a police officer and sometimes parking his squad car or motorbike outside the house when he came home for lunch.

Some of those youngsters have now inherited the properties from their parents and have no desire to move. Of course some have 'done well' and moved to larger properties on the periphery of the town or moved away entirely, but 'moved *to*' an area, rather than 'moved *away*' from Craven Vale.

I have little sense that people were looking to 'escape' the estate either then or now. A few, like my sister and me, were lucky enough to go on to university which meant we left Brighton altogether. But my Mum still lives there and is very happy knowing many of the people who have lived on the estate since it was built. Quite a few of them like my Mum have since bought their homes so it has the feel of more of a mixed community now.

For the Association, there is still a good community spirit, built on the large number of residents who have been there for decades, and it is still an area into which people wish to move.

On ASB: the Community Association's view is that, yes, there is of course some anti-social behaviour, but no more or less than in surrounding areas, whether private, council or housing association.

I was aware that there were one or two families and children who were a little wild and not well cared for who sometimes caused trouble, and were probably responsible for a small amount of graffiti, but they were very much in the minority. Apart from sometimes taking care which way I walked home from school and where we played in the nearby woods (parts of which were used for fly-tipping of old furniture or toys), this had little impact on my life on the estate.

Craven Park is clearly far from typical – in its setting, trajectory or prospects. But it is a fascinating example of how a mixed community can evolve and remain stable, from the ingredients that in some places have gone badly wrong. But we are not just interested in the performance: the attitudes are our concern here. This Brighton estate, crucially, seems never to have got into the self-reinforcing spiral of stigma, rejection and polarization that has increasingly become the problem – and which is explored next.

Figure 8.3. Craven Vale, Brighton. (*Source*: Alan Cooke)

The Worsening Image of Corporation Suburbia

It is clear that from the outset, and right into the 1950s, estates were always seen as something different: a bit different here, a lot different there, perhaps. The differences obviously varied a lot in sharpness of contrast, from area to area. But the important shift seems to have been much later in the post-war period, when things changed markedly and the 'council estate' began its accelerating slide down the social slope. Better-off working-class households increasingly took advantage of the building of millions of new private homes, and of the access to finance offered by a combination of higher incomes and wider mortgage availability. Their exercise of that choice meant that the estates' role, even in corporation suburbia, came more and more to be the housing of those *without* such choice: '...by the 1970s there were the beginnings of a debate about the residualisation of council housing and the increased concentration of lower income and unemployed households on certain council estates' (Jones and Murie, 2005).

This is dramatically illustrated in Liverpool; and in particular, in the Norris Green estate. 'For a generation following the end of the Second World War, Norris Green maintained its reputation as a settled and desirable Corporation estate'. Richard Turkington quotes a 1971 survey: 'Norris Green is the most stable and respectable of the study areas. Only a small proportion of tenants expect to move from the area, and levels of satisfaction are high. Interest in owning is strongest in Norris Green, and levels of income, social class and savings make it likely that a proportion of young families will leave to buy' (Turkington, 1999).

But things got serious, and quickly: 'The estate's subsequent transformation was now to be shaped by a coincidence of Liverpool's economic decline; the changing role and status of council housing; and by the failure to modernize or reshape the estate.' By the time of the 1987 survey, the conclusion was stark, describing Norris Green as a 'community wherein the quality of life is severely eroded and which is, if nothing is done to halt it, set upon a downward spiral of deprivation and communal fragmentation.' And he concludes: 'From the highly desirable model estate of the 1930s, Norris Green is in danger of becoming the suburbia of last resort for the 1990s' (Turkington, 1999).

Perhaps sadder and more salutary even than Norris Green was what happened 25 miles (40 km) away at Wythenshawe. Sadder because the 'garden city' ambitions were so high, and it was seen as so iconic. Salutary because, as the Manchester University researchers observe, these cottage estates turned out not to be immune to the problems that were affecting the slabs and towers of the rest of the social housing stock: '...Le Corbusier cradling his model of the Unité d'Habitation and the demolition of Pruitt-Igoe signal a familiar narrative around the social utopian aspirations of the Modern Movement, and their collapse ... [they] seemed to signify a lack of humanity and social understanding on the part of designers ...where was the privacy in this urbanism, where were the gardens, where were the homes most families aspire to?' Yet this 'earlier style of mass housing that provided privacy and gardens in plenty ... was no better immunised from social failure' (Hebbert and Hopkins, 2012).

Wythenshawe, as noted in Chapter 2 above, was huge and ambitious. Parker designed it for a population of 100,000, in an Arts & Crafts style, in 'out-county' Cheshire: absorbed by the city in 1930. It was to be more than just a big suburban estate: the aim was a self-contained township with its own jobs and services. Social balance would be sought too: aiming for a social mix like Parker's Letchworth or Welwyn, a fifth of the housing was to be owner-occupied.

As in Norris Green, Wythenshawe rents were high, aimed at skilled workers in regular employment, with strict eligibility criteria and a post-occupancy inspection system.

The settlers were aspirational blue-collar families, who seem to have judged that – on balance – home comforts and a clean landscaped environment made up for the various disadvantages of life on the periphery. A 1935 survey found 90% of residents to be happy: some positively revelled in their quasi-rural lifestyle 'playing on the parkway, making dens in the bushes and hiding amongst all the lovely blossom trees'. (Hebbert and Hopkins, 2012)

However its aspirational pre-war character changed after 1945. The design approach changed: pre-fabrication, steel-framed and concrete houses, open-plan fronts instead of private gated gardens; Parker's maximum densities relaxed as cottages were joined by walk-up blocks, maisonettes and then tower blocks; motorway building (M56, M60), and the crude takeover of the Parkway as a traffic-dominated artery, which sectioned parts of Wythenshawe off from each other.

Even more important, it became a receiving area for 'overspill' as Manchester's urban renewal and slum clearance efforts intensified. Coupled with the highway severance, a process of housing differentiation became evident. 'Most of Parker's ten neighbourhoods had a declining reputation, but some were sliding faster… worsening problems of petty crime, rubbish-dumping and vandalism, housing voids, and internecine tensions' (Hebbert and Hopkins, 2012).

The Right-To-Buy accelerated the polarization between owner-occupied and social rented areas. In parts of the estate, rent arrears were leading to evictions which led on to vacancies, so that properties were being 'boarded up' in a visible expression of failure; yet in others house extensions and porches were being added in an individualistic way. But it was the *whole* suburb which was stigmatized by these problems, by chronic unemployment and crime:

It was no longer described as a Garden City. It had become a 'problem estate' – iconic for all the wrong reasons… In the blackly comic television series *Shameless*, first aired in 2004 … filmed on outdoor location in Wythenshawe, [the] characters reinforce every stereotype: … their families are dysfunctional and their alcohol and drug abuse is funded on welfare and crime. (Hebbert and Hopkins, 2012)

As the researchers observe: 'Of course, this reputation was an unfair representation of the everyday reality of life for many Wythenshawe residents and businesses. But iconicity is not about fairness'.

'Manchester in fact has not dealt kindly with its masterpiece' is Peter Hall's judgment in his history of twentieth century planning (Hall, 2002). And indeed the Wythenshawe story seems like a Technicolor illustration of the interaction of policy, practice, attitudes and choices; and the result is a missed opportunity, and a wasted asset, on the grand scale. The efforts to turn things round have begun, as discussed in the final chapter – but four decades of decline and disappointment will not be easy to undo.

In other regions, too, the increased choice of private new-build to move into, the readily available mortgage finance, and the changing aspirations all combined with and reinforced pre-existing attitudes. Thomas Sharp's 1946 warning of the danger of 'social concentration camps: places in which one social class is concentrated to the exclusion of all others…' was becoming true – and two of the places he had named were Becontree and Norris Green (Sharp, 1946).

How fast the change and decline were is underlined not just by the Norris Green experience above ('stable and respectable' in 1971, 'a downward spiral of deprivation' in 1987) but by the early-1980s appearance of a definition of 'residualization':

the process whereby public housing moves towards a position in which it provides only a 'safety net' for those who for reasons of poverty, age or infirmity cannot obtain suitable accommodation in the private sector. It almost certainly involves lowering the status and increasing the stigma attached to public housing. (Malpass and Murie, 1982)

By the late 1980s, these changes were evident in the attitudes on London cottage estates recorded in, for example *Just Like the Country* (Rubinstein, 1991). Mention has already been made, in Chapter 3 above, of the long-time Becontree resident's view, in the 1980s, that '*As for today some of the houses are run down a bit. People aren't taking so much care of them with many of the front gardens left unattended*'. On the same page there, Phyllis Rowden from the Downham Estate is quoted as saying '*The problem about people who have been housed in a council estate is that if they had the money to get on, most of them wouldn't stay*'.

It might be argued that such a narrative, of a sunny former era before a collapse into an unhappy and problematic present, is merely something people always, or often, do with life narratives. The Hodge Hill vicar observed of Bromford that '*established residents will contrast "when I moved here" with how "it's gone downhill", but this long memory actually covers a journey that has had up and down waves, and in reality it's been quieter here in the last five or six years*'. Interestingly, though, Alison Ravetz recognizes but is very cautious about explanations like this: 'Golden age memories are easily put down to nostalgia for a past that never existed, but they are often borne out by examination'. She cites factors such as tighter management, regular rent collection and resident caretakers, as well as authority figures keeping children under control and shared districts of origin, as reasons why estate life was indeed, correctly, 'something to be fondly remembered' (Ravetz, 2001).

Attitudes Today

What are the attitudes today? A cool review of the whole sector (that is, not just of the houses on cottage estates, but all social housing types) can be found in the 2011 British Social Attitudes material presented by Bramley. It starts, perhaps unusually, with a positive question 'asking people to say what they thought were the main advantage and disadvantage of renting from a local authority or housing association as opposed to renting a home privately'. Positive aspects which were particularly valued by existing social tenants were security of tenure (mentioned by 24 per cent), and the option to purchase property through a scheme such as the Right-To-Buy (18 per cent).

On the negative side (the main disadvantage of social housing compared with private renting), two issues cited fairly frequently were having little choice over location (12 per cent) and it being difficult to move to other types of property when needs changed (8 per cent).

But much the most common reply was anti-social behaviour problems on estates.

This is cited by 39 per cent of all respondents, including 31 per cent of social renters themselves. Another seven per cent across all tenures select 'anti-social neighbours'. Taken together, these replies suggest that approaching half the population, and a large minority of social housing tenants, see anti-social behaviour and neighbour nuisance as the main drawback to renting from a local authority or housing association. (Bramley, 2011)

Bramley comments that, despite evidence that social housing quality has improved and that social disadvantage is less concentrated, 'the continued prominence of anti-social behaviour issues in political debate about social housing is, given the strength of public opinion in our survey, unsurprising' (Bramley, 2011).

Thus there is a strong association in people's minds between the estates and anti-social behaviour. This is a clear message about a core aspect in thinking about attitudes to, and the future of, corporation suburbia. But we need to be careful. The associations that people make are not *necessarily* based (though they may be) on accurate or up-to-date evidence, or on actual lived experience.

Another piece of 2011 research which illuminates this difficult area is the study by a Sheffield Hallam team for the Joseph Rowntree Foundation of six quite deprived neighbourhoods across the UK: two of them, on Merseyside and in Anglesey, being estates predominantly of council-built houses. The team started by reviewing research, and observe that:

…there was no evidence from the research of distinct places of difference, dislocated from the world of 'hard-working families' and replete with broken families, poor parenting, lawlessness and dependency. The areas had, to differing degrees, problems with antisocial behaviour, gangs and incivilities, and there were social divisions in these areas. But this was not seen as an endemic and all-consuming syndrome in the neighbourhoods; that is, as inherent in place. (Batty *et al.*, 2011)

They interviewed families and individuals, over a lengthy period, to explore attitudes to living in the places, and to relate their experiences to 'the "broken Britain" narrative, [in which] … The dysfunctional family was presented as the prime culprit behind poor socialisation, antisocial behaviour and low achievement'. Their conclusion is that 'This depiction of family life in more deprived neighbourhoods in Britain was emphatically not supported by this research' (Batty *et al.*, 2011).

On the specific issue of crime and ASB, one of their interviewees, in Grimsby, told the team initially that she felt safe living there, whilst acknowledging that there was a degree of antisocial behaviour; but when she was burgled, her attitude changed dramatically. She felt less safe, was much less likely to go out at night and told the interviewers that 'there is a lot of crime'. She then moved to a different street, still in the same small area, for reasons of affordability and because of her fear of crime, and commented that: *'It's so much better, the area's so much quieter with it being a little off street, there started to be a lot of trouble round Corner Street, we had a drug dealer living down the street and their windows was put in every night cos they weren't getting what they wanted and trouble, fighting and all sorts'*. For a knowledgeable local resident, then, the distinctions within the area, and between those who cause trouble and those who suffer it, were clearly far more important and useful than generalized stigma about a wider area. Later parts of this chapter return to this issue of what the 'knowledge-base' actually is, behind often firmly held attitudes.

World of Balaclavas

Out in the world of the general public 'discourse', of course, few of these nuances apply, to put it mildly. Media treatment, especially, in the popular press, adds the label 'council estate' to an event whether relevant or not. This is not necessarily a stigma in itself, but it forms part of a generally stigmatizing set of attitudes. So 'Teenage thieves targeting vans parked on a council estate forced open the doors of one – and were confronted by four SAS men on a stakeout'. We cannot tell you where because, delightfully, '…The Sun has been asked not to reveal specific details' (*The Sun*, 25 April 2011) On the other hand, in 'Prisoner on run after van is ambushed': 'A manhunt was under way last night after a murder suspect was sprung from a prison van by an armed gang. John Anslow, 31, was freed shortly after being driven from jail on the way to court. A silver Volkswagen Scirocco pulled in front and three men in black balaclavas jumped out' (*The Sun*, 24 January 2012). Presumably, *not* on a council estate.

But what is in the heads of, it seems, many is now also unfortunately at large in blogworld. Lynsey Hanley remarks that 'chavscum.co.uk: a website hosting reams of virulent abuse against the "undeserving" poor, would be shut down if the same dehumanising language were to be directed at people of another colour, or a different religion' (Hanley, 2007). This very widespread e-nastiness often focuses on specific areas, especially the council-built estates, in suburbia as well as the inner city. Prosperous Reading's North Whitley, for example, features in a 2004 'Chavtowns' posting – by, inevitably, 'Anonymous' – as follows:

Reading has been featured a couple of times here but there have only been passing mentions of the source of the chav Nile in Reading: Whitley Wood (Wit-lee, or West Reading, if you are not a scumster and own a house in that area).

Reading would be a tolerable town were it not for the dirt that seeps out from Whitley like maggots from a decaying carcass. All the classics are there, shitty council housing, shitty council scum people, incest, teen pregnancies and more sportswear than even Trisha could handle. (Chavtowns, 2004)

And so on, for several more ill-tempered paragraphs. These may not be facts, but their existence is a social fact.

Even where the commentary is quite friendly, there is undoubtedly still some stigma: the quote below is from 'daisyanne':

Ok a lot of misconceptions about whitley. The bad well there's some rough elements but not in the league of newtown which is not far from old Earley when you think about it. Whitley is the bad parts is like the bad parts of woodley people wise. House wise majority are home owner or private rental. Strong stigma to whitley mostly by those who think their area is better. Now multi racial with whitley street are mostly asian and students. Middle whitley excluding hexham road area don't go there… Rest of middle whitley young familys not so many nowadays/ a lot of african immigrants /some asians some ghurkas/some chinese/some students/but majority mostly middle aged working people of all races. Outer part of whitley round terminus round precint drug hotspot.Homewise some really nice looking houses. All info got from listening to whitley residents experiences of living in the area.[2]

Stigma as 'Pathologization'

Perhaps because so much of this is part of the accepted, if often unspoken grain, of the country's culture, there seem surprisingly few attempts to explain the stigma, as opposed to just describing the patterns and processes. One serious and illuminating study that does try to do this can be found in the work of Annette Hastings of Glasgow University, especially in her 'Stigma and social housing estates: beyond pathological explanations' (2004). Though quite technical and academic, it does try to separate out different types of 'explanation' for problems on estates, and it contains a wealth of interesting material about attitudes and their basis in reality (or otherwise).

Hastings looked first at explanations of urban social problems and of neighbourhood degeneration. She summarizes the main approaches: 'structural' explanations (poverty and neighbourhood change driven by the wider structures of society and the economy); 'area effects' explanations (local factors combining with external forces to create a spiral of decline); and 'pathological' explanations (social and urban problems arising from the dysfunctionality of an underclass).

She then turned to how stigma itself is explained. Before looking at what local residents and other actors say, she looked at the literature, and found that even analysts who would reject a 'pathological' explanation of the actual decline will nevertheless edge towards it in trying to explain stigma. She says, 'it is routine for commentators to note, for example, that a negative image is one of the set of problems afflicting disadvantaged neighbourhoods'. But 'whilst authors tend to explain broad patterns of neighbourhood decline using structuralist and area-effects frameworks, when exploring stigma social, even pathological, explanations seem to come to the fore'. So even when as astute a commentator as Ruth Lupton is discussing the causes of neighbourhood decline, once stigma comes into the frame, economic and structural explanations fade away and it is 'explained as a social phenomenon – as a consequence of a lack of internal social control and the paucity of external relations' (Hastings, 2004). That is, poor behaviours and lack of interaction with the 'outside world' start to be invoked to explain why estates are stigmatized: it's the people, innit?

One study that more clearly separated out the somewhat 'pop' pathological explanations from what was actually testable as evidence was carried out in 1995–1996 for JRF by Cole and Smith on the pre-war cottage estate at Bell Farm in the York suburbs. Whereas many local people had ascribed the estate's notoriety to the high proportion of lone parents, the study authors, in Hastings's words, 'carefully signal a lack of complicity with the idea that there is a link between lone parenthood, social deviation and stigma' (Hastings, 2004).

The case-study part of the research then examined a pairing of *attitudinal* differences and explanations, which she terms 'pathologizing' versus 'normalizing'. Sometimes the interviewees in her study (whether estate residents or external agents or service providers) were what she calls 'normalizers'. They were people who tended to regard residents of stigmatized estates as no different from the general population and largely decent hard-working folk, so did not explain problems in terms of behavioural arguments, or only by way of remarks like 'it's just a few bad apples'. Explanations under this mind-set are likely to be drawn from outside factors: poor services, low pay, under-investment, and so on.

'Pathologizers', on the other hand, are 'behaviourists': the problems are more to do with the different standards of the poor, their different attitudes to crime and work, poor parenting skills or laziness. And while there might be well-behaved people on the estate, the problematic people dominate; and, for some respondents, they should just be locked in behind high walls; or, for others, they are certainly a pretty hopeless case with low employability and no prospects.

Most of Hastings's analysis is of the most deprived estates (as is the more recent work of Ian Cole's Sheffield Hallam team noted earlier – and indeed most others, including some of Hanley's, as at page 180 of *Estates* when discussing the 'wall in the head'). So conditions, and stigma, will tend to be more severe than on the cottage estates of corporation suburbia.

But what her analysis does is to tease apart explanations that are based on actual knowledge and those which are essentially attitude-based. She can then show how and why stigma is so self-perpetuating, and how little direct relationship there is between real knowledge of an area and opinions about it: '…pathologisers were not only less familiar with the estates than normalisers: in some cases they may *never* have visited the estates'. And she adds tartly that 'Interestingly, a lack of direct knowledge of the estates was no barrier to participants offering forthright views about the estates, their problems and their people'. It may be recalled that one of the Bromford residents (Chapter 5) makes exactly this point: nobody comes here, but it doesn't stop them having attitudes to it.

That leads on to an emphasis on the importance of 'external' contributors to estates' reputations. 'The capacity of estate agents to damage perceptions of an estate' features strongly. As part of the study, researchers posing as potential buyers waited to see if agents would raise the issue of estates' poor reputations, and the majority did, with detailed examples quoted from Meadow Well in North Shields and from Edinburgh. In one of the Edinburgh cases it was clear from his description of it during the interview 'that the estate agent had little, if any, experience of the estate' (Hastings, 2004).

As seen earlier, in the 1937 case of an East London chartered surveyor being able to put a precise figure on the devaluation caused by the proximity of the LCC estate, these patterns are very long-established. That they continue to affect attitudes, analysis and decisions could be illustrated from almost anywhere: in this case, from a recent planning study on an outer London suburb (Debden/Loughton), part of which (Debden) is low-density council-built housing of the immediate post-war years: much of it now sold under the Right-To-Buy.

Debden is located within Epping Forest. Whilst the district as a whole is perceived as being both affluent and desirable, Debden itself has often been viewed as Loughton's 'poorer relation'. Arguably, this is partly a marketing/perception problem, and also a reflection of the socio-economic circumstances for Debden. For example, the Loughton Broadway ward has an unemployment rate double that of Epping Forest as a whole (2.8% compared to 1.4%). (CBRE, 2008)

So even an area embedded in comfortable outer suburbia, and with an unemployment rate that would make the North blink twice and look again, is still seen as different and somewhat stigmatized.

Estate agents are not the only players: others included in the analysis were local journalists, police, employers and service providers – and of course local and neighbouring residents themselves. In all cases, the 'knowledge versus ready opinion' dichotomy keeps coming up. There is the at least potentially hopeful conclusion that: 'Finally, and interestingly, it seems that having detailed knowledge of an estate can reduce the propensity to associate stigma with resident characteristics' (Hastings, 2004). An echo perhaps of the line in the Introduction to *Estates*, by Lynsey Hanley, who of course grew up on one: 'Council estates are nothing to be scared of, unless you are frightened of inequality' (Hanley, 2007).

All About Poverty and Class?

It is very obvious that there are strange and strong attitudinal processes at work. Class, and British attitudes to it and its signifiers, are at work here. As usual, the brutal Lynsey Hanley plays it cards-up: 'This book is an attempt to work out how much of the stubborn rigidity of the British class system is down to the fact that class is built into the physical landscape of the country' (Hanley, 2007). And Chapter 2 stressed that John Hills is very clear that how and where council housing was built has been a major contributor to polarization.

On the other hand, this is not a uniquely British issue. Alan Murie notes in his contribution to the LSE comparative study of social housing that there is now emerging a continental European context of increasing residualization (Murie, 2008). And the question might also be posed: are estates, as estates, any more stigmatized than 'non-estate' poor areas such as the coalfield villages in Durham and South Yorkshire? Or struggling inner-city areas where the private rented sector is, or is becoming, dominant, like Abbey Hey in East Manchester or Benwell in Newcastle's West End?

The link to the economy is of course crucial. Jones and Murie look back to the boom years of council building and of the industrial sector:

Significantly, in a period of full employment … the role of council housing was often to house relatively well paid sectors of the working class, and this might create strong local workplace associations among people living on estates. These well-functioning council estates were not necessarily marked by social mix in terms of key social categories… There was a relative homogeneity in the population but a variation in how people behaved… Rather than talking about a degree of mix within the population of a neighbourhood, it is more appropriate to talk about activities and social relationships. (Jones and Murie, 2005)

To some extent, class and perceived class used to matter rather more than poverty or wealth in distinguishing the estates. Now, social tenure is such an indicator for deprivation that both aspects are involved. Even on the more sought-after cottage estates, a key thing that separates them from their market-housing neighbours is generally income levels.

The 'Wall in Your Head'?

One of the central ideas in *Estates* is Lynsey Hanley's insight, based on growing up in Chelmsley Wood, that – as she says on the last page of the book – 'For all its careful planning and proximity to the country, the estate was ringed by that invisible, impenetrable force field: the wall in the head'. Her analogy is with '…the former residents of the communist GDR who can't quite get over the fact that their country has been subsumed… They call it 'die Mauer in Kopf', or 'the wall in the head'… To be working-class in Britain is also to have a wall in the head and, since council housing has come to mean housing for the working class … that wall exists unbroken throughout every estate in the land' (Hanley, 2007).

This is a powerful idea, and it is based directly on her own experience. It raises a question as to how much other, even all, estate residents themselves share the stigmatizing views. As shown in the extracts from Glen Bramley's chapter in *British Social Attitudes 2011*, when the BSA survey asked people about the negatives of social renting, the most common reply was anti-social behaviour problems on estates, cited by 39 per cent of all respondents, including 31 per cent of social renters themselves (Bramley, 2011). And Annette Hastings points out that although her 'normalizer' and 'pathologizer' categories could be found in all groups interviewed, including estate residents, and although 'normalizers' were more likely to know the estates better, 'It is important to note that it was not the case that estate residents *never* explained the estate's problems in terms of resident failings' (Hastings, 2004).

The Sheffield Hallam team's 2011 report on six deprived localities (not all 'cottage' estates) stresses that even with that kind of dissatisfaction, it does not follow that people have given up on their area or estate. 'Many responses demonstrated how participants' sense of self was rooted in place, giving many of them a basis for some security in a context of growing economic uncertainty. Most respondents therefore viewed their future as staying in their neighbourhood, even if they were dissatisfied with certain aspects of living there…'. Indeed '… "neighbourhood" often mattered most to people where both the economic legacy of and future prospects for their community were least favourable'. But the 'normalness' of where you live comes up repeatedly:

> …the research participants rarely identified their neighbourhood as affecting their self-esteem, either positively or negatively. When asked what they were proud about in their lives and how they felt about their own position, respondents compared their current circumstances with other times in their lives, or with other family members, rather than where they lived, which was regularly described as 'just ordinary'. (Batty *et al.*, 2011)

None of this is to invalidate the 'wall in the head' concept. Hanley explains it both as a barrier and as a coping mechanism, and she is not putting it forward anyway as a generalized psychological explanation. On some at least of the estates of corporation suburbia which concern us here, the barriers and the need to find coping mechanisms are, in any event, probably far less acute than elsewhere, and indeed no more serious than the different barriers and problems facing people 'trapped' in other tenures or places, whether it be private renters or young low-pay families in prosperous market towns.

Balancing the Real and the Perceived: 'Sheer Prejudice' or 'Right to be Worried'?

Given how worried many estate residents clearly still are (see the British Social Attitudes material summarized above), we need to be very careful about explaining all the attitudes we encounter in terms of lack of knowledge or of long-established urban myths. Alison Ravetz comments that the 'hypothesis that estates were branded through sheer prejudice was salient in the academic debate for a generation or more'. She illustrates this by reference to Oxford's Blackbird Leys, where the 'rough' reputation arising mainly from delinquent youths terrorizing shopkeepers was analysed as being caused by the 'magnification of those difficulties by authority, and especially by intolerant 'respectable' tenants…' plus 'labelling as a problem estate'.

Her contrast is with the 'careful though less dramatic analysis of the nature of "problem estates"' which was carried out from the late 1970s onwards, where the variables distinguishing 'problem' from 'non- problem' estates were analysed, and factors such as skill levels, unemployment, child densities, turnover rates, newness of estate and arrival of different populations all began to emerge. There *are* real differences – but they still do not explain all the stigma! As Ravetz says in her discussion of attitudes about the now-demolished Quarry Hill flats in Leeds, 'Typically, estate residents explained away any problems by saying "there's good and bad all over" – in effect an acknowledgement that stigmatization was a crude caricature of a living environment that was in many ways satisfactory' (Ravetz, 2001). That caricature is what we need to avoid, or at least work to reduce.

What Residents Think

As to what residents think in the cottage estates of corporation suburbia which are the subject of this book, and particularly in the six case-study locations, these patterns are echoed, though generally in a minor key.

There is no doubt that some residents feel that their estates, and by implication they and their families, are stigmatized, and they may or may not explain that in terms of real-life problems in the area. At Orchard Park in Hull, for instance, discrimination against you because your *'postcode is HU6'* was explicitly mentioned. Becontree – certainly when it is called 'Dagenham' – still seems to carry stigma in the wider London setting. In the Deckham Hall part of the Gateshead cluster, specific streets are clearly stigmatized as problematic, including and especially by neighbouring residents. And in Bromford, locals know that the tower blocks are what mark their estate out, they agree that the flats are the locus of problems, and they oscillate between 'Bromford pride' and wanting away. So stigma is something people have to deal with in their day-to-day lives and choices.

In other places this does not seem to be the case. In Hylton Castle, Tower Gardens, and most of the Gateshead estates (Carr Hill, Sheriff's Hill, Highfield) residents see their area as a pretty normal one, with a normal mix of appeal and problems: no doubt there are posher areas, but that is the case just about wherever you live.

This is in spite of the fact that the price comparisons – for example between Tower Gardens and its tatty Edwardian neighbours, or between private-build and council-build in Hylton Castle – seem to indicate that the external perceptions are still carrying a 'council estate' discount or stigma.

However there is one important area where a crossover between 'external' and 'internal' perceptions may be at work. Anecdotally, young people growing up on some of the estates do not necessarily share their parents' comfortable assessment of the neighbourhood, and will often expect to move to a 'better' area as soon as they are in a position to make their own housing choices. The word 'aspirational' is deployed at this point in the debate by the housing industry… There is not, though, much hard evidence about the issue, which is discussed further in Chapter 9.

One final, and recent, variant on all this arose in both Becontree and Deckham, and it relates to residents of Polish origin. Unprompted, a resident interviewee in London observed, as noted in Chapter 3, that Polish and Lithuanian families see the estate as good value with good schools. And similarly, while discussing a separate topic, the Gateshead councillor said *'when you see more cars than usual outside our community centre, it's a Polish event; they really appreciate the area and its facilities'*. Both shine a bright light on what can happen if you approach corporation suburbia without the preconceptions most English people seem to share.

Figure 8.4. 'pretty normal … with a normal mix of appeal and problems': Tower Gardens N.17, and Heatherwell Green in Gateshead.

Areas of Choice?

This takes things back to some of the questions and thoughts sketched out in Chapter 1. Some, even many, of the estates under consideration have great assets – even if they have some problems too. Can they become 'areas of choice'? – a few probably are already – or will they remain predominantly 'areas to leave' for the foreseeable future, because residents have no belief in the areas' potential to collectively break out of the 'wall'?

It is obvious that there are 'real-life' problems, and it is stunningly the case that there are attitudinal problems; but there is no very straight-line relationship between the two, though they are closely interwoven, in different ways in different places.

Corporation suburbia is far from the only type of area where there has been big social change over the post-war years. If we think about some of the other city neighbourhoods which have changed radically, we see maybe not models (since gentrification is *not* always the answer to every neighbourhood issue) but indicators of what scale of change is conceivable. Less than two generations ago, when new people moved in to start gentrifying Barnsbury, or Kentish Town, or Chorlton-cum-Hardy, they too were 'places to leave', with plenty of 'problem' households and social issues; now they are amongst the most sought-after 'places of choice' in London and Manchester. One of the things this suggests is that attitudes may be at least as important as 'behaviour', as a target for effecting change and improvement on these estates. And Annette Hastings's research suggests that a focus on external actors' attitudes, and on real versus folk knowledge of the estates, could be part of such an effort.

Notes

1. The Craven Vale Community Association kindly sent 'Comments for 'Corporation Suburbia', 19 September 2012.
2. 'daisyanne': these comments are on www.reading-forum.co.uk, 12 May 2011.

Chapter 9

Potentials:
A Lazy Housing Asset?

Potential Assets

The story so far suggests that there is a complex mix of things going on: about place, about the stock, about the mix of residents ... but also about long-run and deep-set states of mind and class relationships. What are the prospects for corporation suburbia now?

To say again: this is not just about 'solving problems'. As one of the *Residential Futures* studies remarked: 'these are not the areas that would typically register on a worst-first analysis' (Urban Studio, 2009*b*): the interest in them here is in the *potential* they have, and the asset they represent. Let us start with what those studies said about that potential.

The studies' conclusion was that:

The *opportunity* for these localities is threefold. Firstly, they can, and indeed should, remain areas of choice for those within the social rented market; secondly, they are well placed to respond to anticipated additional demand for additional units within the intermediate housing market; and thirdly these localities have the potential to more fully integrate into the 'regular' housing market. They would thus play a greater role in the wider city-region offer by offering a viable, desirable, yet affordable product to the lower end of the owner occupier market. In short, the next step for many of these areas is to become a place where households wish to stay given the means, as opposed to leaving as soon as they get a chance. (Urban Studio, 2009*a*)

So the message was of potential, and of effort needed to release it.

Assets – but 'Lazy' Ones?

It was noted in Chapter 1 that when the Northern studies were under way, the team was struck by the potential – and yet by a sense, too, of under-performance. The expression used was a 'lazy asset'. Company analysts use this language to mean property, or a product, or a brand, which may not be loss making, but which is not delivering the sort of results that the shareholders would expect. It is not 'working hard enough'. What is meant here?

Essentially, it means a set of missed potentials – for local people, for the city-region economies, for the nation. It is possible to look at the potential that may be being missed under four main headings:

+ the housing asset;
+ the economic asset;
+ the land and development asset;
+ the community asset.

What it emphatically does not mean is that this property asset (this housing, on these estates) is full of lazy folk, on whom the benefits of this housing are wasted. It will be clear from the previous chapters that the evidence would not support such a thesis even if one were minded to base an approach on it.

Nor is the focus on the financial asset that the cottage estates represent, and whether or not it is being efficiently used. That would be a major study in its own right (the Hills report is a good start). And it would also require an appraisal of the financial shambles which is the whole British housing system, because of the interactions between all sectors of the market.

What *is* being argued is that these places have the potential to contribute more than they currently do to their communities and cities. They are intrinsically a good product, if sometimes rather stigmatized. The measures to help them respond better are affordable, do-able, manageable: they are not 'big-ticket' regeneration programmes with a heavy capital requirement. And the market can be expected to respond to at least some of their potential, once a trend is set: that is to say, in areas like this, we are going with the grain, not trying to redefine troubled areas' whole futures.

But what if these estates are occupied by a mix of people who do not necessarily get the most out of the areas' 'suburban family' potential: say, some who do not really want to be there and would move if they could; some who are out of the labour force but are poorly located to pick up work assuming that they wanted it or could do it; some who no longer really need this size of house, or garden, or nearby open space; and so on? A lot of these things are true of any suburban neighbourhood, of course. But for the municipally-built suburban neighbourhoods, there seem to be additional factors at work: the estates' history, and how you get access to housing in them, combined with stigma and under-investment. The impression is that these things keep them stuck in a position, and a role, that does not reflect their assets and potential.

It could be that if the estates had a more self-selected population (and perhaps more balanced, though this is a contested concept, and needs care), then they would 'look after themselves' more, including economically; they would provide family housing in good locations at reasonable prices/rents; and they would offer an alternative to new build and 'new' locations in many areas.

This chapter explores how far it might be possible to release the potential of these 'assets'. Not by 'reallocation' or enforced moves, but by making them more attractive so that more people with choice would choose them and/or choose to stay. The interest is in the 'churn', about retention and about appeal, and about people's own 'sorting' as in the rest of the housing market; not about measures to move out the poor and unemployed. Though it is also argued that such households *could* drop as a percentage – just as they grew over the 25 years from 1981 to 2006.

A Lazy *Housing Asset*?

The first and most obvious way in which the 'asset' might be being under-exploited is simply as underused housing. There are four main ways in which the national housing stock might be seen to be underused:

◆ housing left empty;
◆ part-time occupation of second homes;
◆ low turnover of the stock;
◆ the homes under-occupied in terms of space versus occupants.

So, Cottage Estate Homes Left Empty?

A look at the Empty Homes issue can illuminate whether this is indeed a significant underused 'asset' in the council-built suburbs. Overall, empty homes account for about 700,000 of England's 20 million or so. According to Shelter, this is made up of about 390,000 short-term private-sector voids (regarded as the normal 2 per cent 'churn' in the market), 288,000 longer-term empty private homes (the focus of Shelter's concern) and 59,000 voids in the social sector (about 1.6 per cent of that stock). But the main variation is not actually in tenure, or type; it is by region, with the North West showing the highest proportion, and Shelter's Bradford case-study, for example, showing a much higher long-term void rate than the average. Their conclusion is that 'The 288,000 long term private empty homes in England could make a contribution to meeting housing need. However, they are not spatially concentrated in the areas of greatest housing need and local authorities face challenges both in getting empty homes back into use and preventing homes from falling empty'. In other words, hard work for only very limited returns (Shelter, 2011).

Second Homes?

Perhaps not surprisingly, England's quarter-million or so second-homes are not a big issue for the estates we are interested in either. It is true that in some country and coastal areas, such purchases of ex-council or ex-Forestry Commission stock have aggravated even further the affordable housing problem, but it is a small component even in these more rural areas.

What about Low Turnover?

The third possible aspect of unused potential could be because of low turnover. This is of real interest, at least in theory, because slower turnover could be leading to less efficient use of housing through 'stickiness' in the stock's response to changing household needs. In fact, though, there is only one big differentiating feature on this aspect, and that is between private rented stock (PRS) and the rest. Nationally, private renters have lived in their homes for an average of one year, social renters for seven; and whereas 36 per cent of PRS households have lived in their home for less than a year, the equivalent for social renters is 8 per cent and for owner-occupiers 4 per cent (DCLG, 2010).

The English Housing Survey (EHS) data for the five years to 2003 shows the percentage of households who moved house, and while a somewhat higher proportion (varying between 9 per cent to 10.2 per cent over those years) shows in the 'most-deprived' band, the similarity between the 'fairly-deprived' (6.2 per cent to 8.9 per cent) and 'most-prosperous' (7.1 per cent to 9 per cent) suggests that this is not a significant variable, nor one which particularly affects the estates of corporation suburbia (Bramley *et al.*, 2007).

Under-Occupation?

This, the fourth possibility for releasing untapped housing 'assets', has of course attracted recent high-profile debate – particularly because of its being cast as an inter-generational issue, with older people's under-occupation of homes seen as shutting out the young.

The EHS gives the national figures:

Around 7.8 million households were estimated to be under-occupying their accommodation in 2008–09, i.e. they had at least two bedrooms more than they needed as measured by the bedroom standard. The rate of under-occupation was much higher in the owner-occupied sector than in the other two main tenures: 46.9% of owner-occupiers were under-occupying compared to 11.2% of social renters and 16.0% of private renters… A further 7.6 million households (35.4%) had one bedroom more than they needed under the bedroom standard; 5.4 million of these households were owner-occupiers, and there were 1.1 million households in each of the two rented sectors. (DCLG, 2010)

These are big numbers. But: the 'bedroom standard' can reasonably be regarded as overstating how much under-occupation there actually is. It is worth looking at one attempt to apply it in practice, in Greater Norwich. There, the study authors illustrate the anomalies, remarking that:

the government definition would identify under-occupation in circumstances most might regard as fully occupied. For our purposes a less minimalist approach is more useful. So we choose to define under-occupation to mean a property with one or more bedrooms not in regular use. This … fits in well with the available data and it is likely to be seen as reasonable. (GNHP, 2007)

Shelter, too, are realistic about the scale, persistence and normal-ness of the phenomenon: '…living in a home that is considered to be technically larger than your needs is extremely common across the whole of England, although there is generally less under-occupation in large urban areas…' (Shelter, 2011).

The Greater Norwich study reports that most under-occupation is in the three-bedroom stock (which would usually include the cottage estates) but that in the social sector it is more a question of two-bed homes being occupied by a single person (which would tend not to be the cottage estates). Not only is it unclear that corporation suburbia is particularly implicated; it is also hard to see how great or rapid change could anyway be engendered. One of the case-studies in Shelter's *Taking Stock* is from a post-war new town:

Under-occupiers tend to be older, often long standing, residents in a community, so any proposals to make them downsize can be a cause of tension or controversy. One of the case study areas, Crawley just south of London, has an under-occupation rate of almost 30 per cent; homes which could potentially alleviate the housing needs of households living in overcrowded conditions. Yet there is a strong feeling from tenants and some local politicians that homes are for life and that no-one should be forced out of their home to make space available for others. Few tenants have downsized... (Shelter, 2011)

The limited contribution of, and measures to affect, the social and socially-built stock can be gauged from Shelter's conclusions: 'The vast majority of under-occupation is in the private sector; 88 per cent of under-occupiers are homeowners... In the social sector, households are less likely to underoccupy from the start – although this does happen – but can become under-occupiers, most commonly because of household changes such as children leaving home'. They do not rule out targeted downsizing policies, but say that 'While a range of policy levers exist to reduce social sector under-occupation, the scope for intervention in the free market is less clear cut and politically more difficult; few policies exist to encourage or facilitate downsizing in this sector' (Shelter, 2011). It will be clear, too, that there is little or no evidence that under-occupation is particularly a feature of corporation suburbia.

Summarizing the Four 'Under-Use' Possibilities

So it looks as though, numerically and proportionally, the cottage estates are not especially underused as assets. Despite this, the political profile has meant that national policy has concentrated on under-occupation of the social rented stock. Measures seek to cap housing benefit payments for under-occupying working-age tenants, and to require them to leave when they no longer 'need' so large a house. Local and regional efforts, too, are under way to 'optimize existing stock';[1] though generally in ways which recognize the reality that the great bulk of under-occupation is in the private, not social, stock. So the balance of national policy attention looks like that politicians' speciality: a sledgehammer to crack a nut. Or, as an academic said the other day, a sledgehammer to squash the tomato next to the nut.

'Misused', Rather than Under-Used?

But the 'inefficient use of stock' issue *might* also be interpreted to mean 'inappropriate' use, in more of a housing-management sense. If the houses on the cottage estates are being occupied by high proportions of non-family households, or by a disproportionate number of households who are not in the labour market, it might still be argued that this is a misuse of the scarce resource which these homes represent, whose initial *raison d'être* was of course the housing of working families.

Chapter 8 showed that there is not really consensus about the purpose of, or entitlement to, social housing (and we have to bear in mind that nearly half these homes are now not 'allocated' by social landlords, they are traded, so only 'allocated' by the market). Theoretically, a change in allocation policies, away from 'need' categories to the 'economically-active' could be implemented for socially held stock. Or alternatively, and a more right-wing perspective, is the argument that the changing role of social housing means that in future, people cannot expect to move in and stay for life any more, and that it is increasingly just a stepping-stone to other tenures.[2] There is an obvious tension here between 'it is social housing so should have poor people in it' and 'it is good housing so get it better used'.

Actually, the full-strength version of the right-wing critique is further on than this fairly common 'housing of last resort'/'transit camp' position. The hard intellectual right argue for shifting *away* from social housing as a safety net, and from *any* specific welfare function: allegedly '…with the aim of ridding rented housing of the artificial divisions that create stigma and discriminate against those unable to access social housing' (King, 2006) This is a logical position if you believe that subsidy is a market distortion liken unto original sin, though it does display a touching faith in the market's ability, in the world we have, to come up with the affordable housing that millions need.

So *are* the 'wrong' people being allocated these homes in some sense? Who actually lives in corporation suburbia can be broadly gauged from the comparisons in John Hills's key report. He compares the people in 'Predominantly council-built areas – mainly houses' (more or less, the corporation suburbs) with those in 'Other areas – not local authority built' (that is, the rest of the stock, much of it the privately-built suburbs). On some measures, there is not much difference: for example, the proportion of couples with dependent children, or people of retirement age. On others, there is a lot of difference: there is more than double the proportion of lone-parent households in this council-built suburban stock, for instance; there is a 16 per cent gap in the proportion of those in employment; and over double the proportion of households who are among the poorest 20 per cent of the population: 32 per cent compared with 15 per cent (Hills, 2007).

This reflects the current role of the socially-owned housing component on these estates: it provides homes for households who are on average more deprived than the wider population. Of course, this is even truer of the other 'non-cottage estate' council-built stock, which is mainly flats. Here the comparisons for lone parents and retired people are about the same as for the 'mainly houses' estates. But the proportion of couples with children is much lower, and the unemployed/inactive and 'poorest fifth' proportions are even higher. However, even in corporation suburbia, and despite the percentage now out of social ownership, the people living there are much more likely to be out of work or poor than in the rest of the housing stock.

Looking, then, at all these aspects of the efficiency of use of the stock: it would be difficult to argue that this housing asset is being under-exploited, or that the people living here are under-using the stock or are inappropriately housed here. 'Under-occupation' is about average; empty homes, turnover and second homes are not issues; and the residents' 'fit' to the stock is comparable to that in the wider community. The possible exception is the employment aspect, which is discussed in the next chapter.

The Issue of Choices

If, however, one moves from this somewhat managerial viewpoint to think about *choices* – there does remain a question about these areas, possibly more in the North than the more sought-after South. This is the question as to whether the estates are being chosen (or not). We have a very constrained market at present, but it is important to remember that it was not always so, even quite recently – particularly outside the South East. Only a decade ago, around the turn of the century, much of corporation suburbia was showing signs of low demand, and even in a few places abandonment. When people *had* more choice, these places performed rather worse than at present.

This is about people wanting to move in, or to stay: which has to do with quality and perception as much as, or more than, housing management, allocations and short-term market behaviour. Chapter 7 noted Jones and Murie's findings that location factors – the estate itself, rather than the home or its size and layout – were most significant in the decisions of new buyers in the former-Right-To-Buy market. Anecdotally, the impression is that young people who grow up on the estates of corporation suburbia move out, to buy, as soon as they can – rather than looking around them for good value in the immediate area they know.

Not Keeping People? Not Attracting People?

The research evidence is copious (researchers have to keep busy), with a long trail from Rossi's original Philadelphia study in the 1950s about why households move and the relative importance of space in the home, the area, and costs (Rossi, 1980). It tells us things about length of stay in home, reasons for moves, turnover rates, and the patterns of young people's moves. Generally, it tells us about national patterns, which may vary a bit regionally but not much, reflecting different regions' tight or slack housing markets and varying degrees of ease of access to social housing. But specific estate accounts are hard to find, and very rarely illuminate the choice issues explored here.

On length of stay, the average is 13 years (for renters 10 years, for owner-occupiers 15 years); it is higher in the North (15 years) and lowest in London (12.3 years). Under-35s have lived in their residence on average about 3 years, compared with 35–44 year-olds at 8 years and 45–54 year-olds at 13 years. Sixty per cent of movers stay within a 5 mile (8 km) radius; 23 per cent move less than a mile (1.6 km), and 17 per cent move more than 20 miles (32 km), especially older people. The main reasons for moving are wanting a bigger or better house, or a nicer location (CML, 2004).

Tony Champion and Tanya Ford's study of movers in Newcastle, from over a decade ago, sheds some light on the relative importance of 'home' and 'place'. The surveys focused on people living in and around Newcastle who had moved home within the last five years or so, and were targeted primarily at households of family-raising age or older moving into owner-occupied housing. The Newcastle market, especially a cluster of inner north wards, interacts strongly with Gateshead, so including the Deckham/Carr Hill case-study area (Chapter 4). Table 6: 'Main reason for leaving previous residence' reports: 'Bigger house' 31.5 per cent (+ 'more space' 6.8 per cent + 'upgrade house' 2.7 per cent) – so over 41 per cent for this issue; 'Better neighbourhood' 11 per cent (+ 'wanted different location' 2.7 per cent) so about 15 per cent here; with all the other reasons below 10 per cent. The conclusion is that 'The survey evidence thus suggests that housing related reasons are central to the decision to move for those moving within the region. Although issues of crime, safety and pollution were mentioned as reasons for leaving the previous residence in Newcastle, housing related reasons were more important for two-thirds of this mover group' (Champion and Ford, 2001).

A survey in East Birmingham/North Solihull, the 'Eastern Corridor' which includes Chapter 5's Bromford Estate, showed a similar pattern. Reasons for moving to current address actually had as the top answer 'allocated the property' (a quarter of respondents), with 'area is a nice place to live' on 6 per cent. The 'why moved from previous home' answers were dominated by wanting or needing a larger place (27 per cent), with 10 per cent having wanted to move to a different area and 9 per cent not liking the area where they had been living (Grimes and Loney, 2006).

These surveys were of movers, in the conditions of a fairly active market. Turnover, though, is falling. Low turnover has been an important feature of the post-2007 downturn. It contrasts sharply with the two earlier peaks (1987, 1.9 million sales; 2007 1.7 million): in 2011, only 820–840,000 private homes were forecast to change hands. At about 4 per cent, this was the lowest level of stock turnover for more than half a century, and the forecasters expected annual housing turnover to stay well below 1 million for the next five years and possibly longer (Hometrack, 2011).

Young people's moving patterns have changed as well. Historically, leaving home was strongly linked to marriage and secondarily to getting a job, but today the reasons for leaving are more varied. The generational differences are really striking. 'Whereas 48% of 65–74-year-olds originally left home to enter marriage, just 22% of 25–34-year-olds left home in order to start a relationship…'. The current reasons given (in an Australian survey of 2008–2009) include 'desire to live independently or with friends… In response to educational opportunities … and as a consequence of personal circumstances…' (Beer *et al.*, 2011).

Work for the Joseph Rowntree Foundation by Sue Heath makes a point of possible relevance to the corporation suburbs, with their long working-class tradition, that:

Young people from middle-class families tend to leave home at a younger age than their working-class contemporaries, largely because of their greater likelihood of leaving home at 18 to attend university. They are also more likely to return home again after first leaving, including on completion of their studies (Jones, 1999; Ford *et al.*, 2002). In contrast, young people from working-class families tend to leave home later, but usually have no intention of returning once having left. If they continue to university, working-class students are also more likely than their middle-class peers to remain living with their parents…'. (Heath, 2008)

Moving from national and cross-sectional patterns to the local level, research giving estate accounts is rare, and sometimes based on few interviews which do not move much beyond the anecdotal. So it is not particularly conclusive or unanimous; it focuses, as we saw in earlier chapters, on 'problem' estates, and it often seems to be weighted by the strong views of ex-residents: for example the former Wythenshawe tenant who told the Manchester University team: 'I'd never want to go back. There are such a lot of problems because there are problem families everywhere, because drug abuse is so rife. I just tend to think that they sort of gather in places like Wythenshawe' (Hebbert and Hopkins, 2012).

An LSE team looked at Old Oak/East Acton in West London – one of the LCC's early wave of cottage estates – and report comments like 'It's generally OK here but I wouldn't want to be further into the estate. People from some areas are wanting to get out…', which is an interesting instance of sub-area differentiation and its possible effect on propensity to move (Lane and Power, 2009).

Data about locationally-based attitudes are not very easy to find. National figures, from the Survey of English Housing, show dissatisfaction in the sense of 'dislike area' hovering around 10 per cent of households in the two most deprived bands (compared with 3 per cent or below on the most-prosperous band). The proportions who actually moved, though, were similar in the most-prosperous and fairly-deprived bands, but somewhat higher in the most-deprived band (Bramley *et al.*, 2007).

A Llewelyn Davies study in urban Hampshire explored levels of satisfaction with urban living in different types of settlement and concluded that 'an important conclusion underlying much of the response received is that the people who live in the urban areas of Hampshire, Portsmouth and Southampton have a positive attitude to urban living. In each type of area studied, from inner city to outer suburb, this was true; around a fifth of respondents said that they would change nothing about their home or area'. Within that overall finding, it noted that 'only 14% of people who were planning to move were moving because they wanted to live in a different area', and this did not appear specially associated with the deprivation score or who had built the estate: the localities where the wish to move was slightly higher were Hilsea in inner Portsmouth and privately-built Hedge End on the outskirts of Southampton (Llewelyn Davies, 1998). The one strong association that affects estates *per se*, is as noted from the 2011 British Social Attitudes material (Bramley, 2011) reported in Chapter 8, '…when it comes to specifying the main disadvantage of social housing compared with private renting, much the most common reply is "anti-social behaviour problems on estates" (39 per cent of all respondents)'.

The Birmingham-Solihull survey also looked at reasons related to neighbourhood.

Three-quarters of the sample claimed to be satisfied with their current neighbourhood, and only 16 per cent were dissatisfied. The Hodge Hill ward which includes Bromford was, however, second highest for dissatisfaction (at 29 per cent). Over the whole survey area, neighbourhood-related reasons for moving were led by 'gangs of youths' (43 per cent), 'high crime level' (36 per cent) and 'vandalism' (33 per cent); but almost a third also suggested 'litter, dirty streets and overgrown bushes' as a major influence: interestingly these ranked higher in Asian residents' responses than in the overall results (they were also less likely then White respondents to say their neighbourhood had got worse). In Hodge Hill ward – and one other, in North Solihull – as many as 50 per cent of the respondents gave not liking the area as the reason for wanting to move. '*It was clear from the responses to these questions that most respondents envisaged their future moves as being local*' because the majority of places that they did, or did not, want to live fell within the conurbation, if not the Eastern Corridor itself. '*Clearly, too, local likes and dislikes were expressed – one area within the Eastern Corridor being acceptable, where others were not*' (Grimes and Loney, 2006).

But little of this material separates out different sorts of place or estate, and so it tends to group the cottage estates in with the totality of municipally-built environments. Nor is it really clear how closely perceptions mirror reality – for example, on actual current levels of anti-social behaviour, or on urban environmental management. And as seen in Chapter 8, this is a question that is at least worth asking – and one where the answers might in some cases point to specific responses to try and change established mind-sets. We are back to the point made in that chapter, which is that what people *think* is an important social fact: though one that it may be possible to influence.

Retention and Attraction

So in trying to answer the question 'are young people/young working families disproportionately moving out of the cottage estates (and not just the *social* housing)?', the research evidence does not really take us very far. The Birmingham-Solihull survey team asked their interviewees about 'emerging households' – predominantly younger members of the household that was being interviewed: those who the respondents expected to want to form a new household soon (Grimes and Loney, 2006). The type of property they would most want to live in was semi-detached (32 per cent; with low-rise flats at 20 per cent) and the type of tenure preferred was buying (38 per cent; social rent 36 per cent). Neither of these responses excludes corporation suburbia, nowadays. And indeed, within their survey area, Chapter 5's Bromford could meet both requirements. So neither this nor the wider research prove or explicitly contradict the anecdotal impression of younger households' propensity to leave. It may be, then, that *retention* is indeed a problem: the estates may well not be keeping people who might have stayed yet are choosing to leave. But on the actual evidence, this is – as Scots law has it – 'not proven'.

On the parallel question 'are these areas left out of housing searches (by particular groups, by non-locals, or whoever)?', the principal evidence is the price differential reported in Chapter 7. Prices on the corporation-built estates are clearly lower than on their near (non-municipal) neighbours of a similar – or even apparently less attractive – nature: for example, Tower Gardens versus the nearby Edwardian terraces on the Tottenham/Wood Green boundary. This is evidence of less pressure of demand, suggesting that the estates are, *ceteris paribus*, less desirable.

As noted in Chapter 4, a property industry view was that – certainly in the North – there are not many areas where an 'incomer' young couple's search patterns would be likely to include ex-council houses. It would generally take local connections, such as family or having been brought up there, to get this stock added to the wide range of housing choice already available elsewhere.

So it seems fair to conclude that they do have the problem that they are not *attracting* people, or as many people as they might; and that this arises as much from attitudes as from real-world factors.

So, *is* This a 'Lazy Housing Asset'?

The answer to the question 'is this a lazy housing asset?', overall, seems very often to be 'no', in two senses: that these estates are doing the job which policy (to the extent that this can be defined) intends; and that they are no more 'underused' (under-occupied, voids, turnover, second homes) than the generality of the stock.

But possibly 'yes' in two ways: in that perception and choices are affecting and maybe even distorting who might live here; and also in terms of what that might mean for the housing and labour markets. The next chapter considers some of these aspects further.

Notes

1. Outline for London by David Lunts in his 'Optimising Existing Stock' presentation to the NLSA Housing Conference, 11 November 2011 at Friends Meeting House (including approaches to mobility, empty homes, under-occupation, Decent Homes).
2. Councillor Tom Davey, Barnet's Cabinet member for Housing, at the NLSA Housing Conference, 11 November 2011 at Friends Meeting House; see also note 1.

Chapter 10

A Lazy *Economic* Asset?

The Housing–Economy Link

Next to be explored is the 'economic' asset which may be being under-exploited. One aspect of the potential that could be being lost is in relation to the competitiveness, or efficiency, of the economy. This might be especially the case in city-regions with a lot of this municipally-built stock – through the impact on labour supply and work incentives.

The scale will no doubt differ from area to area, and probably between the more prosperous South and the poorer North. But we might attempt to estimate how much missed potential is involved, by again looking at the comparisons in the Hills report: between people in 'Predominantly council-built areas – mainly houses' (more or less, the corporation suburbs) and those in 'Other areas – not local authority built'. The difference is most striking in relation to labour market participation; with a 16 per cent gap in those employed (48 per cent on our estates as opposed to 64 per cent in non-council-built); and a 14 per cent gap in those unemployed or inactive: 22 per cent as opposed to 8 per cent (Hills, 2007).

One would expect to see some effects of the Right-To-Buy in action here. The successive waves of RTB purchase, as outlined in Chapter 7, started with existing (usually employed) tenants taking advantage of the deep discounts, but many of them have now left the workforce or sold on. Later waves introduced more earners (by definition, because of the need to get a mortgage), who are younger and often using the stock as a stepping-stone. But the evidence is that this 30-year process has been outweighed by other social changes, so that despite growth of owner-occupation there is a marked gap in the averages of labour market participation, as just noted.

Closing the Employment Gap

Just closing this gap would make a very substantial difference: both to the lives of people on the estates, and to the role that the estates play. So if one imagines an estate of say 2,000 houses, then closing the 14–16 per cent gap could mean 300 or so more households in work there than at present. Such households would be choosing to live there because the 'package' of housing cost (mortgage or rent), travel cost and living environment is as good as or better than the 'package' in the alternative locations they have tended to be moving out to.

This is a 'what if' – but it is not so fantastical. Two comparisons illustrate the fact that change of this kind is not an unrealistic dream. The first is over time. From 1981 to 2006, the nationwide proportion of owner-occupying householders who were in employment fell by 2 per cent – but in the social stock the fall was by 15 per cent (and by 21 per cent if looking at full-time jobs). So this was not the economy at work, or not mainly: it was policy and social change. As Hills says '…the role of social housing has changed… While postwar housing provision was aimed at households with a range of incomes, since the 1980s provision has become more tightly constrained and new lettings focussed on those in greatest need' (Hills, 2007). Obviously the focus here is on one particular segment of the council-built stock, not all social housing; but the message is clear: only a generation ago, these places had a different economic role from the one they have now. That role is not ineluctable or god-given: it might be worth trying to change it.

The second comparison is international. Chapter 2 quoted Hills's European comparison as showing that 'by the late 1990s, the income differences between tenures were greater in the UK…'. The ratios are indeed striking: for the UK, social renters' after-tax incomes are 50 to owner-occupiers' 120 (so a little over 40 per cent); for France, Germany, Netherlands and Sweden they are 75 to 115/130: so around 60 per cent (Stephens et al., 2002). Thus, as with the comparison over time, the comparison over space suggests that current patterns are by no means inevitable or incapable of change.

The Six Estates

Homing in on the six 'case-study' estates, a comparison using 2011 Census small-area data confirms the general, though not ubiquitous, pattern of the corporation estate residents tending to be less engaged in the labour market than those in similar, but non-council-built, areas nearby.

Table 10.1. Case-study estates and neighbours: unemployment.

Area and Comparator	2011 Unemployment %
Tower Gardens	14
Westbury Avenue	8
Becontree	11
Goodmayes	8–12
Deckham / Carr Hill	12
Coldwell Lane, Felling	6
Hylton Castle	12
South Hylton	5
Bromford	17
Erdington south end	7–17
Orchard Park	27
East of Beverley Road	2–6

Sunderland's Hylton Castle showed over double the 2011 unemployment figure that was recorded in mainly privately-built and three-quarters owner-occupied South Hylton on the opposite bank of the Wear. In Gateshead, the picture is similar, with the average rate for the Deckham/Carr Hill estates (12 per cent) comparing with a rate of half that in the majority owner-occupied tract adjoining Carr Hill to the east, around Coldwell Lane, on the borders of Carr Hill, Felling and Heworth.

In Birmingham, the landscape is similar but less sharply drawn. Bromford's two halves differed markedly themselves, with the west recording an 11 per cent unemployment rate and the east (dominated by the towers) 22 per cent. In comparator areas on the other side of the M6, the range was similarly wide: the south side of Erdington around Moor End Lane, which is over three-quarters owner-occupied, showed 7 per cent; the more mixed area off Bromford Lane around Church Road, 12 per cent; and the Birches Green/Round Road tract, which is mainly council-built cottages, 17 per cent.

London's two case-study areas give rather differing results. The Tower Gardens estate, following the perhaps-expected pattern, was noticeably worse placed than its non-council-built comparator. This area, the streets to the immediate southwest off Westbury Avenue, are also predominantly Edwardian, but privately built and with a tenure split now of 40:30:30 between owning, social renting and private renting: here, the 2011 unemployment rate was just above the London average at 8 per cent – well below Tower Gardens' 14 per cent. In Becontree, though, unemployment was around the same level as in the immediately adjoining Goodmayes area: which was built around the same time or slightly earlier, and which has a proportion of owner-occupation 10–25 per cent higher than in Becontree (social renting is much lower, less than 10 per cent compared with Becontree's 35 per cent). So 'council-built' is associated with much *less* difference here in East London.

And then inevitably Orchard Park (Hull), where good news is as ever hard to find… With over a quarter of the economically active population unemployed, it bears no comparison with the predominantly owner-occupied areas just across Beverley Road to the east. But this is not actually much of a comparator, as these streets cannot be regarded as the 'non-municipal' equivalent of the council-built case study. For an estate like Orchard Park there just aren't really any comparators, except maybe in the inner city.

The case-study estates, then, do tend to show an 'employment gap' of the kind identified in discussion of John Hills's figures. However the story inevitably differs from place to place, according to local conditions. Overall, they could be argued to be something of an 'anomaly' in the general pattern of economic activity, in the sense that, given where they are and what they are like, one would expect them to have fewer people out of work than they do – and this 'anomaly' seems to be associated with the tenure.

However the comparison with Goodmayes suggests that Becontree is much *less* of an 'anomaly'. It is in the hot London labour market (but so is Tower Gardens); it has a notably dynamic private-rented sector; and it seems to be attracting young working families, many non-British, who either ignore any stigma or reckon that they have no other choice.

The comparisons probably also reflect how in parts of the North people in the cottage estates, as well as in the flatted developments, are very badly dislocated from what work there is. It also reflects the greater choice of homes, which means that people who *are* in work are much more likely to be able to afford to move out to areas they see as more desirable.

It is not however just North versus South. In the Midlands case study, the western, mainly 'late-period cottage estate' part of Bromford is also less of an 'anomaly' in the labour market/housing market pattern than is the eastern section. Its unemployment rate is worse than average, and worse than more-or-less contemporary, or slightly older, privately-built stock in surrounding areas: so it does conform to type to some extent. But the difference is less striking than in many other places (and certainly much less marked than in eastern Bromford with its tower-blocks and more inner-city feel). Birmingham, like London, is a big complex city with all sorts of social and economic pressures interacting, so it is hard to draw definitive conclusions. But like Becontree, the most 'corporation estate' part of Bromford suggests that these areas *can* edge back towards a more 'normal' relationship between the housing offer and the labour market response, in certain conditions at least.

Implications in North and South

So if the country's corporation estates did come closer to the 'non-council-built' average in attracting and retaining people, what might be the implications of their providing family housing in good locations at reasonable prices/rents? Clearly some already do: we saw in Chapter 7 that in areas of high housing demand (such as Mole Valley south of London, and some of the Birmingham estates) they are filling a gap in the regional housing market as, for example, first-time buyers move out of London. But in many parts of the country this stock is not contributing all it could to the range and choice in the housing market. In a lot of areas, the people who might move in, or stay, are going elsewhere, often further afield.

The implications for city-region economies seem to relate to the way in which these estates could, potentially, offer employers a pool of labour in reasonable locations who could afford to work at hireable wages. This is complex: the questions include: At which margins do these choices bite? What alternatives do movers have and not have? What quality-of-life 'offer' makes it worthwhile for households, at the price and wage levels operating (and this is quite likely to show a sharp North versus South difference)?

As housing is such a large component of overall living cost (about a third), competitive housing costs feed indirectly into labour market responses, including wages. In a low-wage regional economy with plenty of housing, the cost of living is low and housing is very affordable. Conversely when house prices were rising rapidly, wages needed to follow suit just to keep employees at the same quality-of-life level.

This impacts on the locational advantages of a given region/city, and over time may erode a location's competitive advantage.

In the London & South East case, the movers to Mole Valley are trading a longer average journey to work for more space/better quality-of-life at an affordable price; their alternatives (if not staying in Croydon or Merton) are even further out, where prices are lower but travel costs higher. The council-built stock here is offering more or less the same deal as is its privately-built counterpart – maybe at a slightly lower price because of residual stigma, but essentially doing the same job. In other parts of the South East, though, this is not necessarily happening. Becontree, for example, is still a long way from substituting in the marketplace for inter-war or post-war 'private' suburbs in housing search patterns. Hence many of the estates, even in the pressured South, are *not* operating as one of the options in the work-travel-home-cost-wages package, as in the case of Mole Valley. That must impact on the labour market, even if indirectly: some working-household 'travel+home' costs are higher than they need to be, and the salary they need to make the equation work has to be higher than it otherwise would be.

In the North – say in Sunderland, and thinking about the Nissan plant there and its workforce, quite a few of whom live in the Hylton Castle locality considered in Chapter 4 – the point is a different one: for Nissan, wage inflation is likely to be moderated if their reasonably well-paid staff can afford to access a range of housing options within a short commute of the factory. Contented staff are also more likely to be productive and turnover to be low. The cost-package aspect will tend to be less important to these housing markets, with more choice and lower prices relative to wages.

Employers' experience of these choices is therefore indirect. But in normal economic conditions, wage levels and the ease of hiring good staff will be influenced by the size of the labour supply within a given travel distance. Companies' performance depends on a lot of factors, but in many sectors, especially modern service industry and growth sectors, quality staff, and their retention, are critical to sustained success. The Heriot-Watt/Rowntree study demonstrates one of the interactions (labour demand with house prices, broadly a proxy for housing demand): 'The measure of "change in access to jobs" is based on travel to work data for 1991 and 2001… This has a consistently positive effect on price change, as expected. Wards where accessible job numbers increased saw bigger price rises' (Bramley *et al.*, 2007). So the housing market was showing clear effects of good job access.

How?

What then are the sorts of measures that might help to rebalance the cottage estates towards 'normal' integration into the labour market and city-region economies? Chapter 14, which discusses the issue of greater social mix, raises four possibilities. These are the use of selective Right-To-Buy, to restrain the market trend where this might be a threat; or second, to encourage it, the sort of 'mixing' strategy applied in the Rowntree SAVE programme (Martin and Watkinson, 2003), of selling alternate vacant properties on the open market; with, third, actual allocations policies for social landlords' rental properties – the 'who' of housing, adjusted to try and avoid over-concentration of households with no-one in employment; and fourth, drawing on an example in Darlington, mortgage support for on-estate buyers: carefully encouraging tenure mix and building on people's neighbourhood commitment.

Some of this would be controversial. But historic allocations policies completely dominated by need definitions have helped to contribute to residualization and area disadvantage: they should be at least reviewed and probably often altered, in the interests of a sustainable future for the cottage estates and the people who live on them.

So – a Lazy Asset?

Again: what is the answer to the question – are the cottage estates a lazy (economic) asset? It looks as though the answer is yes – the potential of these estates to play a full part in the range of housing on offer is not being wholly used, and this must work through to labour market costs and choices.

Chapter 11

An Untapped *Land/ Development* Asset?

The third exploration is of the physical and spatial assets that may be under-exploited. Here, the nature of the potential was sketched out in the *Residential Futures* city-region case study in Sunderland (Tyne & Wear), starting with the issue of too much and too low quality open space.

In common with many developments of the same period, there is random 'amenity' open space … having little or no practical use-value and serving only to create areas of indeterminate ownership and potential (or actual) forums for anti-social behaviour. The quantity, quality and utility of public open spaces in such localities needs to be aggressively reviewed, with a view to rationalising and revitalising the most important spaces. Simply put, quality is far more important than quantity. (Urban Studio, 2009*b*)

It went on to suggest ways of exploiting the asset: 'There is an argument that these spaces might be made to "work", becoming locations for activities or being developed for various uses (including residential), while the retained open space is actively managed … [and] … re-styled as community parks, allotments, play areas, safe zones for older residents, ecology areas and secure dog-walking areas, for example'.

The two Sunderland estates which were reviewed in that study (Hylton Castle, see Chapter 4, and its immediate neighbour Castletown) are notable for the scale of such open land. The estates cover some 175 hectares, of which about 50 hectares is open space, much of it as described above. The map from the *Residential Futures* study reprinted in Chapter 4 identifies ten more corporation-suburbia estates strung out along the A19, from Herrington south-west of Sunderland to Annitsford across the Tyne near Cramlington: a lot of potential spare land.

Other city-region case studies in the series made similar points. For Kirkholt in Rochdale, the commentary notes that 'The quality of open space is low, and in some instances is perceived as leftover rather than positive, lacking designated uses' (Llewelyn Davies Yeang, 2007*a*). The study of the Mereside estate on the edge of Blackpool says that 'On some larger spaces some limited development could bring in new housing, as well as providing overlooking and activity near to open spaces' (Urban Studio, 2009*d*).

Chapter 3 earlier recorded one Becontree resident's view that there is in fact too much open space, and that quality rather than quantity should be the focus ('*they should break Parsloes Park up and develop some of it, and make nice little spaces like in Bethnal Green, with cafés and so on…*'). This is even more the case with the sterile swathe of Goresbrook open space alongside the A13 trunk road, and the local council could usefully consider these parks' functions and potentials in a much more strategic way.

Inevitably many of the estates do not have opportunities of this kind and on this scale. It depends on their initial layout and subsequent history. In Liverpool's Norris Green, 'the inflexibility of an estate environment in which almost every square metre was developed' constrains opportunities markedly (Turkington, 1999). The same is largely true of tightly-planned early estates like Beech Hill in Wigan, or Tower Gardens in Tottenham described in our Chapter 3 estate study.

But even in Norris Green, space of a kind was opening up: 'many residents were finding it difficult to cope with the generous provision of back gardens, and responded by abandoning their lower length'. Coupled with the need to deal with 'several thousand non-standard houses whose physical condition is now a massive liability', substantial elbow-room was starting to emerge, albeit in a very problem-driven way (Turkington, 1999).

And although the underused green space seems often to be the main opportunity, all the areas examined in the Northern Way work had at least some other potential. An example is in Hull's outer estate of Bricknell, where a surplus school site and a local shopping parade cleared after a gas explosion total something like 8 hectares, out of an estate which is at most 80 hectares in total (Urban Studio, 2009*e*). Not all the areas will have anything like 10 per cent of their area having development potential, but put together with the smaller parcels of left-over land and disused facilities, this is clearly a resource of some substance.

Figure 11.1. Sunderland's Hylton Castle: two out of many such 'amenity' spaces – what *are* they doing?

Figure 11.2. Another 'lazy asset': underused garage site – actually on a popular cut-through in Hylton Castle.

The Scale of Available Land

The release of such potential is not however straightforward. Certainly the idea of just filling-up every corner on the cottage estates, as is sometimes suggested by local politicians (understandably) desperate to meet housing need, is liable to be counter-productive in an effort whose aim is quality more than quantity, and choice rather than constraint. The raw total of notionally available sites has to be factored down to recognize objectives of good design and community cohesion. It must also build in realism about the constraints of likely local opposition, and the complexities of ownership and acquisition. So the numbers will not be as big as a 'capacity' calculation might suggest.

Table 11.1 below takes the six estates from Chapters 3–5, plus four of the 'Type 2' estates from the *Residential Futures* studies, as a basis for thinking about the type and scale of potential that might be available. A judgement is made about how much of each 'source' of potential might be unlocked, given constraints such as existing block layout and local acceptability. This is compared with the total area of the estate, by way of giving an indication of the proportional addition that might be possible.

On the basis of the – admittedly heroic – assumptions here, the implication is that these ten estates could find 110 hectares of additional housing land: ranging between 0 per cent and 30 per cent of their total area, at an average of about 6 per cent. At say 30 dwellings per hectare – more or less the 12 per acre of the interwar years and the Tudor Walters report – this looks like space for 3,300 new houses, in just ten locations.

There are all sorts of caveats. Table 11.1 gives the strong impression that the less successful estates tend to have the most space: Orchard Park versus Hylton Castle, for example. So the space may be most available where it is least sought – no great surprise there. It is worth noting, though, that in Bromford, the space becoming available

Table 11.1. How much development potential? Ten estates.

Location	Nature of Potential				Estate total (ha)	%
	'Spare' open space	Vacant facilities etc	Former housing sites	Possibly available (ha)		
Tower Gardens	✗	✗	✗	0	16	0
Becontree	✓	✓	✗	10	1,000	1
Deckham/Carr Hill	✓	✓	✓	4	93	4
Hylton Castle	✓	✗	✓	3	62	5
Mereside (Blackpool)	✓	✗	✓	4	55	7
Kirkholt (Rochdale)	✓		✗	16	175	9
Bricknell (Hull)	✗		✗	8	80	10
Lakes (Redcar)	✓		✓	22	120	18
Bromford	✗	✗	✓	9	40	22
Orchard Park	✓		✓	34	120	28

is largely from the removal of the form that *has not* worked there (tower blocks), potentially releasing land for more of the two-storey house form that seems much more sustainable and popular there. So in at least some places, the approach would be going with the grain.

Estates' age, and tightness of layout, clearly play an important role. The older less loosely-planned neighbourhoods have less 'space left over after planning', and fewer windy tracts of pointless grass mown to within an inch of its life every fortnight. Hence Tower Gardens is assessed as having no space for more housing: as planned, it was a tight little grid, and it still is. But even here, there is something of a definitional issue: the study in Chapter 3 takes just the little (16 hectare) estate itself – its immediate neighbour, the interwar Roundway area, is rather looser and would probably throw up at least some developable space if reviewed.

In Deckham, there are several sorts of opportunity: a redundant housing depot, unsafe-feeling open space, gap sites where flats have come down. But the Deckham Hall part is already pretty tight, and filling *all* the gap sites would mean closing up an estate that may at last have got some of the breathing space it needs (there was certainly a very enthusiastic game of scratch football with 'jumpers for goal-posts' on the Bayswater Road corner site, on one visit…).

Councillors in both Gateshead and Sunderland gave specific examples of such difficulty: in Deckham, a site in Avon Road which has been vacant for 12 years at last has a development proposal (for rent and sale) by the RSL and a commercial partner. But 12 years as one of the few bits of flat land above the steep 'Bankies' means it has been local play space for two generations of kids, and the scheme has run into opposition. And in Hylton Castle, the importance of playing pitches (formal and informal), as part of stopping inter-estate gang rivalry, means that building on open spaces, while a real potential, needs to be very carefully handled.

So the responses will be different strokes for different folks, and different cases in different places. But the strong suggestion is that there *is* something here. Grossing up from individual unique estates to a national figure is impossible. But the scale of the potential is obviously significant. Probably it will not often go beyond 5 per cent addition in the earlier and more stable estates; but in places it will be up above +20 per cent.

A National-Scale Potential

And there *are* a lot of these estates. In just two of the regions of the North, the *Residential Futures* studies analysed how many 'Type 2' estates there were in total. For Tyne & Wear, as Chapter 4 noted, it was ten. For the Sheffield city-region, though, it was thirty-six: half of them in Sheffield itself, half spread across the surrounding districts such as Chesterfield and Barnsley (Llewelyn Davies Yeang, 2007*b*).

Nationally, this shows that there must be thousands of 'houses' worth' of land in corporation suburbia. The land will generally be in public ownership already, so that there will be one less constraint on development. And it is in locations that already have infrastructure: roads, schools, utilities, etc. So the marginal cost to society of its development must be well below that of newly released land.

The Demand Side, and the 'Actors'

How much available space is not the only issue. The potential is not just a function of the supply (raw or adjusted). It is also 'demand-pushed'. Sites will work harder, including attracting developer interest, when a whole area is seen positively, rather than negatively because of long-run stigma. So the development market can be expected to respond to at least some of this potential, once a trend is set. And an approach which is working on 'TLC', on relatively small-scale opportunities and on improving perceptions will in general be less complex and demanding (and costly), because it will increasingly be going with the grain; it is not trying to redefine troubled areas' whole futures as in the major regeneration schemes.

This is not just a 'private developer market versus council ownership' question. The registered social landlords (RSLs, housing associations etc) have an interest in the success of the estates where they have stock. They need to think out how they respond and manage in areas where the tenure balance is changing, in sometimes-unpredictable ways. RSLs are interested in investment and diversification as a way of protecting the longer-term value of their assets – and their stock is not as valuable as it could be, including as an asset that they can borrow against for further development, if the area is struggling. So there obviously is a role here for the social landlords themselves in getting the most out of a 'lazy asset' as landowners, and using the potential to generate finance by using the value from sales to fund borrowing at a multiple. Doing schemes themselves, joint-venturing with the private sector, mixing in both sales and rental – all are ways of exploiting the development potential of the corporation suburbs.

In some areas, the market may be sufficiently active, and perceptions favourable enough, for such potential to be explored by private developers or individuals. Noted earlier were the examples from Surrey and Birmingham where council-built estates appear to be functioning almost indistinguishably from the rest of the market. Some parts of Becontree (see Chapter 3) may be similar. However, it is essentially in terms of house *sales* that they are responding so far; there is little evidence that the *development* market is interested. It is unclear what private schemes, even in the pre-2007 boom, were going into such areas without the inducement of public-sector support.

It is interesting to note the contrast with the privately-built interwar suburbs which are the subject of the analysis of development and change in *Changing Suburbs*:

It is perhaps surprising that the notion has gained credence that interwar suburbs have not undergone great physical change. Like the myths about their creation, this partly reflects the paucity of attention that interwar suburbs have received ... the piecemeal changes that characterised suburbs have, when added up, often resulted in substantial change. (Whitehand and Carr, 1999)

Here, as these authors note, the market has been active for many years in spotting capacity and opportunity: not necessarily with very happy results, as handsome 1920s villas are replaced with dull five-storey apartment blocks in a sea of parking: but opportunities nonetheless.

In the other, less pressured, city-regions, the question is rather: could such interest be helped or accelerated rather than just waiting for it to turn up? The *Residential Futures* case study of Crumpsall in Manchester (Llewelyn Davies Yeang, 2007a) suggested a shopping-list of the sort of relatively low-cost measures which might be used to encourage activity, including landscape improvements to better link the area to its more sought-after neighbours, more prominence for the metro stop, quality upgrade to local shopping and targeted public realm works at key sites. The main Northern Way study report stressed that 'there are many inner urban areas, suburbs and tertiary former industrial towns in the north that could be transformed as attractive places to live and could accommodate sustainable housing growth...'. Recognizing that a change of emphasis towards releasing potential and attracting private investment interest (rather than just 'problem solving') would need direction and assistance, it proposed 'A "Next Generation Communities" initiative ... for the North of England to provide support for city-region local authority partners to realise the potential of untapped inner areas ... [with] similar characteristics to the New Growth Points initiative operating in the South and Midlands' (Urban Studio, 2009c).

A 2011–2012 initiative, 'Good to Grow', from the GLA and HCA, has some of these aims and characteristics, probably reflecting the very acute supply position in London and so the search for all sorts of opportunity.

Yes to this 'Lazy Asset' Question

Is there, then, a 'lazy development asset'? It certainly looks like it. The brief review here has suggested that supply potential could indeed exist. It is not going to be enormous, but it must be in the tens of thousands. Substantial enough, if released, to help take some of the pressure off new-build and newly-allocated locations as the only 'solution' to demand pressures. There may be an absence of such pressures in many parts of the country in the short-term, post boom and bust. But this should not obscure the need to seek out useful and creative ways of returning house-building to levels nearer to 200,000 new units per annum, sharply up from the post-crash reality of less than 100,000 annually.

Chapter 12

Are We Missing on *Community* Assets?

The fourth set of 'assets' questions relates to the communities who live in corporation suburbia. This is partly about what residents themselves feel is possible or desirable. It is also partly about the argument that corporation suburbia could 'look after itself' more: that is, if the estates had a more 'balanced' and self-selected population, they would be not only more economically but also more socially sustainable, and less dependent on external, public-sector support. After all, 'ordinary' (non-council-built) suburbs do not expect to have special local provision like community centres and so on laid on, do they? Is that part of what distinguishes the estates, perhaps unnecessarily?

The Idea of Community Assets

What might be the ingredients of the community assets that the cottage estates have or have not got? They include local people's own resources and organization, and the consequent ability to handle the challenges the areas face, and isolation – neighbourhoods may find it difficult to interact with other surrounding areas. There is also, potentially, the question of stability, commitment and churn in the households in the area.

And this may be related to attitudinal aspects like comparative levels of hope and self-confidence – as between areas where fewer than half the households have an employed member, and areas of fuller employment. Or could it simply be a question of household poverty, with poorer neighbourhoods needing more support and intervention because people just have not got the wherewithal to keep the area going without external support?

We need to be a bit careful about what our 'tests' are for community activity and organization. Peter Cowan, writing about suburban London in the 1970s, observed that 'it is as well to be aware that these suburbs are likely to be as varied as any other group in their social organization' (Cowan, 1973). Alison Ravetz's thoughtful review of 'Community on Council Estates' points out that the '…activities chosen by tenants and their associations were not always, however, what middle-class professionals had hoped'. So – 'It was natural for outside observers, not finding the kinds of cultural activity they thought valid, to conclude that estates had failed as communities'. And she quotes a 1974 study concluding that twenty-three out of thirty estates studied 'appeared to have a divided community or to lack community spirit'.

Her more sympathetic view is that there was in fact 'a lot of vitality in estate culture. It would for instance have been difficult to find a poorer and more derelict estate than Sheffield's Manor in the late 1980s...' but actually there was 'pigeon fancying, boxing, weightlifting, pool, CB radio, a touring drama group, and the 'Manor Militaires' with band and resplendent uniforms...' (Ravetz, 2001). CB radio, eh? Now there is a time-specific slice of instant nostalgia...

The data and research tell you, as might be expected, that the estates are not all the same, and that their potentials – and possibly capacities – vary, even quite locally. This may seem an obvious point. But what Ravetz calls the 'Bethnal Green' view of working-class life (because Young and Willmott's seminal study (1957, 2007) had seen that area as a one-class neighbourhood) has tended to lead to a conventional view of a unitary working-class with an in-built cohesive 'community'. And so explanations then needed to be sought for the apparent absence of this desirable attribute on real-life estates. Actually, 'a divided tenant population ... corresponded better to the Victorian notion of layered and plural working classes than to the twentieth-century concept of a single, unified "working class"' (Ravetz, 2001).

A lineal descendant of the Bethnal Green study, the Young Foundation, has collaborated with the Homes & Communities Agency and the Chartered Institute for Housing to try and define the case for investing in social sustainability. Mainly focusing on what is needed for new communities, it covers four main themes, summarized as:

♦ *Amenities and social infrastructure*: Social infrastructure and amenities are crucial to creating sustainable communities. Experience from the post-war New Towns to more recent new housing settlements has repeatedly shown that local services like schools, shops and public transport, are needed at an early stage in the life of new communities.

♦ *Social and cultural life*: Good relationships between residents and a range of local activities – formal and informal – are key to thriving communities.

♦ *Voice and influence*: Involving local communities in decisions that affect their lives throughout the stages of new developments is vital if public investment is to be effective.

♦ *Space to grow*: Adaptability is one of seven core objectives of urban design identified by CABE. If a new community is to be successful and sustainable, the place – the physical space, the amenities and the social infrastructure – needs to be able to adapt over time to new needs and new possibilities. (Future Communities, 2009)

This may look a bit like what an over-busy chief planner once described to the author as 'applehood and mother pie'. In fact the four-part structure then opens out into thoughtful and interesting advice on how to interrelate questions of physical design, say, with people's perceptions of an area, and its capacity to support their daily and community life. The site argues that:

There is an important role for agencies in providing support, especially in the early years, to work with local people to generate the social and cultural infrastructure that is essential for quality of life. If this does not happen, there is a danger that residents will feel alienated from their new homes, mental health problems increase, people do not invest for the long term and move away when they have the option to do so. (www.futurecommunities.net/socialdesign/social-and-cultural-life)

For the cottage estates covered here, this looks right, even though it is mainly aimed at new communities. They need places, structures and funding which enable them to work out their own ways of living as a community, and they do not always have them. Some of the estates are better designed than others, for example, to meet the needs for places to meet casually ('third places'), or for adaptability. Others, like Deckham Hall, benefit from supportive and 'listening' organizations that work in the direction of social sustainability; others do not.

A Sheffield Hallam University study for the Joseph Rowntree Foundation says of one of these aspects:

Public places such as local shops, pubs, cafés, clubs and community centres have been described as being 'third places' of social interaction after the home (first) and workplace (second). The research confirmed a range of third places as important and valued mediums for interaction in lower income neighbourhoods, with shops and markets emerging as most important. (Bashir *et al.*, 2011)

The team recognize that of course some people do not *want* to interact, so choose to avoid third places precisely for that reason. But they point out that generally, such places are seen by locals as a marker of their area's health; and that partly as a result of the recession, such public places for interaction are reduced in number and availability. A trend remarked on by their respondents, one of whom said: 'It's sad that there are no more little shops and cafes because there aren't enough places to socialise now'. They therefore make the explicit case that neighbourhoods which are on average poorer *do* need the support that better-off places do not: 'Policy and practice, especially in the context of regeneration, need to recognise the importance of the broader social and physical contextual attributes of neighbourhoods subject to intervention'.

Residents' responses and attitudes in this book's own case-study areas tend to support this. Deckham Hall, in Gateshead, for example, has no residents' association, despite Home Group having tried to set one up. On this fairly poor estate, it seems that local people's 'community' reflects the role of family connections as an essential part of the estate's appeal – responses will be issue-by-issue, often from regularly-outspoken tenants, but community organization is not a priority. In Tower Gardens, in contrast, with much more penetration of 'incomers' as a result of the Right-To-Buy, the local councillor saw the existence of a strong (though small) residents' group as evidence of commitment to the area, including by longer-standing residents. On the Becontree estate, the threshold of perceived usefulness of community organization seems to be reached only where there are management issues best dealt with en bloc: that is, in the flatted developments, not the main body of cottage housing. In the rest of the estate, people clearly do not think it is worth investing the effort: which may reflect lack of time or resources, and/or no perceived need, and/or an absence of much sense of local community at neighbourhood level – which was the explanation offered by a local resident. When Sheffield Hallam argue that estates which are on average poorer need more support than better-off places, they are not saying that *every* cottage estate needs special local provision like community centres and so on laid on. But they are pointing to the need to recognize that the availability of communities' own resources varies markedly, and requires area-specific response.

Community by Community Variation

The estate communities do, of course, vary a lot, and often over quite small geographies. There have been some attempts to map and analyse this. Research for the *Manchester Independent Economic Review* (MIER) looked at local area differences in quite a detailed and localized way (Amion/CUPS, 2010). It tried to sort out which of Greater Manchester's deprived areas were, in their terms, 'isolate', 'transit', 'escalator', or 'gentrifier' areas. Some of the neighbourhoods analysed are cottage estates, but many of course are not, being in the (often-poorer) inner city. Their study thus principally targets poverty-reduction strategies, rather than being place-focused and looking for opportunities. A look at the MIER study's information tends to confirm the fairly obvious point that the corporation suburbs are indeed not all the same; and the more interesting and important point is that some *may* be so badly stuck as to be 'isolate'. But it is unfortunately not possible to use their detailed mapping to draw conclusions which link differences in their data to differences in actual places on the ground, so it does not provide a ready route to understanding how neighbourhoods' reported variations relate to their success, popularity or otherwise.[1]

Fragility and Churn

Moving on from the question of variation, one can deal quickly with the idea that the communities of corporation suburbia are particularly characterized by 'churn', leading to problems of instability or community fragility. In fact, as remarked in an earlier chapter, 'this is not a significant variable either, nor one which particularly affects the estates of corporation suburbia' – a point underlined by Jones and Murie's observation that a common assumption about the Right-To-Buy, that it would act to *increase* stability, has not been borne out: '…resales have also not stabilized the more desirable neighbourhoods, especially where resales act as starter homes and form part of the segment of the housing market with the highest turnover' (Jones and Murie, 2005). Thus the cottage estates are in a sense only now approaching the levels of turnover seen in the wider market; so not many conclusions can be drawn about the relationships in these places between stability, churn and turnover.

What about the aspect of community strength or fragility in terms of the cottage estates' own resources, especially as they may be seen to be 'isolate'? The Sheffield Hallam research does shed considerable light on this. They remark that:

There is a tendency in policy discussion and academic debate about poverty-related behaviours and associated impacts to assume that people live spatially bounded (neighbourhood-based) lives. Lower income neighbourhoods can be portrayed as spaces of difference, where internally cohesive and segregated communities nurture dispositions and behaviours that deviate from wider social and cultural norms. (Bashir *et al.*, 2011)

A related SHU report connects this to the 'broken Britain' idea 'implying that residentially segregated and economically deprived communities were by definition socially isolated; these places were therefore problematised for nurturing cultures and associated behaviours at odds with the dominant moral order' (Batty *et al.*, 2011).

Their studies, though, did not support any idea of dramatic difference or isolation: 'The spatial routines of daily life among interviewees … in the vast majority of cases … extended beyond the local neighbourhood on a regular and frequent (often daily) basis. This is a simple but important finding because it challenges the assumption that people in deprived neighbourhoods follow tightly bounded spatial routines rooted in their immediate locality' (Bashir *et al.*, 2011). So 'The idea of a gap between "broken" and (presumably) "cohesive" communities that has underpinned some policy rhetoric in recent years found little echo in the accounts given by respondents in our research' (Batty *et al.*, 2011).

Neighbourhood, as seen in Chapter 8, often mattered most to people where both the economic legacy and the future prospects were least favourable. So 'deprived neighbourhoods can be home to sets of relationships that constitute a resource pool from which people can draw support and that help them to "get by" in the face of disadvantage and inequality' (Bashir *et al.*, 2011).

But this does not mean they are all ready to join tap classes or stand for the parish council (or, in the words of a Becontree respondent, '*bake cakes and go to community do's*'). The Sheffield Hallam team observe that:

Many of the problems facing households in our case studies were rooted in the consequences of economic restructuring rather than some form of cultural malaise, and the challenges of getting by on a daily basis were often quite a sufficient test of their resourcefulness … the assumption that there is a considerable latent commitment to 'help out' just waiting to be ignited would seem to be wide of the mark. (Batty *et al.*, 2011)

The stories in Chapter 5 from Birmingham's Bromford estate emphasize how a local informal network of family and friends is what characterizes the local 'community' there (even if the 'Bromford Pride' video's brother and sister could not agree if there *was* a community). The ward councillor pointed out how residents had actually come together on a couple of occasions, about the 'Comet Park' and about the tower blocks, but also commented how fragile the process was and how quickly people could become disheartened by knock-backs like damage to the newly-installed park equipment. The 'visible' community activity in Bromford seems to rely on a very small core of committed folk, some of them (extremely un-in-yer-face) Christians, doing very specific locally-targeted projects.

There is real concern over the impact of 'austerity'-induced cuts. A Gateshead councillor has in his 17 years on the Council seen vast improvement, but saw a real danger of losing it: Neighbourhood Wardens going, CPSOs removed by police funding cuts, worries about the elderly centre which is a real focus for the community: *'it all threatens what's been put in place and what residents asked for'*.

The limited nature of the resource seems to be the reality in Tower Gardens too. There is a SureStart (well, there is at the time of writing). There is a rather besieged-looking community centre in Tower Gardens Park, where the residents group meets, the ward councillor holds monthly surgeries, and Haringey run some park activities. So this largely working-class, not desperately deprived, neighbourhood is getting some 'external' support, is not making unusually high demands on public services, and has a degree of local organization. But any idea that it might have the capacity to take on a greater role in shaping its own destiny seems pretty unlikely.

Figure 12.1. An Edwardian SureStart...

Figure 12.2. ... and a target-hardened community centre.

The neighbourhoods studied by Sheffield Hallam were all very deprived, and they are not all cottage estates. Still, their conclusions seem to suggest that it is unlikely that corporation suburbs are notably socially isolated or short of the 'asset' of community resources and effort. But it also looks as though, to the extent that they are on average somewhat poorer than equivalent non-council-built areas, they may have that much less available time and energy for any activity which is not part of 'getting by'.

'Lazy Community Assets'? – Probably Not

So, are there 'lazy community assets', in any sense? Not really: perceived issues such as isolation or high levels of churn turn out not to be particularly important, and communities' own resources do generally exist, albeit with no spare 'capacity'. This suggests that if policy did seek to release the cottage estates' potential in terms of housing, economics and land development, many of the resident communities could need careful support through any such change process.

At the same time, there is one sense in which potential might exist, untapped. This is the question, in an era of 'Localism' and 'Neighbourhood Planning', of whether communities can play more of a part than hitherto in managing and changing their own affairs at estate level. Chapter 13 considers 'Who might do these things?' in dealing with the possible actions which could help release the potentials of these suburbs.

Note

1.   For the limitations of the MIER mapping see the MIER website, for example at www.manchester-review.org.uk/projects/view/id?id=723. A close look at the results for, as an example, the west side of Wigan (Pemberton, Norley Hall, Worsley Mesnes, etc) shows distinctions between small 'isolate', 'escalator' and 'gentrifier' areas which have no reflection on the ground and which lead nowhere in terms of possible conclusions or responses.

Chapter 13

The Potentials, and the Things We Might Do

It seems, then, that there *are* assets here waiting to be unlocked. The key argument, though, is not only that they exist. It is also that there are things that can be done to unlock them – and that many of them are relatively straightforward and reasonably low-cost.

However, they have to be placed in the context of strong external factors at work as well. Bramley and his colleagues remark, about areas' relative performance, that 'despite the extreme differences between areas, certain types of factors dominate the explanation – the wider economy and labour market, regional market dynamics, poverty, and local market dynamics' (Bramley *et al.*, 2007). So none of the suggestions here are the magic wand to transform estate after estate.

What, nonetheless, might be tried? In Chapter 6 it was argued that 'We can make much more of the asset represented by the cottage estates via initiatives which are rather more low-key: the sort of "TLC" measures suggested in the *Residential Futures* studies: local upgrading, small targeted grants to improve the quality of neighbourhood facilities, work on image and stigma, employment access, infill housing, and so on, each package specific to each estate's needs and potential'. And earlier, in Chapter 11, mention was made of four themes from the Crumpsall (Manchester) *Residential Futures* case study which aimed to capitalize on specific features of the area and use them to help make the locality more attractive.

Although each estate's needs are different, one can still list out some of the kinds of thing that could make a difference. This draws on the *Residential Futures* city-region case studies already quoted.

Action in the Local Centres

The local centres first: for some areas, a high priority is to 'lift' the local shopping experience. Not just for functional reasons, but because the initial impression it gives to anyone who might be thinking about moving into the area can be very positive – or terminal. The *Residential Futures* team's shorthand for this was the 'Costa grant': trying to induce a national brand into your area… So that study's case study in Hylton Castle (Sunderland) suggested a redesign of the local centre, its feeble 'square' of amenity space and the parking. But as the Bricknell (Hull) case-study stressed, it is only worth doing this if the centre is *visible* – one of the problems for on-estate parades all over the country is that they are buried within the housing, known only to nearby residents, bereft of passing trade.

Visibility and 'Gateways'

And that relates to the general issue of the ways that the estates announce themselves to the world. 'Gateways' are of course beloved of, and overrated by, urban designers. But an attractive entry point – one *Residential Futures* example of a missed opportunity being the Crumpsall metro stop, discreet to a fault – or a well-designed series of façades to the main road can act as a marker for an area that looks successful and interesting, rather than dull and apologetic. In Crumpsall, too, another 'gateway' issue was the failure of an area of open space to link the locality to neighbouring areas which are more sought-after and whose success ought to be replicable by ease of connection and so familiarity.

The Open Space Asset

It has been shown that this is an issue almost everywhere in corporation suburbia. Chapter 11 pointed out how much of Castletown/Hylton Castle (Sunderland) is public open space, and how indeterminate a lot of it is. Here, and in Kirkholt (Rochdale), Mereside (Blackpool) or Becontree (London), the potential is to get quality rather than quantity out of the open areas, to get some of the land thereby released into use as housing (and maybe for new sports centres, if needed) – in development which frames the parkland attractively and gives it safety through overlooking.

Movement and the Public Realm

Many of the estates, because of when they were developed, need a rethink of how people get about. In Hylton Castle, a car-dominated road system needs to be made more pedestrian-friendly, including on the main roads, if it is to be safe and attractive in daily use. For Kirkholt, the studies recommended a clearer hierarchy of streets and spaces: to help way-finding, to give more identity to individual parts of the estate, and to improve the relationship between the roads, paths and the open spaces used as routes. Smaller pieces of the 'public realm', too (corner plots, space outside shops, etc), all need attention. This should be done in a targeted way, in places where it can work in step with other actions to make a real difference. Some of this starts, inevitably, to creep from 'low-cost' to 'medium-cost', and will be competing with many other priorities for investment.

New Development – Of Quality

It is not just that there is a lot of development potential in poorly used open space, and that change can help with visibility and area presentation. It is also vital that new development is of good quality, not 'anything'll do here': because the whole purpose is to raise expectations and attract people to choose the estates. It is important too that new schemes act as linkage not blockage. There is a real danger that where developers are twitchy about surrounding areas, their housing development schemes will be designed in ways which cut off through routes, even on foot: so people who do not live on the new scheme itself cannot use its streets as part of a wider street network offering 'normal' easy access along and through the whole area.

'Soft' Measures

So far, these are all about physical change. There is also a raft of things to do that are not: so-called 'soft' actions. Much of this is about image, not surprisingly given the importance of the stigma issue (Chapter 8). The *Residential Futures* Sunderland case-study report pointed out that 'often it is the stigmatisation of these localities that can be the hardest aspect to address. The role of place-branding initiatives to sell a story of change is an important one … a crucial soft measure to bring marginalized communities back into the mainstream' (Urban Studio, 2009*b*)

Re-branding is well-established as a tool in major high-spend regeneration schemes, and indeed is almost a stereotype as high-rise estates regularly reappear as 'villages'. But for the less-problematic cottage estates, thinking about this aspect is less familiar, though just as necessary in many cases. As the Northern Way's Bricknell and Kirkholt case studies noted, this should include the issue of internal differentiation, between the separate sub-areas of what are sometimes rather monotone and endless-seeming estates.

Urban Management

There are many other non-physical aspects that need thought: starting with the basic issue of urban management. Chapter 8 outlined some of the issues facing the Manchester estate of Wythenshawe. In his *Cities of Tomorrow*, Sir Peter Hall comments that 'Manchester has not dealt kindly with its masterpiece… The place looks down-at-heel in that distinctively English way, as if the city has given up on it' (Hall, 2002). And Doreen Massey, who grew up there, is quoted as writing 'perceptively of how "that open spaciousness of the fresh air can be closed down in a myriad of daily ways" – the cracked kerbstone, the vandalized bowling green, the security grill on the *kitchen window*' (Hebbert and Hopkins, 2012). These may seem to be commonplace observations – but they point the finger at the need for constant attention and care, not just assuming that places will look after themselves. They will not.

A strong impression from Chapter 4's north-eastern case studies in particular is that the social housing landlords in Gateshead and Sunderland *do* get this. Whether 'arm's length' council, long-established housing association or expanding non-profit group, all three regard their role as wider than just running their own stock – they are engaged in neighbourhood management in a variety of ways. And this is true even in localities where a lot of houses have been sold under the Right-To-Buy. In contrast, the visitor to the giant Becontree estate can easily come away with the impression that the local council's agenda has *not* really caught up with this potential and need.

The Leader of Sunderland Council argued, though, that while it may be true that councils are less single-issue-focused on the housing than RSLs or ALMOs, that is because you *cannot* just limit the aim to 'making the estate nice' and forget about social aspects: there is a social care job to do, and the councils have to do it. This is a really difficult equilibrium to reach, but it ought not to be impossible to balance the two requirements.

The Northern Way case studies also mention other 'soft' issues: better linkage to employment, training and education; the private rented sector; and 'town-centre-management' type initiatives with local traders. Of course finance will be a serious constraint on many of them. What is needed, though, are two things: first, for the initiatives that there are to take on the corporation-suburbia dimension, and not just always focus on 'worst first'. And second, for British local government to deliver, and be expected to deliver, and be financed to deliver, the standard of urban management care that is provided across the rest of Western Europe, from Lapland to Lanzarote.

Who might do these Things?

The earlier discussion of 'community' potential raised the possibility that, in a climate at least notionally favourable to Localism and Neighbourhood Planning, the residents themselves might play more of a role in shaping their estates. Alison Ravetz's perhaps optimistic take on this, a decade ago, was 'it may be both possible and legitimate to recapture some of the early idealism that inspired council housing...' (Ravetz, 2001) – by a fusion of strands such as tenant participation, communitarianism, co-operatives and community professionals working *with* residents rather than *on* them.

Interestingly, though, her most vivid example is Hulme. As she says, its unique history and large scale meant that it might well not offer a pattern that many estates across the country could follow: 'Hulme mattered to its authority... No culture mix like Hulme's was likely to be found anywhere else, unless perhaps parts of central London ... [there was] a dogged working-class population with a long memory ... [with] an impressive capacity for self-improvement'. She describes a 'rich mix of traditional tenants' cheek and outrageous creativity, with much imaginative support from the housing associations and the Rowntree Foundation...' (Ravetz, 2001).

Chapter 12, in considering the likelihood of residents getting involved in local organization, sounded a note of caution – people are busy, pressed, short of money and time. Attempts to set up residents' associations and so on have often floundered. Yet with sympathetic leadership and support, as in the Home Group's Neighbourhood Management Initiative in Deckham, it is possible to see how landlords and councils might respond to the inherent potential of, and pride in, neighbourhood and place.

Obviously a crucial element has to be, and was in Hulme, the sustained commitment of the local authority. This needs stressing. It needs stressing in Britain in particular:

a country where the democratically-elected and properly-funded municipality has for many years been regarded, it seems, as a luxury a poor struggling nation cannot afford. So the local leadership role that is taken for granted in French or German cities now has to be argued for – or regarded as a wonder when, as in Manchester under council leader Leese and chief executive Bernstein, co-ordinated and effective political leadership and executive action actually happen.

The estate communities could very likely be much more involved, and on many of them that potential may indeed be there. But they need the 'Corpo' to be there alongside them, and to be resourced accordingly.

OK, That's 'Things': But What about People?
The Issues of 'Gentrification' and Housing for the Poor

But if you *do* these things and they work, is this always a 'gentrification' agenda? Or perhaps only in the South? This is a fraught topic, and this is not an attempt to write a sociology text. But trying to trigger or accelerate, or direct, social change is bound to raise questions of this kind.

And it does not necessarily have to mean gentrification in the London 'middle-class invasion of dear little terraces' sense. The MIER study quoted earlier uses the term 'gentrifying area' rather differently from this common usage, more like a term for a statistically-observed 'move from richer to poorer area', and largely as a category within the deprived neighbourhoods only (Amion/CUPS, 2010). This is quite like the moves described in Chapter 7, where Jones and Murie's work was used to show who actually *has* been buying, and what 'place in the market' some of the cottage estates are now finding (Jones and Murie, 2005). It is sometimes 'incomers', but they are not necessarily very different from many of the people already on the estates.

And on some, possibly many, of the cottage estates 'gentrification' – however defined – is a pretty remote prospect. In Gateshead's Deckham Hall, for example, with its tight street layout and rather stark houses, and the range of other places which would attract incomers long before it did, the agenda is far more about careful work to avoid the downward spiral, not worries over pressure from outside.

Anyway, what is of interest is as much or more what (to stick with the amateur sociology) one can call 'embourgeoisement'. That is, change in terms of those who are already there. Yes, we want the cottage estates to be as attractive to outsiders, and as little stigmatized as their non-council-built equivalents. But even more, we want the young employed couples who are growing up on these estates, and then leaving them, to stay. This is how the 15 per cent gap in the employment rate, highlighted in chapter 10, is most likely to be closed.

Glen Bramley and colleagues home in how complex this is, and how carefully each area's conditions will need to be considered, in what they call:

a much bigger dilemma for local housing policies. Much of the thrust of policies, notably in HMR areas, is to make areas 'better'. In housing market terms, that means making them more attractive and more valued by the market, i.e. raising house prices. But sooner or later that runs up against the other overarching aim of housing policy, which is to promote housing affordability. It is a difficult balancing act to achieve both of these things simultaneously. In different areas and time periods, the priority may be more towards one than the other. (Bramley *et al.*, 2007)

What this then takes us on to is the question of 'where *do* the poor live, then?' (if there are going to be fewer poor, unemployed, older households on these estates as is suggested above). The ideal answer would presumably 'look where they live in Holland':

those that live in social housing are older, live in smaller households, have lower incomes, are less likely to be in employment…' [etc] … [but] Most neighbourhoods in the country are fairly mixed, although in areas with a lot of social housing the lower middle class often predominates. There is no stigma attached to living in social housing, unlike in some other western countries… (Elsinga and Wassenberg, 2007)

Rents are controlled (in both sectors) though moving slowly towards deregulation, with about 21 per cent of social tenants on benefit. So the answer for the Netherlands seems to be: 'everywhere, with their rent covered'.

In Britain, it hardly needs saying that we are very far from this answer, given the combination of welfare reforms/caps with the critical need for more housing in total and more subsidized housing in particular. In the longer term, as argued above, the capacity in corporation suburbia can be a part of a package contributing more housing. And that capacity is more likely to be released if the estates' attractiveness increases, with some population changes. But in the immediate future, and irrespective of what happens on the cottage estates, the British answer to the question will increasingly be: 'in the private rented sector, in very overcrowded conditions'.

Releasing Potential

The last part of Chapter 6 argued that the cottage estates offer a potential release of value through what can often be quite low-cost investment. So which assets *are* in any sense 'lazy', with prospects of such release?

Housing? Yes, but only in the sense that the estates of corporation suburbia are not wanted enough, not sufficiently 'places of choice', mainly because of stigma. Not in the sense of under-occupancy, empty stock, or household composition.

Economic? Yes, there are fewer working families than there need to or could be, in well-located homes and places that could suit them (i.e. have the attributes they want, but which they currently seek elsewhere); this is potentially less efficient in labour market terms than it could be.

Development? Yes, there is substantial unreleased housing capacity: a specific form of the urban capacity which the Urban Task Force identified and for whose release it urged policy shifts (Urban Task Force, 1999).

Community? No, little spare 'capacity'. These estates are not notably socially-isolated, the churn is not high, and there is considerable community resource there – but what they have tends to be needed just to 'get by', and is not available to substitute for public-sector support. Any programme aimed at releasing the housing, economic and development capacities of the cottage estates would need to be accompanied by support that engaged with that existing capacity and augmented it through the change period.

Things to do? Yes, there are things that can be done to unlock the potential – many of them relatively straightforward and reasonably low-cost. A mixture of physical and 'soft' measures could focus on turning more of the estates into the 'locations of choice' they have the potential to be.

People to do them? – Yes, potentially, but it will need a place-by-place alliance of residents, their council and key landlords to agree what to do, why and how.

So there *is* potential; it *is* worth releasing it; and given the right intelligent and locally-targeted tactics for each locality, corporation suburbia could again become the place of choice in the 'garden city' dream.

Chapter 14

The Corporation Suburbs
in the Twenty-First Century

Looking Forward

This final chapter takes a look at what the future might or could hold for the corporation suburbs. This could be seen as impossibly ambitious. Housing policies and markets in the UK are a shambles; and they have been for years, it is not just a problem of the post-2007 bust. Current policies are if anything set to make things worse (Leather *et al.*, 2012; Housing Justice, 2012; Fitzpatrick *et al.*, 2012).

So it is with extreme diffidence that one suggests anything. However, starting with reflections from the places themselves, it is possible to identify some 'threats' and some 'potentials' for the future of these estates. And to conclude with the positive case for a rediscovery and celebration of what we have inherited.

Lessons from the Places?

Looking at the cottage estates themselves has thrown up quite a few clues about the potential and the threats. Tottenham's Tower Gardens, for example, shows the importance of distinctiveness – its houses and its layout differentiate it from its close neighbours in the rest of the Roundway estate, and a virtuous circle of conservation and resident commitment seems to be defining it as a place of choice.

The Right-To-Buy can be seen to work in a similar way – localities emerging as areas of choice – on quite a few estates, and at least some of the time: as we saw in Becontree and Gateshead, where small clusters may be gelling as groups of established and popular market homes. But Becontree also shows one of the possible threats which RTB has unlocked: in other patches, some of its streets seem to be tipping into an unstable and uncared-for niche dominated by private renting, where area disadvantage could actually be on the rise again.

Another of the lessons is about the possibilities, and limitations, of physical intervention. A thoughtful consideration of possible lessons from the garden city movement observes that:

It is tempting to look at somewhere like Letchworth or Hampstead Garden Suburb which remain popular and to believe that our problems would be less if only all housing were built like this. Yet

Wythenshawe is almost identical in design ... and this classic Parker-designed Manchester garden suburb is nonetheless poor and sometimes problematic. (Rudlin and Falk, 2009)

And it *is* easy to go round and think of 'stuff to do' to each of the estates examined. Indeed earlier chapters have suggested quite a lot of possible actions which might be seen as generic solutions to shared problems or opportunities. However, each one needs its own package, based on its own conditions. Birmingham's Bromford shows this: it is a 'Radburn' layout, and it does have problems to do with that form – the rear access courts, safety on foot and at night, and so on. The Llewelyn-Davies study mentioned in Chapter 5 suggests a menu of interventions, some quite drastic. Some young urban designers, who regard Radburn as the spawn of the devil, might be tempted to sweep it all away. That might be right on some Radburn estates. Yet in Bromford one of the mature central pedestrian avenues is a real success, and the actions needed are surely more about capitalizing on that, to add other elements which would secure the Bromford that we have, as a popular location for working families with choice.

As noted in Chapter 6, the size of the houses is another factor that will affect estates differently. Places like Gateshead's Deckham Hall, with its generally smaller homes, and the streets in Becontree which are mainly two-bedroom houses will appeal less nowadays to families (as well as to the private-rented sector).

Looking at several of the estates also illustrates the 'land asset' potential. Hylton Castle in Sunderland and Kirkholt in Rochdale, for example, look like they have useful land reserves, and as though they could benefit from having them intelligently developed. Again though, each estate is different, and so is its market context. Bromford has a lot of sites, but serious constraints. Some authorities in the South have been tempted to fill every small 'spare' plot with a new house; but it is important to be careful as well as positive, not just adding anything anywhere. Some in the North might regard in-estate land as too difficult, and release new greenfield sites for another round of housing: they need to take a more rounded view too.

Each estate is therefore facing its own questions. But there are nonetheless some shared potentials and common threats that can be identified, and they tend to need thought and response at national as well as local level.

Threats?

Long-Term Threat No. 1 – in the North

The possible threat in the North is the danger of a return to 'low demand' or even abandonment. Nationally, government policy is for a lot more housing to be built, assisted by the package of incentives like New Homes Bonus and deregulation via the Planning Framework and Localism Act. The main target is clearly the high-pressure southern half of the country. Yet it is possible that this will have only limited impact in the South East because of resident resistance: whether you call it Nimbyism or a sense that yet more development will just add another twist to the cycle of pressure.

But it will have much more effect in other areas – where ironically the overall market is much slacker, and the development pressure ought to be less.

In those conditions, given a lot of new supply in fairly flat demand conditions, there is a danger that some of the cottage estates in the North and Midlands (even quite reasonable ones) will start to shed earners and owner-occupiers again; and/or start dropping into the bottom end of the private-rented sector. It is after all only a decade since cottage estates like Walker in Newcastle or the Old Fold in Gateshead, in the low-powered Tyneside housing market, were running at 30 per cent voids and undergoing piecemeal demolitions.

At present, all the housing markets, in all three main tenures, are tight, with few areas anywhere experiencing any slackness on the demand side. However, as markets creep back to more like 'normal' conditions over the next few years, such low-demand symptoms could restart, and completely reverse some of the positive trends identified in earlier chapters, in at least some of the non-South-East regions. This is not just a locality-by-locality problem, or a regional one: a serious worry would be that, as in for example Liverpool's Norris Green (see Chapter 8), area failure and its costs will come back to haunt future governments as they did before.

Long-Term Threat No. 2 – in the South

In contrast, the threat in the South could be not 'too little' but 'too much' demand. It could lead to the end of these estates' role as (almost the only) affordable housing in the 100-kilometre radius London regional hinterland. Different trajectories, roles and issues will apply across this enormous and varied southern territory, and the speed of the effects could also vary a lot. Nonetheless, even in the case of Becontree (Chapter 3's 'type' for the huge inter-war estates, but set within an always-pressured regional market), the expectation could be that over time less and less of it will be available as affordable and social housing.

An eventual complete merge into its surroundings would then be restrained, as in the example of Debden (again, Chapter 8), only by residual stigma. Over the long term, in the London-region market at least, even 'real' gentrification, with the 'discovery' of such areas by incoming middle-class households rationalizing their economic choices with cultural references and justification, is not inconceivable. The model in that case would be Barnsbury – which after all was poor Irish private-rented inner-city not much more than a generation ago; now the same plain but handsome Georgian and early Victorian terraces are, or have been, home to barristers, bankers and Tony Blair. Even without such an extreme switch, the South's corporation suburbia could quite soon have little or no role as cheap and starter housing. There would be less and less social mix, no damper on the increasing polarization, and no economic role of the kind suggested in earlier chapters as stable places for working families on modest incomes.

Potentials?

This final chapter has begun with two 'threats', and those threats are undoubtedly serious concerns for the future of the cottage estates in both the North and South. But this book has repeatedly stressed the need to also look at the *potential*: to take off the 'problem-shaped glasses', for a while at least, and to try to understand what we can release in corporation suburbia if we take a positive and locally-focused perspective. The potentials outlined here draw on the evidence from the case-study estates, on the thinking in the *Residential Futures* studies, on the experience of skilled social landlords across the country, and on things we can learn from our European neighbours. They cover issues like greater housing mix; the need for 'TLC' on estates which have tended to be taken for granted; the possible contribution to the stock of new homes; and a 'celebration' of the positives, coupled with realism about tackling real-life problems. There is a lot here, and it is an exciting agenda for change.

Potential No. 1: Mix

On the positive side, the estates *could* offer potentially greater social mix and stability. One idea, for example, would be to vary the application of the Right-To-Buy. It could be ended, selectively, in areas which have partly gone upmarket. This, coupled with other measures, could help to achieve the aim discussed in the Hills report of countering the polarization between areas, regions and neighbourhoods which has been created by the UK's particular combination of market effects, social attitudes and local geography.

Hills, quoting Nye Bevan's lyrical vision of '...the lovely feature of the English and Welsh village, where the doctor, the grocer, the butcher and the farm labourer all lived in the same street ... the living tapestry of a mixed community', argues that '... in the current state of English social housing ... the market may operate in a way that leads to sharp area segregation and polarization, and to the emergence of low-income ghettoes...'. He stresses '...the *potential* for breaking the strength of the links between household incomes and location, in a way that could make it much easier to sustain mixed-income neighbourhoods than systems relying exclusively on market provision' (Hills, 2007). In the cottage estates at least, some of the ingredients are already there to make this work: we are not starting from scratch.

The Rowntree study by Glen Bramley and colleagues, already referred to, also includes a discussion of social mix:

Poverty emerges as being very important for the market status of neighbourhoods ... the big question is how to change the poverty status of neighbourhoods. The evidence shows that changing the housing supply can make a difference, with more owner occupation reducing poverty in a neighbourhood and more social renting increasing it. This provides support for notions of tenure mix and mixed communities... (Bramley *et al.*, 2007)

Obviously defining 'mix' (of tenure? social class? employment status? etc) is not straightforward. Managing the balance would be a complex process, and a different one in each locality. The tools deployed would vary from place to place.

Mention has been made of the use of selective Right-To-Buy as one tool (though current attempts to sell off even more of the stock will clearly make this more difficult). At the other end of the spectrum, where the aim is less to restrain the market trend than encourage it, is the sort of 'mixing' strategy deployed in its most hands-on way by the Joseph Rowntree Housing Trust, with their SAVE (Selling Alternate Vacants on Estates) programme, selling alternate vacant properties on the open market (with the proceeds reinvested in replacement property). Their view is that the benefits associated with mixed tenure justify the sales. Rowntree are far from the only landlord to apply some form of thinking like this – a study for their Foundation reports that 'over 70 per cent of a sample of social landlords have taken some initiative to "rebalance the communities" on their single-tenure estates by introducing a mix of tenures and incomes (other than occurs through the "Right to Buy")' (Martin and Watkinson, 2003). The same research found, consistently, overall improvement in property prices, reduced turnover, increased demand, tenant satisfaction and improved area reputation, associated with the mixing.

A third tactic is landlords' actual allocations policies for their rental properties – the 'who' of housing, adjusted to try and avoid over-concentration of households with no-one in employment, aiming to close the '15 per cent employment gap' discussed in Chapter 10. This no doubt has overtones, for some, of the pre-war policies whereby only the respectable working class got the new homes. On the cottage estates now, though, the results of historic allocations policies completely dominated by 'need', however defined, have helped to contribute to residualization and area disadvantage: they should be at least reviewed and probably often altered. Changing this balance is bound to be difficult, especially now when key elements of the national 'housing settlement' are being eroded by welfare reform (Fitzpatrick *et al.*, 2012); however it is a real issue for the future of the cottage estates and indeed social housing more generally.

A fourth, and positive, sort of measure – and an attractive one because it can be locally based and incremental – is mortgage support for on-estate buyers. It can be illustrated by an example in Darlington, in the North East. Here the Fabrick social landlord group is working with the (still mutual) Darlington Building Society to provide some of its tenants who want to buy with the means of doing so: again, carefully encouraging tenure mix and building on people's neighbourhood commitment. This is an initiative which seems like a small-scale British version of the pattern, much more common in northern Europe, where local institutions combine to provide locally-relevant solutions for local people.

If this all looks like a plea for micro-managed social engineering, the answer is perhaps twofold: first, that not doing anything except apply unsympathetic national policies, and letting the market do your social engineering for you, is a (non-)policy too; and second, that the position which the estates of corporation suburbia are now in means that they can respond well to carefully-planned local initiatives, informed by excellent local knowledge: see the examples from estates in the North East, in Chapter 4.

Nor are these suggestions blind to the realities of class in the UK, or to what the academic sociologists call 'path dependency' and 'segregation theory' – meaning that most people prefer to live near people who are like them (Lee and Liu, 2009). What *should* be possible, though, is intelligent use of tools and interventions to keep places as balanced as they reasonably can be, to meet the Hills aims of less polarization, diminishing stigma, and de-concentration of location-specific poverty.

Potential No. 2: Integration and TLC

Integrating the outer estates economically, improving them and caring for them, so that they are places that working families can and will choose (and stay in): this is at the heart of the argument for the 'rediscovery' of corporation suburbia. The measures outlined at the end of Chapter 13 above fit well with the further conclusions of the Bramley/JRF work: 'Local practitioner perspectives are broadly consistent with the statistical analysis... Common themes include the importance of environment/quality of life, of status/reputation, and of access to opportunities...' (Bramley *et al.*, 2007).

Identifying which local shopping centres have potential – they do not all – and 'lifting' them; reshaping parks and open space to get quality rather than just quantity; new development on spare land, and work to improve areas' images. There is a menu of actions here that can help to move more of the cottage estates towards becoming the attractive neighbourhoods that the best of them already are.

This is a menu that need not break the bank. Unlike the major regeneration initiatives, these measures can be done gradually, affordably, and in step with private investment.

It should also be in step with careful management of the neighbourhood and the environment. Chapter 4 remarked on how, in Gateshead and Sunderland, the social landlords clearly see their role as wider than just their own houses and tenants. In the case of Home Group, they have a specific dedicated Neighbourhood Management operation for Deckham Hall, very hands-on and quite impressive. Not all areas will require this intensity, and not all landlords will be able to afford it. Still, the case studies do argue strongly for a 'manage, manage, manage' approach to caring for the whole place – which, in different ways, the people at Home Group, Gateshead Housing and Gentoo Sunderland all apply.

Two places reviewed – Bromford and Becontree – seem to have lacked this sort of dynamic. Their streets and housing were described in earlier chapters as looking somewhat 'tired'. It may be a coincidence that they are both run by council housing departments. But it may not. We do need the local authorities to be very strongly involved and proactive. Yet we also seem to need the focus of a dedicated 'housing operator'. It could be that the 'ALMO' (arm's-length management organization) model provides this within some sort of democratically accountable framework. But as a Birmingham city staffer pointed out, their tenants had the opportunity to vote for an ALMO, and did not: they may moan, but they appear to trust the council that much at least.

It might perhaps be argued that this runs counter to the critique at the start of Chapter 12, which suggests that the cottage estates might do more to 'look after themselves' if they are to become more like the rest of suburbia. The answer, though, is that given where corporation suburbia is now at, after some three decades of residualization and neglect, the *laisser-faire* of private suburbia will not yet do. Other than in a few locations, 'hands-on' is still needed, with coherent locally specific responses and knowledge.

Potential No. 3: New Homes

Building new housing, of the right kind, is also an important opportunity. These 'garden city' estates are often already examples of good British urban design. Applying 'what works' lessons can include encouraging intelligent 'infill' and building twenty-first century versions of the original idea within the existing grain: there is no reason why new housing could not be built in these areas, which are generally quite 'loose' in form. The tenure balance would need to be worked out place by place. In some areas, it might be preferable to build only for the owner-occupier and private-rented markets; in others, RSLs might also be encouraged to build more good-quality low-cost social housing as well.

As to their design and layout: let us not get carried away by theory. Let us look at targeting what worked and what did not work on cottage estates over the years. A shorthand version is provided by Alison Ravetz:

Larger estates were in general less popular than smaller ones, especially when the latter were located near existing centres used by a range of social classes... Most popular of all were the 'miscellaneous properties' acquired piecemeal, and also the postwar 'prefabs' typically clustered on small blitzed sites... It is easy to account for the popularity of houses that were part of the ordinary street scene, or small infillings that blended into their surroundings. 'People liked living in an ordinary house on an ordinary street'. (Ravetz, 2001)

Potential No. 4: New Homes in the Right Places

As well as more new homes, and well-designed ones, we need them to be intelligently located – and capable of being delivered. The Birmingham study referred to in Chapter 2 draws lessons from that city's experience to argue that 'Urban extensions, not new settlements, are the way forward' and that 'There are other housing models apart from statism and *laissez-faire*'. The nature of Birmingham's economy was such that:

Creating small-sized new settlements away from the city would have destroyed some of its qualities. The solution was to create garden suburbs – what might be called 'sustainable urban extensions' by practitioners today. They would be close to infrastructure running out of the city - tramlines - as well as sources of employment. Then, as now, and has been demonstrated by studies of continental exemplars, [this] is the most sustainable and obvious way to allow cities to continue to grow economically, while providing high-quality housing. (Neale, 2012)

Persuasive, if not completely proven. Probably not the same answer everywhere, anyway. As to the business of actually getting them *built*: Neale's argument is that endless debates about market versus state-led miss the point:

The Birmingham example demonstrates that there are other solutions which combine public and private… Plans specifying road lines, and minimum qualities for housing can regulate land values and ensure a minimum standard for privately provided housing. Limited municipal land purchase, and the use of covenants, can help promote competition among developers. (Neale, 2012)

The mechanisms can vary (Bournville was long-term landownership, Harborne was a co-operative venture), and so can the extent of involvement of public sector leadership and funding.

Potential No. 5: Hearts and Minds

Hearts and minds: this is about rediscovering and celebrating the cottage estates and corporation suburbia; and about making them both better performing and better perceived. In the second half of the twentieth century, Victorian terraces went from being a pitiful blot on the landscape to the height of urban chic. By-pass semis, once the nadir of lower-bourgeois ghastliness, have been elevated by books like *Dunroamin* (Oliver *et al.*, 1981) to an appreciation of what Paul Barker calls 'The Freedoms of Suburbia' (Barker, 2009). Rediscovery is possible and, surely, necessary. Chapter 8, drawing heavily on Annette Hastings's work, showed both how persistent is the stigmatization of the estates, and how it ought to be possible to target some at least of the explicit ways in which this stigma is transmitted (property trade, local media, police, etc.).

Undoing years of stigma will need clarity of thought about what the situation is on each estate. Places that were predominantly social housing but are not now; places that still are; places in either category that have or have not got real-life problems of ASB, neighbour problems, acute poverty, high benefit-dependency… Each requires a slightly different approach to changing people's 'hearts and minds'. For all of them, though, there is the underlying John Hills's point about our British estate experience: a product of place being so closely aligned with tenure, and tenure with poverty (Hills, 2007).

A concerted – though rather conventional – attempt in this direction can be seen on the massive Wythenshawe estate in south Manchester. A PR initiative by a partnership including the city council, a developer and two housing trusts runs a website dedicated, since 2008, to shifting the area's downbeat image.

We listened to the local community – the people who live and work here. We also talked to people living in the surrounding areas. It soon became clear that the image people outside Wythenshawe have is often untrue or at very best 10 years out of date. But the people who live here are proud of Wythenshawe – it is a good place to live. It is important that we take control of image and tell people the real story of Wythenshawe. Quite simply people should see much more of what is the

'Real Wythenshawe', hear about the real lives of people who live here, understand the real facts, see the real picture. (Real Lives Wythenshawe, 2012)

The site itself still gives off the 'regeneration area' ambience which it is in a sense trying to move the place beyond: the most difficult bit of the trick, of course. But the Manchester University authors' recent review of Wythenshawe does strike an optimistic note: they describe the city's aim:

to regenerate the estate through an economic strategy based on proximity to the regional airport, and reaffirmation of its 'garden city' identity as a place of natural greenery, local food and healthy living.

And add the gloss that:

It is in this context that Barry Parker's garden city is being revalorized. Lost in middle age to a vast and fractured housing estate, its regeneration returns to the tangible assets of the Arts and Crafts design with its retained woodland, gardens, allotments and out-of-town ambience. As Doreen Massey writes, it is 'green and spacious still: the clarity of the air, the freshness of the (constant) breeze still strike me each time I arrive'. (Hebbert and Hopkins, 2012)

Rediscovery needs more than local boosterism, of course. National media that is interested and intrigued by the potential could be very important. So: as well as the local authorities' worthy initiatives, a hearts and minds effort could probably do *not* with an ad campaign, but with TV programmes in the genre of *Changing Rooms, Trading Places* or *Flip that House*: something more at the national popular-cultural level to show this part of suburbia as interesting and full of potential and individual opportunities, stories and life.

Potential No. 6: Realism about Tackling Problems

> **THE INSPECTORS ARE COMING**
>
> When we moved to Downham we had inspectors every so often to come and see if you were keeping the place clean. The word would go round, 'the inspectors are coming!' When you moved you had loads of rules to keep. The windows had to be washed every fortnight and the front step cleaned once a week. No mats were to be shaken after ten o'clock. No cats, no dogs, no pets of any kind. Then indoors there used to have to be a fireguard for the children. You had to keep your children under control at all times, you couldn't let them run about and do as they liked. They couldn't go on the greens or climb trees or anything like that. If you didn't abide by the rules in the rent book, you'd get a real severe letter from the council. They didn't give you many warnings and they'd take action against you...
>
> Beatrice Kitchen of Downham, quoted in Rubinstein, 1991

Coupled with the 'hearts and minds' effort has to be honest confrontation with any problems the estates *do* have: in particular the anti-social behaviour and bad-neighbour problems that feature so heavily in the reports of the views of estate residents themselves. There is no going back to the era of 'The inspectors are coming!' – yet better urban management and social control, including by landlords, seems to be a key requirement before at least some of the estates can turn the corner and unlock their potential as places of choice.

The celebration of corporation suburbs as the 'Garden Cities of Tomorrow' might be a start. But it has to be backed up with realism, and measures, to tackle what existing residents see as problems.

Potential No. 7: Celebration

The 'celebration' should not just be done *to* the estates and their residents. And it is far from being just about media and trendiness – though that can help, by interacting with what local people themselves feel and think. It is vital that they be part of it. Local pride and the local sense of community, possibly supported by explicit community development skills, ought to be an important element in rediscovering, reaffirming, and celebrating the value and appeal of the cottage estates.

In one of Chapter 2's French comparisons – the *cité-jardin* in Stains just north of Paris – there is a real sense that people are now proud of, and powerfully aware of, the aspects of their place that make it not only a special piece of the Île-de-France's heritage, but also a great place to live. The elderly resident quoted in Chapter 2 as having visited it with her children years ago spoke enthusiastically about the features and advantages of the *cité-jardin*: not just the individual houses, the neighbourliness and the gardens whether shared or private, but also, amazingly, its block structure (*l'îlot*). A local residents' group (*Amicale des locataires*) and a social landlord (OPH93) are involved, there is a shop-window – '*Mémoires du cité-jardin*' – in a former ironmongers' shop, and there is obviously serious public-sector support for the whole effort and the related community engagement from the (communist-led) municipality, from the inter-authority grouping Plaine Commune, and from the Seine-Saint-Denis *département* and Île-de-France region (Site officiel de la ville de Stains, 2012).[1] The feel is now that the 'celebration' is self-sustaining. In Stains hundreds, maybe thousands, of residents value and appreciate their garden suburb as a unique and well-loved place – and will tell you all about it if you come across them in the street.

Britain's miserabilist public-sector ethos cannot be expected to go very far down the route offered by that French model. Still, it would surely not be impossible for proud and active landlords like Home Group or Gentoo to link this sort of appreciation of place and local heritage to the very good neighbourhood management work they are already doing on the estates they run.

The Positive Case, and What Can Be Done

A Lot of Positives

Very few of these ideas and potentials are about, or solutions to, the longer term questions of how to get and finance more housing. Or about how the social (subsidized) sector is to be built and funded and what its long-term role is to be. Or about what a modern private-rented sector could be like and should do; or indeed about the ultimate balance between the three tenures, whether nationally or locally.

But there *are* a lot of positives here, and they do not all cost huge budgets to release the much-needed potential. On many of these estates – though not all of them – the sort of 'things to do' that are suggested in Chapter 13 could help make them into real places of choice for the twenty-first century.

The argument throughout this book has been that although celebrating the estates of corporation suburbia is not perhaps the most fashionable of causes, the total achievement shows that this is a thing that Britain did a lot of, and in many places did very well. It was a variant of the widely admired garden city/garden suburb concept, with many of that idea's strengths and attractiveness.

The current role of the cottage estates is not eternal or inevitable. An open-ness to the potential for change is reinforced by the history of other areas which used to be 'places to leave', but which are now amongst the most sought-after 'places of choice' in the country.

Thanks in large part to the Right-To-Buy, the estates' role in the marketplace has changed, and is still changing. The direction and the strength of the change varies from place to place, and it is not always just towards more integration, or greater stability, or a settled mix. A lot of what is involved is to do with attitudes and image. It is clear that attitudes may be at least as important as 'behaviour', as a target for effecting change and improvement on these estates.

Potential of the 'Assets'

The approach here has been to look at the potential that seems to be locked up in corporation suburbia: the 'lazy assets'. Chapters 9 to 12 looked at four sorts of underused potential:

♦   *Housing*: The key here is that the estates of corporation suburbia are not wanted enough, not sufficiently 'place of choice', mainly because of stigma. They are not, however, markedly underused in the sense of under-occupancy, empty stock, or household composition.

♦   *Economic*: There are fewer working families than there need to, or could, be in well-located homes and places that could suit them, and this is potentially less efficient in labour market terms than it could be.

♦   *Development*: There is substantial unreleased housing capacity on the estates, with real potential to help the housing effort as well as the suburbs themselves.

♦   *Community*: There is a considerable community resource here – but what they have tends to be needed just to 'get by', and is not available to substitute for public-sector support, which would be needed in any change programme.

There is a menu of things that could be done to unlock the potential. Many of them are straightforward and reasonably low-cost. A mixture of physical and 'soft' measures could focus on turning more of the estates into the 'locations of choice' they have the potential to be.

And Finally...

A bizarre image rears up of an alliance between Nye Bevan (with his vision of a shared community future) and Margaret Thatcher (with the changes her Right-To-Buy unleashed): between them providing the underpinning for an intelligent rediscovery of these fascinating places.

The cottage estates were, and are, garden suburbs. The best of them already show this country's twentieth-century architecture and planning heritage at its most appealing and successful. Their next 100 years should be based on a reinvigoration, and a celebration, of that birthright.

A world where Becontree, or Bromford, or North Whitley, are places where people are happy and proud to live is not *dramatically* different from today's world. But it *is* a different world. And it would be a world where we would be getting the most out of the assets presented by this great British invention – corporation suburbia.

Note

1.   The Ville de Stains newsletter *7 jours à Stains* (jeudi, 13 Septembre 2012, p. 8) has a feature on 'Journées du Patrimoine de cite-jardin' which illustrates this shared endeavour.

References

Note: Socio-economic data have been drawn primarily from the 2011 Census, supplemented by the 2001 Census where relevant, and also other standard government sources.

Amion/CUPS (AMION Consulting and Centre for Urban Policy Studies, University of Manchester) (2010) *Manchester Independent Economic Review: Sustainable Communities*. Manchester. Available at: http://www.manchesterknowledge.com/knowledge-bank/manchester-independent-economic-review.

Atkinson, R. and Kintrea, K. (1998) *Reconnecting Excluded Communities*. Edinburgh: Scottish Homes.

Atkinson, R. and Kintrea, K. (2000) Owner-occupation, social mix and neighbourhood impacts. *Policy and Politics*, **28**(1), pp. 93–108.

Barker, K. (2004) *Review of Housing Supply: Final Report (A: Summary of Interim Analysis)*. London: HM Treasury. Available at: http://www.barkerreview.org.uk/.

Barker, P. (2009) *The Freedoms of Suburbia*. London: Frances Lincoln.

Barton, L. (2009) Barton's Britain: the Becontree estate. *The Guardian*, 9 October.

Base Mérimée (2012) *Monuments historiques et bâtiments protégés de Notre-Dame-de-Gravenchon*. Available at: www.actuacity.com/notre-dame-de-gravenchon_76330/monuments.

Bashir, N., Batty, E., Cole, I., Crisp, R., Flint, J., Green, S., Hickman, P. and Robinson, D. (2011) *Living Through Change in Challenging Neighbourhoods: Thematic Analysis*. York: Joseph Rowntree Foundation.

Batty, E., Cole, I. and Green, S. (2011) *Low Income Neighbourhoods in Britain* CRESR for Joseph Rowntree Foundation. York: Joseph Rowntree Foundation.

BCC (Birmingham City Council) (2012a) *Core Strategy 2026, Consultation Draft* (Chapter 8 East Birmingham). Birmingham: Birmingham City Council.

BCC (2012b) *Hodge Hill District Strategic Assessment*. Birmingham: Birmingham City Council. Available at: http://fairbrum.files.wordpress.com/2012/11/hodge-hill-strategic-assessment.pdf.

Beer, A., Faulkner, D., Paris, C. and Clower, T. (2011) *Housing Transitions Through the Life Course: Aspirations, Needs and Policy*. Bristol: Policy Press.

Birmingham Mail (2011) Notorious Bromford tower blocks are finally demolished. 8 April.

BNG (Bridging NewcastleGateshead) (2010) *The Changing Place*. Newcastle: BNG.

Bramley, G. (2011) Housing: homes, planning and changing policies in *British Social Attitudes: The 28th Report*. London: NatCen Social Research, chapter 8. Available at: www.natcen.ac.uk/BSA2.

Bramley, G., Leishman, C., Karley, N.K., Morgan, J. and Watkins, D. (2007) *Transforming Places: Housing Investment and Neighbourhood Market Change*. York: Joseph Rowntree Foundation. Available at: http://www.sbe.hw.ac.uk/documents/Bramley_et_al_Transforming_places_FULL_REPORT.pdf.

CBRE Ltd (2008) *Debden Town Centre & Broadway: Final Report*. London: CBRE Ltd for Epping Forest District Council. Available at http://rds.eppingforest dc.gov.uk/Published/C00000500/M00006991/AI00037310/NWA004Broadway RegenerationAppI.pdf.

Champion, T. and Ford, T. (2001) *Who Moves Where and Why? A Survey of Residents' Past Migration and Current Intentions: Results of the Newcastle Case Study*. Newcastle upon Tyne: Department of Geography, University of Newcastle.

Chavtowns (2004) Reading-Whitley-Wood. Available at: http://www.chavtowns.co.uk/2004/10/reading-whitley-wood/.

Chavtowns (2005) Bromford Bridge (da Bromford), Birmingham. Available at: http://www.chavtowns.co.uk/2005/04/bromford-bridge-da-bromford-birmingham/.

CML (Council of Mortgage Lenders) (2004) *A Moving Experience: How often do People Move Home and Mortgages?* London: CML.

Cole, I. and Smith, Y. (1996) *From Estate Action to Estate Agreement: Regeneration and Change on the Bell Farm Estate*. Bristol: Policy Press.

Comité Départemental du Tourisme de Seine-Saint-Denis (2012) *Mettre les villes à la campagne avec les premières cités–jardins*. Pantin: Comité Départemental du Tourisme de Seine-Saint-Denis. Available at: http://www.tourisme93.com/document.php?pagendx=831.

Cowan, P. (1973) *Some Views of the Suburbs*. Working Note 2. London: Joint Unit for Planning Research.

CPRE (Council for the Preservation of Rural England) (1937) *Building in Lancashire*. Preston: CPRE Lancashire.

CPRE (Campaign to Protect Rural England) (2012) *Sir Patrick Abercrombie 1879–1957: CPRE co-founder, Honorary Secretary (1926–1938) and Chairman (1938–1957)*, Display panel at HQ, London.

DCLG (Department for Communities and Local Government) (2010) *English Housing Survey 2008 to 2009: Household Report*. London: DCLG. Available at: https://www.gov.uk/government/publications/english-housing-survey-2008-to-2009-household-report.

DCLG (2011) *Live Tables on House Building*, Table 241, *Permanent dwellings completed, by tenure: United Kingdom historical calendar year series*. Available at: https://www.gov.uk/government/statistical-data-sets/live-tables-on-house-building.

DCLG (2012) *Live Tables on Household Characteristics*, Table 801, *Tenure Trend from 1918*.

Available at: https://www.gov.uk/government/statistical-data-sets/live-tables-on-household-characteristics.

Dennis, N. (1970) *People and Planning: The Sociology of Housing in Sunderland*. London: Faber.

Donegan, L. (1960) *My Old Man's A Dustman*. London: Pye Records.

Droste, C. and Knorr-Siedow, T. (2007) Social housing in Germany, in Whitehead, C. and Scanlon, K. (eds.) *Social Housing in Europe*. London: LSE.

Elsinga, M. and Wassenberg, F. (2007) Social housing in the Netherlands, in Whitehead, C. and Scanlon, K. (eds.) *Social Housing in Europe*. London: LSE.

Fitzpatrick, S., Pawson, H., Bramley, G. and Wilcox, S. (2012) *The Homelessness Monitor: England 2012*. London: Crisis. Available at: http://www.crisis.org.uk/data/files/publications/HomelessnessMonitor_Scotland_2012_complete.pdf.

Ford, J., Rugg, J. and Burrows, R. (2002) Conceptualising the contemporary role of housing in the transition to adult life in England. *Urban Studies*, **39**(13), pp. 2455–2467.

Forrest, R., Murie, A. and Gordon, D. (1995) *The Resale of Former Council Homes*. London: HMSO.

Fribourg, A.-M. (2008) *Regards sur une demi-siècle de politique de logement en France*, in *Crises et politiques du logement – en France et au Royaume-Uni*. Paris: Presses Sorbonne Nouvelle.

Future Communities (2009) *The Case for Investing in Social Sustainability*. Available at: www.futurecommunities.net/case-investing-social-sustainability.

Galonska, C. and Elstner, F. (2007) *Gartenstadt Hellerau/Garden City of Hellerau*. Chemnitz: Palisander-Verlag.

Gateshead Council (2011) *Urban Character Assessment/Central: Carrhill Estate, Deckham East, Sheriff Hill*. Gateshead: Gateshead Council. Available at: www.gateshead.gov.uk.

GHDI (2012) *Row Houses in the Garden City of Hellerau c.1910* (German History in Documents & Images). Washington DC: German Historical Institute. Available at: http://germanhistorydocs.ghi-dc.org.

GNHP (Greater Norwich Housing Partnership) (2007) *Greater Norwich Housing Market Assessment: Under-Occupation of Housing*. Norwich: GNHP.

Green, O. (2004) *Metro-Land: British Empire Exhibition Number, 1924 edition with new introduction by Oliver Green*. London: Southbank Publishing.

Grimes, R. and Loney, S. (2006) *Understanding Housing Demand in East Birmingham and North Solihull (The Eastern Corridor)*. Birmingham: CSR Survey Ltd.

GVA Grimley (2006a) *Urban Design, Heritage & Character Analysis Report: Deckham*. Gateshead: Gateshead Council.

GVA Grimley (2006b) *Deckham Neighbourhood Action Plan, Executive Summary*. Gateshead: Gateshead Council.

Hall, P. (2002) *Cities of Tomorrow: An Intellectual History of Urban Planning and Design in the Twentieth Century*, 3rd ed. Oxford: Blackwell.

Hall, P. and Ward, C. (1998) *Sociable Cities*. Chichester: Wiley.

Hanley, L. (2007) *Estates – An Intimate History*. London: Granta.

Haringey Council (1997) *The Tower Gardens Estate Repair & Conservation Guide: Supplementary Planning Guidance SPG 3.1*. London: Haringey Council.

Haringey Council (2012) *A Life in the day of a Tower Gardens resident*. London: Haringey Council. Available at: www.haringey.gov.uk.

Harris, R. and Larkham, P. (eds.) (1999) *Changing Suburbs: Foundation, Form & Function*. London: Spon.

Hastings, A. (2004) Stigma and social housing estates: beyond pathological explanations. *Journal of Housing & Built Environment*, **19**, pp. 233–254.

HCC (Hull City Council) (2010*a*) *Draft Planning Brief – Outline Business Case for Private Finance Initiative*. Hull: HCC.

HCC (2010*b*) *Orchard Park – Strategy & Delivery (Draft submission to HCA Housing PFI Programme)*. Hull: HCC.

Heath, S. (2008) *Housing Choices and Issues for Young People in the UK*. York: Joseph Rowntree Foundation. Available at: http://www.uk.ecorys.com/pdfs/2325-young-people-housing.pdf.

Hebbert, M. and Hopkins, J. (2012) Wythenshawe Garden City. Paper presented to the International Planning History Society Conference, Sao Paulo.

Hills, J. (2007) *Ends and Means: The Future Roles of Social Housing in England*. London: CASE (Centre for Analysis of Social Exclusion, London School of Economics). Available at: http://eprints.lse.ac.uk/5568/.

Home, R. (1997) *'A Township Complete in Itself' – A Planning History of the Becontree/ Dagenham Estate*. London: London Borough of Barking & Dagenham/ University of East London.

Hometrack (2011) *Prospects for the Housing Market in 2012*. Available at: http://www. hometrack.co.uk/our-insight/commentary-and-analysis/prospects-for-the-housing-market-in-2012.

Housing Justice (2012) *The Housing Crisis in London: Mobilizing the Church*. Report of Conference held on 10 October 2012. London: Housing Justice. Available at: http://www.housingjustice.org.uk/data/__resources/580/Housing-Crisis-Report -FINAL.pdf.

Inventaire général du patrimoine culturel (Base Mérimée) (2012) *Notice no. 94000452, Cité-jardin de l'Aqueduc*. Ministère de la Culture, Paris. Available at: http://www. culture.gouv.fr/public/mistral/dapamer_fr?ACTION=NOUVEAU&nt.

Jackson, A.A (1991) *Semi-Detached London*, 2nd ed. Didcot: Wild Swan.

Jones, A. (1999) No cardboard boxes, so no problem? Young people and housing in rural areas, in J. Rugg (ed.) *Young People, Housing and Social Policy*. London: Routledge.

Jones, C. and Murie, A. (2005) *The Right to Buy: Analysis and Evaluation of a Housing Policy*. Oxford: Blackwell.

Kerr, M. (1988) *The Right to Buy: A National Survey of Tenants and Buyers of Former Council Houses*. London: HMSO.

King, P. (2006) *Choice and the End of Social Housing*. London: IEA.

Lane, L. and Power, A. (2009) *Low Income Housing Estates*. A report to Hammersmith United Charities on supporting communities, preventing social exclusion and tackling need in the London Borough of Hammersmith and Fulham. London: Centre for Analysis of Social Exclusion, London School of Economics and Political Science. Available at: http://eprints.lse.ac.uk/28343/.

L&LP (Leicester & Leicestershire Partnership) (2010) *Leicester & Leicestershire Economic Assessment*. Leicester: Leicester & Leicestershire Partnership.

LCC (London County Council) (1944) *The Greater London Plan* (the Abercrombie Plan). London: LCC.

Leather, P., Nevin, B., Cole, I. and Eadson, W. (2012) *The Housing Market Renewal Programme in England: Development, Impact and Legacy*. Sheffield: Sheffield Hallam University.

Lee, P. and Liu, X. (2009) *Northern Way: Residential Futures, Tyne and Wear Demonstration Project*. Birmingham: Centre for Urban and Regional Studies, Birmingham Business School, University of Birmingham.

Llewelyn Davies (1998) *Urban Living: Perception, Realities and Opportunities*. Winchester: Hampshire County Council.

Llewelyn Davies (2005) *Options for Remodelling Terraced and Radburn Housing in Areas of Low Demand*. London: CABE.

Llewelyn Davies (2006) *Bromford Estate Area Planning, Final Report*. Birmingham: Birmingham City Council.

Llewelyn Davies Yeang (2007a) *Quality of Place: The North's Residential Offer – Residential Futures, Phase IIIa Consultation Draft Report*. Newcastle on Tyne: The Northern Way.

Llewelyn Davies Yeang (2007b) *Residential Futures: Planning for Opportunity*. Newcastle on Tyne: The Northern Way.

Lupton, R. *et al.* (2009) *Growing Up in Social Housing in Britain: A Profile of Four Generations from 1946 to the Present Day*. York: Joseph Rowntree Foundation. Available at: http://www.jrf.org.uk/sites/files/jrf/social-housing-britain-FULL.pdf.

Malpass, P. and Murie, A. (1982) *Housing Policy and Practice*. London: Macmillan.

Martin, G. and Watkinson, J. (2003) *Rebalancing Communities: Introducing Mixed Incomes into Existing Rented Housing Estates*. York: Joseph Rowntree Foundation.

Mason, M. (2011) *Walk the Lines: The London Underground, Overground*. London: Random House.

MORI, Urbed and School for Policy Studies, University of Bristol (1999) *But Would You Live There? – Shaping Attitudes to Urban Living*. London: Urban Task Force. Available at: http://media.urbed.coop.ccc.cdn.faelix.net/sites/default/files/But%20Would%20You%20Live%20There_0.pdf.

Murie, A. (2008) Social housing privatisation in England, in Scanlon, K. and Whitehead, C. (eds.) *Social Housing in Europe II*. London: London School of Economics.

Neale, J. (2012) *Birmingham and the Garden City Movement*. Unpublished monograph. Birmingham.

Neave, D. and Neave, S. (2010) *Hull: Pevsner Architectural Guide*. London: Yale University Press.

Olechnowitz, A. (1997) *Working Class Housing in England between the Wars: The Becontree Estate*. Oxford: Clarendon Press.

Oliver, P., Davis, I. and Bentley, I. (1981) *Dunroamin: The Suburban Semi and Its Enemies*. London: Barrie & Jenkins.

Osborn, F. and Whittick, A. (1963) *The New Towns: The Answer to Megalopolis*. London: Leonard Hill.

Oudenampsen, Merijn (2010) *Retracing the Garden City*. Available at: www.overtreders-w. nl/publicaties/cookfarmerwifeneighbour.pdf.

Panerai, P., Castex, J. and Depaule J.-C. (1997) *Formes urbaines: de l'îlot à la barre*. Marseille: Editions Parenthèses.

Parker Morris Committee (1961) *Homes for Today and Tomorrow*. London: HMSO.

Pevsner, N. (1985) *The Buildings of England: County Durham*. London: Yale University Press.

Pevsner, N. (1991) *Pioneers of Modern Design*. London: Penguin.

Power, A. and Houghton, J. (2007) *Jigsaw Cities: Big Places, Small Spaces*. Bristol: Policy Press.

Priestley, J.B. (1934, 2009) *English Journey*. Ilkley: Great Northern Books, 75th anniversary edition.

Ravetz, A. (2001) *Council Housing and Culture: The History of a Social Experiment*. London: Routledge.

Real Lives Wythenshawe (2012) www.realliveswythenshawe.com.

Richards, J.M. (1965) *An Introduction to Modern Architecture*. London: Pelican.

Rightmove.co.uk (2012) *Property for Sale in Hylton Castle, Sunderland, Tyne & Wear*. Available at: www.rightmove.co.uk.

Rossi, P. (1980) *Why Families Move*, 2nd ed. Beverly Hills, CA: Sage.

Rubinstein, A. (ed.) (1991) *Just Like The Country: Memories of London Families who Settled on the New Cottage Estates 1919–1939*. London: Age Exchange.

Rudlin, D. and Falk, N. (2009) *Sustainable Urban Neighbourhood: Building the 21st Century Home*, 2nd ed. Oxford: Architectural Press.

Samuels, I., Panerai, P., Castex, J. and Depaule, J.-C. (2004) *Urban Forms: The Death and Life of the Urban Block*. Oxford: Architectural Press.

Shannahan, C. (2012) *Bromford Dreams, 'Social Exclusion and Urban Youth Spiritualities'* – *Graffiti Art Project*. Available at: http://www.birmingham.ac.uk/schools/ptr/depart ments/theologyandreligion/research/projects/social-exclusion.aspx.

Sharp, T. (1946) *The Anatomy of a Village*. London: Penguin.

Shelter (2011) *Taking Stock*. Policy briefing. London: Shelter. Available at: http://england. shelter.org.uk/__data/assets/pdf_file/0008/346796/Shelter_Policy_Briefing_-_ Taking_Stock.pdf.

Site officiel de la ville de Stains (2012) *Boutique <<Mémoires du cité-jardin>> chantier-école* www.ville-stains.fr. Rubrique 'Découvrir Stains'.

Stephens, M., Burns, N. and Mackay, L. (2002) *Social Market or Safety Net? British Social Rented Housing in a European Context*. Bristol: Policy Press.

SYAS (South Yorkshire Archaeology Service) (2009) *Early to Mid 20th Century Municipal Suburbs* (South Yorkshire Historic Environment Characterisation Project Part III: Sheffield Character Zone Descriptions). Sheffield: SYAS.

Taylor, S. and Lovie, D. (2004) *Gateshead: Architecture in a Changing English Urban Landscape*. London: English Heritage.

Thompson, D. (1976) The British new towns revisited, in Apgar, M. (ed.) (1976) *New Perspectives on Community Development*. New York: McGraw-Hill.

Turkington, R. (1999) British 'corporation suburbia': the changing fortunes of Norris Green, Liverpool, in Harris, R. and Larkham, P. (eds.) *Changing Suburbs*. London: Spon.

Urban Studio (2009a) *Residential Futures, Final Report*, Vol. II, *Research Report*. Newcastle: The Northern Way.

Urban Studio (in association with CURS) (2009b) *Residential Futures, Tyne & Wear City Region Report*. Newcastle: The Northern Way.

Urban Studio (2009c) *Residential Futures, Final Report*, Vol. I, *Summary Report*. Newcastle: The Northern Way.

Urban Studio (2009d) *Residential Futures, Central Lancashire City Region Report*. Newcastle: The Northern Way.

Urban Studio (2009e) *Residential Futures, Hull & Humber Ports City Region Report*. Newcastle: The Northern Way.

Urban Task Force (1999) *Towards an Urban Renaissance*. London: Routledge.

Urbed (2006) *Orchard Park – The Book*, for Gateway/Hull City Council. Manchester: Urbed. Available at: http://media.urbed.coop.ccc.cdn.faelix.net/sites/default/files/Orchard%20Park%20Photography%20Study.pdf.

VCH (Victoria County History) (1958) *The City of Leicester: Social and Administrative History since 1835, A History of the County of Leicester*, Volume 4: *The City of Leicester*. Available at: http://www.british-history.ac.uk/report.aspx.

VCH (2012) *Durham Housing & Rehousing from 1918, Victoria County History - Durham: Sunderland*. Available at: victoriacountyhistory.ac.uk.

White, J. (2008) *London in the 20th Century*. London: Vintage.

Whitehand, J.W.R. and Carr, C.M.H. (1999) England's garden suburbs: development and change, in Harris, R. and Larkham, P. (eds.) *Changing Suburbs*. London: Spon.

Whitehand, J.W.R. and Carr, C.M.H. (2001) *Twentieth-Century Suburbs – A Morphological Approach*. London: Routledge.

Whitehead, C. (2007) Social housing in England, in Whitehead, C. and Scanlon, K. (eds.) *Social Housing in Europe*. London: LSE.

Young, M. and Willmott, P. (1957, 2007) *Family and Kinship in East London*. Harmondsworth: Penguin Modern Classics.

Index